THE ROCKY MOUNTAIN FUR TRADE JOURNAL

VOLUME 10   2016

Editor
Jim Hardee

Publications Director   **Editor Emeritus**
Angie Thomas   Dr. Fred R. Gowans

Design and Production
Sommers Studio, Pinedale, Wyoming

Authors
Don Arp, Jr.   Michael M. Casler   Jim Hardee   Carol Kuhn
Clay J. Landry   Larry E. Morris

Reviewers

J. Ryan Badger	John W. Fisher	Dr. Darby Stapp
Stephen V. Banks	Todd Glover	Dr. William R. Swagerty
Vic Nathan Barkin	William Gwaltney	Tim Tanner
Nathan E. Bender	Gene Hickman	Melissa Tiffie
Dr. Roger Blomquist	Keith Moki Hipol	Dale Topham
Barry Bohnet	Mark William Kelly	Dr. Mark van de Logt
Dr. Jay H. Buckley	Mike Moore	Scott Walker
Allen Chronister	David F. Morris	E. Rick Williams
O. Ned Eddins	Dr. David J. Peck	David Wright
Jerry Enzler	Dean Rudy	Dr. Ken Zontek
	Dr. Mark Schreiter	

Published by the Sublette County Historical Society
and the Museum of the Mountain Man, Pinedale, Wyoming
Angie Thomas, Director
Laurie Hartwig, Assistant Director
Elizabeth A. Watry, MA, Curator
Mindy Seehafer, Business Manager
Arlaina Goddard, Media Resources Specialist

Board of Trustees:
John Anderson, President
Jim Gehlhausen, Vice President
Kimberly Ervin, Treasurer   Dawn Ballou, Secretary
Travis Bing   Jon Gibson   Ty Huffman   Paul Jensen
Ken Marincic   Jeness Saxton   Rob Tolley   Paul Ulrich

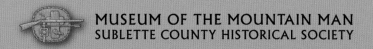

MUSEUM OF THE MOUNTAIN MAN
SUBLETTE COUNTY HISTORICAL SOCIETY

The Rocky Mountain Fur Trade Journal

An annual academic peer-reviewed publication intended to further the knowledge and discussion of the Rocky Mountain fur trade era and provide an avenue for researchers to showcase their work.

The Rocky Mountain fur trade era is defined as beginning in 1824 and ending in 1840. In March 1824, Jedediah Smith led a party of trappers into the Green River Valley, finding an abundance of beaver and few hostile Indians. Following this discovery came brigades of mountain men, then the rendezvous and overland supply systems to support them. These aspects characterize the Rocky Mountain fur trade era.

The 1840 rendezvous proved to be the last classic rendezvous. While fur trade ventures existed before 1824, and endured for a time after 1840, those years bracket the rendezvous system. The geographic boundaries of the Rocky Mountain fur trade are roughly defined as the Rocky Mountains of Idaho, Montana, Wyoming, Colorado and Utah, the region worked by the mountain men and Indians who depended on and were supplied by the rendezvous system.

Cover image:
Estate of Hugh Glass, American Fur Company Ledger,
Upper Missouri Outfit, 1830-1834
MISSOURI HISTORY MUSEUM, ST. LOUIS, MO

ISBN: 978-0-9973143-0-4

The Rocky Mountain Fur Trade Journal is published annually by the Sublette County Historical Society/Museum of the Mountain Man, a non-profit organization in Pinedale, Wyoming. Subscriptions are available through membership in the Society. Back issues can be purchased by contacting the Museum.

SCHS/MMM
P.O. Box 909
700 E. Hennick Lane
Pinedale, Wyoming 82941
307-367-4101
www.MMMuseum.com

©2016 Sublette County Historical Society

Articles and images appearing in this journal are copyrighted to the authors, Sublette County Historical Society/Museum of the Mountain Man, and other organizations. All rights reserved. No part of this journal or its cover may be reproduced without written consent. The presentation and opinions expressed by the authors and contributors are not necessarily those of the SCHS/MMM organization.

THE ROCKY MOUNTAIN FUR TRADE JOURNAL

SUBMISSIONS
Annual deadline: September 1

The Museum of the Mountain Man in Pinedale, Wyoming, publishes the award-winning *Rocky Mountain Fur Trade Journal* each July. The 2016 volume marks its tenth year. Our academic peer-reviewed publication showcases new ideas and discoveries related to the Rocky Mountain fur trade era in American history.

The *Journal* continues to increase knowledge and bring fresh perspectives by encouraging research and debate in the academic arena. Likewise, we welcome exploration into innovative topics as well as defensible challenges to previously accepted theories. The peer-review process ensures quality, and thus the *Journal* extends this invitation to non-professional and student writers in addition to professional scholars.

Up to ten articles are selected for inclusion in each issue. Selected authors may be invited to make a presentation when the volume is introduced to the public during the annual Green River Rendezvous Days, held the second weekend in July at the Museum of the Mountain Man.

WRITER'S GUIDELINES:
www.MMMuseum.com • journal@MMMuseum.com

MUSEUM OF THE MOUNTAIN MAN
SUBLETTE COUNTY HISTORICAL SOCIETY
P.O. BOX 909 • PINEDALE, WY 82941

ALFRED JACOB MILLER, *HUNTING THE BEAR* [DETAIL], 1858-1860. THE WALTERS ART MUSEUM, BALTIMORE, MD #37.1940.107

Introduction

by Jim Hardee

In 2007, the Museum of the Mountain Man and the Sublette County Historical Society set out to create a venue that would encourage research and debate about the fur trade era. The concept of an annual collection of well-documented, peer-reviewed articles to keep that period of history engaging and relevant in academia became *The Rocky Mountain Fur Trade Journal*. At the time some declared, "There's nothing left to research, the fur trade has been examined to its fullest." Yet a decade later, the *Journal* continues to receive submissions from the cutting edge of investigation into one of the most memorable eras of American history.

In its ten years to date, the *Journal* has brought to light a lost diary that William Ashley kept in 1826, and surveyed other important documents heretofore unknown to historians. It has reconsidered the art of Alfred Jacob Miller. It has addressed fur trade material culture in new, enlightening ways that have become mainstays of understanding the era. It has introduced new information about Jedediah Smith and Jim Bridger, among others, and consistently proven that there is still much to learn about the Rocky Mountain fur trade of the Far West. In pursuit of this goal, the *Journal* has received multiple awards for excellence from the Wyoming Historical Society.

Focused on increasing knowledge of the fur trade, the *Journal* brings professional historians, academics, and history enthusiasts together to raise the bar for promoting study of this intriguing segment of Western expansion. Our tenth anniversary issue is no exception.

The recent Hollywood production of *The Revenant*, a fictionalized account of mountain man Hugh Glass's great survival story, reimagines oft-told fragments of Hugh Glass lore. This volume's first article, **Hugh Glass: The Rest of the Story,** investigates new and rarely-considered data to build a more complete, and no less remarkable, picture of the man and his circumstances, especially in his later life. Clay J. Landry, well known to *Journal* readers and historical consultant for the movie, uses period account books and letters to bring a fresh and informative look at Glass.

Michael M. Casler investigates the epidemic that struck the upper Missouri in **"This Outrageous Desease": Charles Larpenteur's Observations of the 1837 Smallpox Epidemic.** Casler uses Larpenteur's first-hand account, other primary sources, and modern understanding of the pathogen to advance a nuanced picture of how fur traders dealt with the scourge that annihilated so many Native Americans and devastated families in the fur trade.

Complementing the topic of the smallpox epidemic of 1837, Don Arp, Jr., considers a contemporaneous infestation of vermin at a fur trading post. **The Rats at Fort Clark** compiles statistics recorded by Francis Chardon from 1834 to 1839, revealing how these pests affected daily life at an American Fur Company post on the Missouri River.

Most readers will recognize John Sutter as the man who owned the California sawmill where gold was discovered in 1848, setting off a massive rush to the Pacific coast for riches. But who can make the connection between Sutter and the fur trade? **The Influence of the Fur Trade on John Sutter,** by your *Journal* editor, will trace the myriad ways in which Sutter's trip west in 1838, rubbing shoulders with mountain men, affected the history of what became the Golden State.

Fur trade enthusiasts are undoubtedly familiar with numerous scientists who went west in company with trapping forays. Author Carol Kuhn offers a unique angle on the business of studying western flora and fauna in her paper **Naturalists in the Rocky Mountain Fur Trade Era: "They are a Perfect Nuisance."** This new perspective examines in detail not just how, but why these men ventured into the Rocky Mountains. The answers may surprise historians.

Finally, Larry E. Morris continues excavating the fur trade's effect on greater events in US history in **Mountain Men and the Taking of California, 1845-1847**. With the decline of the beaver trade, many trappers got involved with American military ventures. Morris explains the integral roles that mountaineers played in the Mexican-American War.

Who would have thought ten years ago that *The Rocky Mountain Fur Trade Journal* would have impacted how historians view the story of the beaver trade? Yet, magical as it seems, after ten volumes of eclectic, informative articles, the *Journal* has proven its worth. None of this would be possible without the support of the Editorial Board, the Museum's staff, and the people of Sublette County, Wyoming. Enlarging upon the past events of the Green River Valley and the Rocky Mountain fur trade will continue to be an exciting, educational, and dynamic mission.

One of many specimens collected by British botanist David Douglas on his 1824-25 journey in the American West is the western white pine (*Pinus monticola*). This important timber tree is particularly valuable for building construction. See Carol Kuhn's article for more on early botanical discoveries and naturalists in the fur trade. ©THE BOARD OF TRUSTEES OF THE ROYAL BOTANIC GARDENS, KEW. REPRODUCED WITH THE CONSENT OF THE ROYAL BOTANIC GARDENS, KEW

THE ROCKY MOUNTAIN FUR TRADE JOURNAL

VOLUME 10   2016

Contents

iv   Introduction

1   **Hugh Glass: The Rest of the Story**
by Clay J. Landry

18   **"This Outrageous Desease": Charles Larpenteur's Observations of the 1837 Smallpox Epidemic**
by Michael M. Casler

37   **The Rats at Fort Clark**
by Don Arp, Jr.

49   **The Influence of the Fur Trade on John Sutter**
by Jim Hardee

Naturalists in the Rocky Mountain Fur Trade Era: "They Are a Perfect Nuisance"   **73**
by Carol Kuhn

Mountain Men and the Taking of California, 1845-1847   **94**
by Larry E. Morris

Reviewers   122

The Museum of the Mountain Man   126

View on the Gila (1852) was sketched by US Boundary Commissioner John Russell Bartlett following the Mexican War. For more on mountain men's participation in this war, see the article by Larry Morris, page 94.

THE JOHN CARTER BROWN LIBRARY AT BROWN UNIVERSITY

298

Dr. Hugh G...

	1831			
August	21	To Ledger A. Page 261		221
		" Bal A/c at Ft. Union		34
	1832			
April	30	" Transfer from Ft. "		118
Jun	30	" Acc.t at — " — "		288
				662
	1834			
Jun	30	To Balance		548
	1833			
Jun	30	" Advances at Ft. Union		13
				560

Hugh Glass's account page from the American Fur Company Upper Missouri Outfit shows his debits (Dr.) and credits (Cr.) for 1831-33, through the closing of his account at Fort Union. The heading describes Glass as a "Freeman," meaning that he was not an AFC employee. This ledger was kept at the AFC offices in St. Louis, compiling reports from the company's Missouri River posts. MISSOURI HISTORY MUSEUM, ST. LOUIS, MO

Hugh Glass: The Rest of the Story

by Clay J. Landry

In 1963, John Myers Myers published a book on the life of Hugh Glass and the known facts about the savage grizzly bear attack and Glass's survival saga.[1] Myers's book presented a comparative analysis of the published historical accounts of the mauling and Glass's life in general. To refrain from covering old ground, this essay will set the scene for Glass's bear attack, summarize his quest for revenge, then use details from old and new historical sources to construct a narrative for the life of Hugh Glass. This narrative will present previously unpublished information about Glass's later life and details about his death in 1833.

Prelude to meeting *Ursus arctos horribilis*

Hugh Glass was a member of the Henry/Ashley Company's second expedition, in 1823. The venture consisted of two keel boats, seventy trappers and the necessary boatmen and crew that departed St. Louis on March 10 of that year. They were headed to Fort Henry, a fur trade post the partnership had established near the mouth of the Yellowstone River the year before, during its first expedition.[2]

On May 30, 1823, the two keel boats dropped anchor downstream of the Arikara villages near the mouth of the Grand River. The next morning, though the Arikara's initial reception was indifferent, by offering gifts and following proper Indian trade etiquette, Ashley was able to trade for nineteen horses and two hundred buffalo robes. In the early morning darkness of June 2, 1823, the men on the shore were awakened by Arikara war cries and Edward Rose running into camp saying that Indians had killed trapper Arron Stephens. At dawn a hail of fusee balls and arrows rained down upon the shore camp, hitting both horses and men. The Arikara attack resulted in 14 men killed and 10 wounded. Ashley's list of men wounded in this conflict is the first historical record of Hugh Glass as a member of the Henry/Ashley Company.[3]

After waiting two months, a force composed of military, trappers and Indian allies waged an unsuccessful campaign against the Arikara. About all that was accomplished was the burning of the deserted Arikara villages and the deaths of chief Grey Eyes and a few Arikara warriors.[4] At some time during these events, Ashley and Henry determined the Missouri River route to the mountains was no longer feasible or cost effective due to the hostile, unpredictable nature of the tribes residing along the river. The price in lives, capital and time had become too great.

The partners decided a land route would be the best way to avoid further conflicts with hostile tribes along the Missouri, so two groups left the river, taking a westward course to the mountains. One group, led by Jedediah Smith, traveled west along the White River. The other group, with Andrew Henry in charge, made haste northwesterly to Fort Henry, to reinforce a small band of trappers remaining there. Ashley returned downriver to St. Louis.[5]

Glass, a grizzly and the legend begins

Hugh Glass went with Henry's group, which by late August of 1823, was traveling up the Grand River in present-day South Dakota.[6] Glass, working as a hired hunter, encountered a sow grizzly bear with two cubs. The bear charged and severely mauled the mountaineer.[7]

Glass was so badly mangled that everyone in the party, including Henry, believed that he had only hours, or at most a day, to live. Henry did not want to endanger his entire party as well as the shorthanded group at Fort Henry by waiting around for Glass to die. He asked two volunteers to remain with Glass, provide as much comfort to him as circumstances would allow, give him a decent burial once he expired, and then proceed to the fort.[8]

The events associated with this bear mauling would become one of the most epic stories in the annals of the Rocky Mountain fur trade. The earliest and most succinct account of the three men at the center of this episode came from one of Henry's men. In a July 7, 1824, letter, Daniel Potts summarized the Hugh Glass bear story this way: "one man was also tore nearly all to peases by a White Bear and was left by the way with out any gun who afterwards recover'd."[9]

The two men stayed with the suffering Glass only a few days, then deserted him in a semi-helpless state, taking his gun, knife, and possibles bag. Fortunately for Glass, and unfortunate for the two scoundrels who deserted him, his will to live was strong and he was able to heal enough to start crawling toward Fort Kiowa, some 200 miles away. Aided by luck and determination, he found berries, insects, small animals and carrion to eat along the way and eventually hobbled into Fort Kiowa by late fall of 1823. Once recovered from his wounds enough to be mobile, he set out to exact revenge from the cowardly caregivers and retrieve his gun and accoutrements.[10]

Knowing that these two men were likely still with Henry on the upper Missouri, Glass left Fort Kiowa for the mouth of the Yellowstone River during the winter of 1823. Glass had covered nearly 2,000 miles of the Yellowstone and upper Missouri River region by the time he reached Fort Henry.[11] Finding the post deserted, Glass went on to the Bighorn River, where he located Henry's party and the younger of the two men who deserted him. Glass ended up forgiving him because of his youth.[12] The second man, John Fitzgerald, had left the fur trade and enlisted in the Army at Fort Atkinson. When Glass appeared at the fort in June of 1824 demanding to see Fitzgerald, the Officer of the Day denied his request, but returned Glass's rifle and belongings.[13] The Army's position was that despite what he had done, Fitzgerald now belonged to them. Any punishment due would be meted out by them, not by a civilian.

The troopers at Fort Atkinson and other men he encountered along the way were quite impressed by Glass's story of the bear mauling, wilderness survival, and the extraordinary quest to gain revenge on the men who had deserted him. So much so that, by frontier American standards, the Glass story spread like wildfire. The first printed version, titled *The Missouri Trapper*, appeared in the March 1825 edition of the *Port-Folio*, a periodical published in Philadelphia.[14] By June that year, the article had been republished in several St. Louis newspapers, the first being the *Missouri Intelligencer*.

Within seven months of its debut, *The Missouri Trapper* had been reprinted by newspapers in Maine, Vermont, North and South Carolina, Virginia, Massachusetts, and New York.[15] Evidently, people all over the United States were interested in the life and death struggles encountered by men working in the Rocky Mountain fur trade.

Trapping and trading in the Southwest

Once his dealings at Fort Atkinson regarding the fate of John Fitzgerald were concluded, Hugh Glass persevered in his life as a Rocky Mountain trapper. Funded by a $300 purse, paid to him at the fort to appease his vengeance and to partially compensate him for the hardships he had endured, Glass traveled to the western settlements of Missouri. By the spring of 1825, the Santa Fe trade was in full bloom and Glass became a partner in a trading venture traveling the Santa Fe Trail to New Mexico.[16]

Another person interested in improving his prospects by relocating to the Santa Fe and Taos areas was a young man who had apprenticed in medicine for several years in St. Charles, Missouri. Convinced that he could establish a lucrative medical practice in New Mexico due to the lack of competition, Dr. Rowland Willard departed St. Charles on May 6, 1825, headed to Lexington, Missouri, the rallying place for the Santa Fe Trail caravan he had selected.[17]

Arriving at Lexington on May 15, Willard soon learned that the caravan would travel in two groups. Because of their slower pace, the heavily loaded wagons would form one party, while a faster group, mounted men trailing pack animals, would lead the way. These thirty-three mounted men would meet at the Blue Springs campground the next day to organize and elect their own leaders. Willard rode ahead to that meeting place, joined the "packers," and traveled to Mexico as a member of that group.[18]

During his trip to Taos and throughout the two years he lived in New Mexico,

Willard kept a daily record in a pocket or "travel diary," noting his experiences and the people he met.[19] While traveling with the packers, Willard encountered "Mr. Glass," a hunter who supplied meat to the party. Willard mentioned Glass just three times in his diary during the forty-eight-day trip from Blue Springs to Taos. On May 24, he recorded that Glass killed some elk, and on June 1, Glass went buffalo hunting. Willard's last diary entry about Glass was on June 21: "Mr. Glass had a severe turn of the colic which required my attention for several hours."[20]

In about 1867, when Willard was in his early seventies, he wrote an autobiography. The pages about his trip to Taos and his time in Mexico were based on his travel diary and reminiscences. This memoir contained more detailed information about Hugh Glass than the travel diary had, including that he first met Glass in the company of a man named Solomon Stone at the Blue Springs campground near Fort Osage in May 1825.[21] Willard described Glass as "quite advanced in life probably 75" and "was by birth a Highland Scotch man, & still retained the kilts & cap of his native country."[22] He explained that Stone and Glass were beaver trappers with many years of experience in the mountains and men who liked to spend all of their hard earned fur money on liquor as soon as they reached the settlements. Once out of money, they would head back to the beaver streams and restart the cycle of debauchery.[23]

Willard's memoir also contained a bear mauling story which he claimed he had heard directly from Hugh Glass. In Willard's version, Glass is with Stone and two other free trappers out on their "own hook" trapping. Glass, on camp duty one morning while the other men went to check traps, was attacked by a large white bear as he was bent over the fire cooking.[24] The bear was on top of Glass chewing away at him when Stone happened to return to camp with rifle in hand and dispatched the bear.

In his memoir, Willard also implied that shortly after meeting Glass he was able to examine the old trapper's scars and observed "large chasms upon right arm & shoulder blade the crest of which was wanting, also the upper portions of the thigh."[25] He also claimed that he visited with Glass one last time in Taos, where the old man thanked the doctor for saving his life with the colic treatment while on the Santa Fe Trail. Willard concluded his story about Hugh Glass by stating that the veteran mountaineer was killed while trapping on the waters of the Colorado River. According to the doctor, mountaineer Glass was in a party of French trappers, all of whom were clubbed to death one night by a group of Indians the trappers had carelessly allowed into their camp.[26]

Other than verifying that Hugh Glass traveled the Santa Fe Trail in the summer of 1825, Willard's travel diary contains no information relevant to the Glass story. The doctor's diary entries do support and coincide with George Yount's account, which states that Glass left western Missouri as part of a commercial venture headed for Mexico between fall of 1824 and spring of 1825.

Several versions of the Hugh Glass story were printed and reprinted in the Missouri newspapers between 1825 and 1842. In addition to the newspaper coverage, the story was retold in two different books published in 1846 and 1847.[27] The availability and common local knowledge of the Glass bear mauling story in western Missouri of the mid-1800s makes one wonder whether Dr. Willard was either wholly ignorant, or contriving to claim his version as the "real" truth. His rendering is so far removed from contemporary published accounts that it seems doubtful Willard obtained his bear story firsthand.

Neither do the remembered personal details about Glass in Willard's autobiography correlate well with the historical record. One historian evaluated the memoir as an "illusion" in which "Willard zoomed in on [Glass] from the distance of his own advanced age."[28] None of the trappers who knew Hugh Glass mentioned him wearing a kilt or Scotch cap. Moreover, given that Glass was trapping the upper Missouri country five years later, Willard's calculus would make Glass an unlikely eighty years old at that time. Willard may have examined Hugh Glass's scarred body but it certainly appears that "time, memory lapses, and fabrications crippled the doctor's account."[29]

In Santa Fe, Hugh Glass formed a partnership with a Frenchman named DuBreuil, and the two men went on a trading and trapping venture along the Gila River.[30] After a year of trapping and trading southwest of Santa Fe with only marginal success, Glass relocated to Taos and there met Etienne Provost. Provost engaged Glass to lead a party of trappers into the southern Colorado territory of the "Eutau" (Ute) Indians. While trapping and canoeing down a river, Glass's group spotted a lone Indian woman along the bank.

This woman was a Shoshone, a tribe at war with the Utes at the time, and hostile toward any whites who traded with their enemy. Glass and his men beached the canoes and approached the woman with an offering of beaver meat, however their sudden presence startled her and she let out a horrendous yell. The scream alerted Shoshone braves resting nearby and numerous arrows were fired at the mountaineers. The attack resulted in one trapper killed and Glass with an arrowhead embedded in his back. Glass endured the pain of an inflamed wound while the party traveled 700 miles back to Taos. Once there, the metal arrowhead was removed by a fellow trapper using only a straight razor.[31] After spending several months in Taos allowing the wound to heal and recuperating his health, Hugh Glass ended his three-year New Mexican sojourn by joining a group of trappers headed for the beaver grounds of the Yellowstone River country.[32]

Return to the upper Missouri

No documentation has yet come to light revealing the regions of the Yellowstone visited by Glass during 1827-28. However, the story of Phillip Covington's employment with William Sublette's rendezvous caravan from that time provides new information regarding Glass attending the 1828 Bear Lake Rendezvous.[33] Published in a Colorado newspaper during the 1870s, Covington's story was virtually unknown until an edited version was republished by John Gray in a 1982 issue of *Colorado Heritage* magazine. Covington wrote that at the 1828 rendezvous, Glass told the story of his run in with Ol' Ephraim and "to prove the facts in the case, pulled off his shirt and showed the scars on his back and body."

One of the hot items of discussion at the 1828 rendezvous among free trappers was the exorbitant prices for goods being charged by Smith, Jackson and Sublette. In an effort to bring about more competition, the free trappers asked Hugh Glass to represent them to American Fur Company (AFC) man Kenneth McKenzie and invite the AFC to send a trade caravan to the 1829 rendezvous.[34] As a result, Glass left the 1828 rendezvous bound for Fort Floyd, an AFC post located on the upper Missouri River near the mouth of the White Earth River, to palaver with McKenzie.[35] To date, no record of the meeting between Glass and McKenzie has surfaced. Because McKenzie had dispatched Etienne Provost to the 1828 rendezvous to sell the free trappers on the idea of bringing their furs to AFC posts on the Missouri River to trade, McKenzie was clearly already anxious to do business with the freemen.[36]

Glass's movements during 1829 are not certain, but it can be assumed that he made it to either of the dual rendezvous in 1829, at Pierre's Hole or the Popo Agie River, to report to the free trappers the results of his visit with Kenneth McKenzie. The free trappers' special envoy may have actually

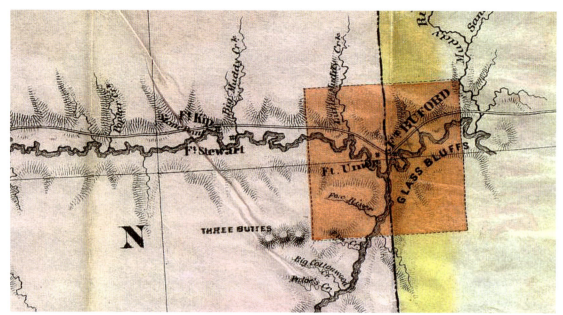

This detail of W. W. DeLacy's 1872 "Map of the Territory of Montana with Portions of the Adjoining Territories," shows the confluence of the Yellowstone and Missouri rivers (brown box), with Glass Bluffs across from forts Union and Buford. RUMSEY COLLECTION, DAVIDRUMSEY.COM

influenced AFC management, because a trading caravan under the leadership of Lucien Fontenelle and Andrew Dripps was scheduled to attend the 1830 rendezvous.[37] Whatever the specific outcome of Glass's representation of the freemen, subsequent events indicate that he and McKenzie developed a mutually respectful relationship.[38]

By the spring of 1830, Hugh Glass was working for Kenneth McKenzie's Upper Missouri Outfit (UMO). A branch of the Western Department of the American Fur Company, the UMO was based at Fort Union, near the mouth of the Yellowstone River. In a letter dated May 5, 1830, McKenzie wrote "to the Gentleman in charge of Fort Tecumseh," that "I send Francis & old Glass with other men to you to bring up as many horses and mules as you can spare."[39]

A comment penned by McKenzie at the end of this letter indicates an elevated regard for Glass: "Francis and Mr. Glass merits more attention than the common men."[40] AFC records also show that in 1831, three keel boats, named the *Assiniboine*, *Blackfoot*, and *Old Glass*, delivered goods to the company's upper Missouri trading posts.[41] Naming a company keel boat after Glass is another indication of McKenzie's admiration and fondness for the old trapper.

The UMO Ledger Book contains a credit and debit page titled "Hugh Glass – Freeman," for the years 1831 through 1833 (see first two pages of this article). This ledger page shows occasional purchases of goods by Glass at Fort Union over those years totaling $662.69.[42] According to historian Hiram M. Chittenden, Glass worked as a hunter for Fort Union and hunted bighorn sheep on the hills opposite the fort. Those hills became known as Glass Bluffs.[43] As early as 1870, a map of the Territory of Montana showed the bluffs near the mouth of the Yellowstone identified as "Glass Bluffs."[44]

The UMO ledgers also show that Johnson Gardner, another famous free trapper, migrated to Fort Union during the same time period. Gardner had been with the first Henry/Ashley party, in 1822, and had been an independent Rocky Mountain trapper and trader since that time.[45] Considering that both men came to the upper Missouri country as Ashley men and endured many of the same hardships, they were most likely friends, and at the least, respectful of one another's accomplishments.

Kenneth McKenzie planned to monopolize the trade in the upper Missouri region, and built Fort McKenzie to capture the Blackfoot trade. With the establishment of his post in the Brulé Bottom near the mouth of the Marias in 1831, McKenzie was then able to refocus his attention on the land of the Crows.[46] He explained his Crow Country interests in a letter to AFC management in St. Louis:

> *I intend to build [another] fort next summer on the Yellowstone at the mouth of the Bighorn for the Crows, and for many years some straggling white hunters will stay in the Crow country from whom we may expect a little beaver.*[47]

In the summer of 1832, Samuel Tullock was sent to locate a site and construct a new trading post. By late fall of the same year, Fort Cass was open for business. Nathaniel Wyeth visited Fort Cass in 1833 and described its location as being three miles downriver from the junction of the Bighorn and Yellowstone rivers.[48]

The final episode – death and vengeance

Not long after the completion of Fort Cass, either by his own choice as a "freeman" or at McKenzie's request, Hugh Glass relocated to the new post.[49] A few miles down the Yellowstone River from Fort Cass, Glass's uncanny wilderness luck ran out. John Myers Myers and Aubrey Haines were two of the first historians to write about the circumstances of Glass's death in any detail. Myers and Haines were contemporaries, and because their accounts are similar, it appears they relied on the same source documents for their research.

The common thread of the Myers and Haines accounts states that one morning during the winter of 1832-33, Glass accompanied two men named Rose and Menard departing Fort Cass. As the trappers were crossing the ice of the frozen Yellowstone, they were ambushed by a large party of Arikara who had been concealed on the opposite bank. All three men were shot, scalped and plundered.[50] Unfortunately for the trappers, the Arikara war party had been scouting the area around the fort, bent on stealing horses, when they spotted the trio. While Myers and Haines each concluded that Edward Rose was one of the men with Glass that fateful day, they were unable to determine the first name of Mr. Menard.

It is not surprising that both historians fixed on the well-known Edward Rose as the Rose who died with Glass. Edward Rose was a multi-racial man, born of a half-Cherokee, half-black mother and a white father. Often referred to as a mulatto in the historical record, Rose grew up around Louisville, Kentucky. A later knife cut across his nose would earn him the moniker of "Nez Coupé" or Cut Nose.[51]

Rose entered the fur trade as a member of the St. Louis Missouri Fur Company's 1807 expedition to the mouth of the Bighorn River to construct Fort Raymond.[52] His preference for living with the Indians developed into a relationship with both the Crow and Arikara tribes. Having learned the Crow language, Rose's services in the country between the Big Horn Mountains and the Missouri River were quite valuable to many of the fur companies. Thus, despite his reputation as a hot-tempered troublemaker, Rose was hired as a guide and interpreter for the Andrew Henry party in 1809, the Astorians in 1811, William Ashley in 1823 and the Atkinson-O'Fallon Expedition in 1825.[53]

Interestingly, historian Hiram M. Chittenden disregarded the story that Edward Rose died near Fort Cass, citing the narrative of mountain man Zenas Leonard, who never named the "old negro" he met in a Crow village, as proof that Rose was still

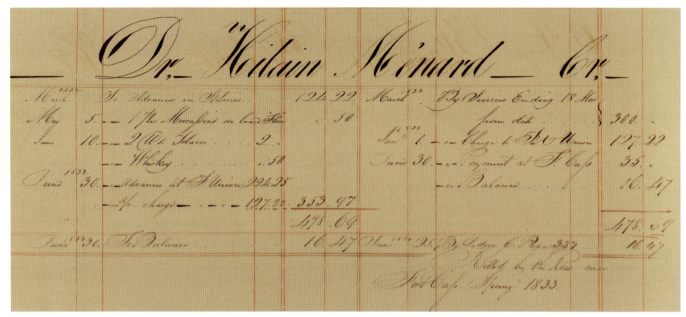

Figure 1: Hilain Menard's account page notes "Killed by the Rees near Fort Cass Spring 1833" near the bottom right. American Fur Company Ledger, Upper Missouri Outfit, 1830-1834.

MISSOURI HISTORY MUSEUM, ST. LOUIS, MO

living among the Crows in 1834.[54] Chittenden also claimed Rose was buried on the Missouri River, nearly opposite the mouth of the Milk River. His only support for this was that in "any of the old steamboat itineraries of the Missouri River may be seen among the names in that vicinity, 'Rose's Grave.'"[55]

Three dead men at Fort Cass

Contemporary analysis of the historical record in regard to Hugh Glass generally agrees that he died on the Yellowstone River, but the year of his death is in question. This has caused historians to hedge on the exact year by saying Glass was killed sometime during the winter of 1832-33. Most modern published accounts also state Glass died along with two hunting partners, the infamous Edward Rose and "a trapper named Menard."[56] This essay brings to light overlooked documentation that provides some certainty as to the year Glass died, provides trapper Menard with a first name for the first time, and examines the question of whether Edward Rose was actually the same man named Rose who died with Glass.

Two of the ledger books for the UMO contain pages for Hilain Menard.[57] Ledger Book B, 1830-1834, contains Menard's account page (Figure 1). This record shows a final entry dated June 30, 1833, indicating that the account is balanced or closed. A hand-written notation made on the credit side of Menard's account book page states, "Killed by the Rees near Fort Cass Spring of 1833." The word "Rees" was mountaineer slang for the Arikara tribe.

A standard bookkeeping practice of the fur companies was to post a closing balance entry to an account in the same year in which a man left employment, whether by death, changing employer or other reason. Applying knowledge of this procedure to the entries on Hilain Menard's account page indicates that he died sometime between the end of 1832 and the June 30, 1833, account close-out date.

Ledger Book C, 1833-1836, contains an account page (Figure 2) titled "Estate Hilain Menard."

Figure 2: Estate of Hilain Menard. American Fur Company Ledger, Upper Missouri Outfit, 1830-1834. MISSOURI HISTORY MUSEUM, ST. LOUIS, MO

Estate accounts were also a bookkeeping method used by the AFC to settle a man's financial affairs with the company if he died. It closed a deceased employee's or customer's account and provided a record for any heirs as to the man's financial standing with the company at the time of death.

Menard's estate account page contains a one-line entry dated June 30, 1833, and refers to a $16.47 final balance, as shown in Ledger B. The fur company's clerk setting up a ledger page titled "Estate" is also a certain indication that this man is deceased and that he died prior to June 30, 1833.

The Upper Missouri Outfit's Ledger B also contains an account page (Figure 3) for a man named Colin Rose. The entries on this account page indicate that Colin Rose owed $17.58 on purchases at Fort Clark on July 3, 1832, that were subsequently transferred to Fort Union. The credit side of this man's account shows he was paid for services rendered beginning October 28, 1831 through 1832. Like Menard's account, this page contains a final balancing entry and the notation "Killed by the Ree Indians near Fort Cass Spring of 1833."

As in the case of Menard, an estate account was established for Colin Rose (Figure 4) in UMO Ledger C. This account contains a one-line closing entry dated June 30, 1833, like the entry on the Hilain Menard estate page.

A thorough search of the Upper Missouri Outfit's 1830-1833 records found no other account pages under the surname of Rose. The question is whether the Colin Rose listed in the UMO records, and clearly shown to have been killed alongside Hilain Menard and Hugh Glass, is the same person as the veteran trader and interpreter Edward Rose. It was not uncommon for a man to be referred to in the records of the fur trade by different first names. The Fort Hall records, for example, show Osborne Russell listed predominantly as John Russell and, in one instance, as William, but he was never listed as Osborne.[58] By contrast, if Edward Rose was using an alias or randomly assigned one by a UMO clerk, such a practice contradicts past fur company relationships in which Rose is uniformly listed in the records of the Missouri Fur Company, the Pacific Fur Company (Astorians) and the Henry/Ashley Company as Edward Rose.[59]

James Beckwourth, another mulatto mountain man known to have resided with the Crows, knew Edward Rose and referred to him as "one of the best interpreters ever known in the whole of Indian country." Beckwourth claims to have been at Fort Cass in the spring of 1833 and acknowledged "poor Rose" as one of the three trappers who died on the ice of the Yellowstone River.[60]

On the other hand, Chittenden may have been correct in concluding that Edward Rose died and was buried on the Missouri River across from the mouth of the Milk

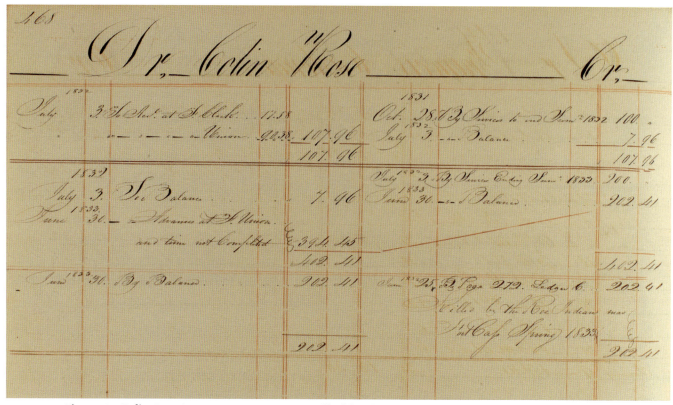

Figure 3: Colin Rose's account page notes "Killed by the Ree Indians near Fort Cass Spring 1833." American Fur Company Ledger, Upper Missouri Outfit, 1830-1834.

MISSOURI HISTORY MUSEUM, ST. LOUIS, MO

River. The records, journals and information reviewed for this essay found no information to contradict Chittenden's claim. The documents presented in this study provide proof that Hilain Menard and Colin Rose were the two UMO men who were killed in the spring of 1833 near Fort Cass. The true identity of Colin Rose will be better determined by a separate and focused research endeavor.

In addition to ledger pages for Colin Rose and Hilain Menard, the same two UMO ledger books contain account pages for Hugh Glass. The aforementioned credit and debit record from Ledger B, shown on pages viii-1 of this article, begins with an entry dated August 30, 1831. Like the Hilain Menard and Colin Rose account pages, there is a closing balance entry posted June 30, 1833. The figures on this ledger page indicate that Glass was indebted to the UMO in the amount of $544.50 at the end of 1832. This suggests that he was still alive in December of 1832.

A second account page (Figure 5) found in Ledger C is titled "Estate Hugh Glass." The only entry on this page, posted June 30, 1833, shows total purchases up to that date of $560. The account was made to balance by a credit of the same amount from Fort Union on the same date. This one-line entry, like the ones posted to Menard's and Rose's estate account pages, means this man is deceased, so the account was closed, and the books were balanced.

Thus, research in the ledger books of the American Fur Company's Upper Missouri Outfit proves that Colin Rose, Hilain Menard and Hugh Glass were killed by Arikara Indians near Fort Cass within the first six months of 1833. Two other contemporary historical sources describe the circumstances related to the death of Hugh Glass.

Figure 4: Estate of Colin Rose. American Fur Company Ledger, Upper Missouri Outfit, 1830-1834. MISSOURI HISTORY MUSEUM, ST. LOUIS, MO

One rendition of the story comes from Indian Agent John F. A. Sanford's letter written to Superintendent of Indian Affairs William Clark, dated July 26, 1833. Sanford reported that on his visit to "the remote tribes of the Upper Missouri," he learned the Arikara had abandoned the Missouri River in the fall of 1832 and their new location could not be ascertained. Sanford went on to state,

> During the last winter a war party belonging to that nation came on the Yellowstone below the Big Horn where they fell in with three men belonging to A. Fur Co. who they treacherously killed. Two of these men had been dispatched from Fort Cass (a new Fort mouth of Big Horn) in the morning with the express to go on to Fort Union; (mouth of Yellowstone) The third was a <u>free</u> man, a veteran Trapper who was accompanying the others as far as a camp of White Hunters some short distance below the Fort. They scalped them and left part of the Scalps of each tied to poles on the grounds of the Murder … The Names of the men killed are Rose, Menard & Glass.[61] [Emphasis in original]

While Sanford indicated the men who died with Glass were delivering an "express" to Fort Union, nowhere in the letter does he give their first names.[62] It is assumed Sanford's informant was Kenneth McKenzie, because Sanford visited Fort Union the summer of 1833. Sanford's comment that one of the dead trappers was a "free man," meaning a free trapper, and the other two men were employees of the fur company is verified by the UMO ledger pages which include "Freeman" in the title of Glass's account. The accounts for Rose and Menard show them earning wages.

During the years 1832-34, German aristocrat Alexander Philip Maximilian, Prince of Wied, traveled to the United States as part of his study of the Americas' natural history. Part of this excursion included a trip to the fur trading posts of the upper Missouri region. Accompanying the prince on this trip was artist Karl Bodmer.[63] The drawings, paintings and written narratives executed by these two men left a record which has proven invaluable to historians, naturalists and ethnologists.

The Prince's journal shows that on May 14, 1833, he and McKenzie encountered four men in a canoe coming down the Missouri River. These trappers brought news to McKenzie that Indians along the Yellowstone had killed three of his men. In an addendum to this journal entry, Maximilian later added that one of the trio killed along the Yellowstone was "Old Glass."[64] The timing of this encounter and McKenzie receiving news of three dead trappers coincides with the time of year recorded in the UMO ledger account pages for the death of Hilain Menard and Colin Rose.

Figure 5: Estate of Hugh Glass, American Fur Company Ledger, Upper Missouri Outfit, 1830-1834. MISSOURI HISTORY MUSEUM, ST. LOUIS, MO *

This concurrence provides additional verification that Hugh Glass and his companions were killed by the Arikara near Fort Cass in the spring of 1833.

Avenging Hugh Glass's death

Almost exactly a year later, Prince Maximilian heard mountain man Johnson Gardner's own story concerning Glass's death.[65] On his return trip to St. Louis, Maximilian fortuitously encountered Gardner near the Vermillion River in present day South Dakota. Maximilian's journal entry for May 8, 1834, records the seasoned trapper's tale of subterfuge and revenge:

> *We lit our fire on the beach in front of the forest, and Gardner told me about his various dangerous expeditions into Indian country and his skirmishes with the Indians. He was the one who killed the two Arikaras – from one of whom I have the scalp. The day before [he did so], the [Arikaras had] killed old [Hugh] Glass and his two companions. Old Glass went beaver hunting with two companions from Fort Cass on the Yellowstone River. As they crossed the ice of the Yellowstone farther downriver, all three of them were shot, scalped, and robbed by a war party of about eighty Arikaras hidden on the opposite bank. From there these Indians – so dangerous to the white men – moved to the sources of the Powder River. It so happened that Gardner, with about twenty men and some thirty horses, was camped there just then. While the Americans sat at several fires in the dark, the Indians appeared suddenly, greeted them in the Hidatsa language, surrounded the fires, and dried their shoes. Gardner, a man experienced in dealing with Indians, took safety precautions right away, especially since a Hidatsa woman with him informed him that the strangers were Arikaras.*[66]

Maximilian's account goes on to explain that the trappers suspected these Indians were trying to steal horses, and were thus on the alert for trouble. Gardner's men were able to capture three Arikara during the horse thieving attempt. The trappers observed that "One of them had old Glass's knife; the rifles of the murder victims had also been seen in the group." Some unsuccessful bartering between the trappers and Indians then took place over the stolen horses in exchange for the captives. One Indian hostage escaped and the remaining two were ultimately killed by the trappers. Seeing the Arikara with guns and knives known to belong to three fellow trappers had put Gardner and his men in a mood for vengeance rather than trade. Maximilian added that both hostages were "scalped, and I now own one of these scalps. I received the scalp mentioned above later from Mr. Chardon of Fort Union."⁶⁷

Maximilian's version indicated the two Arikara prisoners were shot and stabbed to death by the mountaineers. In his letter to Clark, Indian Agent Sanford explained that when the Arikara would not swap the stolen horses for the two prisoners, the trappers

> *killed those they had in possession – Good!! – Is it not time that the Government should put in execution some of their numerous & repeated threats against this band of Robbers & Murderers?*⁶⁸

Maximilian would write a later journal entry on May 21, 1834, with a revised version of the same series of events. Here he changed the ownership of the weapons:

> *The whites had seen the rifle of old Glass as well as the knife of another of the three slain men. The captives chanted their death songs, after they had stated their names and declared that they were brave men ... The two Indians were killed, and I own the scalp of one of them.*⁶⁹

Historian Aubrey Haines, in his biographical essays on Glass and Gardner, stated that the two Arikara were scalped and then burned alive by Gardner. While Prince Maximilian's May 1834 journal entry specified that Johnson Gardner, as the avenger of Hugh Glass, scalped and killed the Arikara prisoners, neither he nor Indian agent John F. A. Sanford said anything about the two Indians being burned to death. Glass biographer John Myers also related that Gardner burned two Arikara in revenge for the death of Glass and his fellow trappers. Both historians cited Sanford's July 26, 1833, letter to Clark as the source. Myers quoted Sanford writing "John Soy Gardner caught up with a couple of the murderers a few weeks later and burned them to death."⁷⁰ A thorough examination and study of Sanford's original letter found no such comment, but, based on the Haines and Myers publications, many historians still attribute such an act to Johnson Gardner.

Sanford's original letter indicates that the trappers killed the two Indians when the stolen horses were not returned. He made no mention of them being scalped or how they died. Sanford's report is also silent on the name of the trappers' leader. Haines used a quote from George Catlin to indict Gardner for burning Indians alive. According to Haines, Catlin allegedly stated that a few weeks before departing Fort Union, he was told by McKenzie that a group of trappers had burned two Arikara to death on the prairie.⁷¹ Catlin visited Fort Union the summer of 1832 and was returning to St. Louis by the end of July, arriving there in late October 1832. Therefore the burning of the two Arikara, as reported to him, would have happened in the summer of 1832 when Hugh Glass was still alive and Fort Cass was still under construction.

A lost manuscript

In addition to providing greater detail to the historical narrative on the death of Hugh Glass and Johnson Gardner's revenge upon the Arikara, the Prince of Wied's journal also contributed two other interesting tidbits. During his stay at Fort Union in October 1833, the Prince often socialized with the post's chief clerk James Archdale Hamilton.⁷² At these evening gatherings, Hamilton

> *would read to us from his manuscript of the life story of old Glass, who, together with two other white men, had been shot by Indians near the Yellowstone in spring 1833; most likely [the Indians were] Arikaras. During the previous winter, Glass had told Mr. Hamilton the story of his whole life, which would make a very interesting book. Mr. Hamilton collected in this manuscript many a fascinating*

note about these Indians, and Catlin made me a drawing of old Glass.[73]

In addition to reaffirming the spring of 1833 as the time of Glass's death, this passage reveals that Hamilton wrote an account of the life of Hugh Glass and that George Catlin sketched a likeness of the old mountaineer and presented it to the Prince. To date, no such manuscript on the life of Hugh Glass authored by a former Fort Union clerk has come to light, nor has a drawing of Glass executed by George Catlin yet been discovered.

Beckwourth's tales

James P. Beckwourth also provided an account of Hugh Glass's demise in which Beckwourth stated that he was at Fort Cass in the spring of 1833 and found the bodies of the trappers lying on the ice. Beckwourth's account comes from a book of reminiscences published in 1856 about his adventures in the Rockies which he had related to writer Thomas D. Bonner. Beckwourth's book has been shown to include several inaccuracies stemming from his mixing dates for certain events and placing people at places in the wrong year. His tendency to glorify his own exploits also clouds the facts of some actual events.

Beckwourth's version began with his arrival at Fort Cass in 1833, and a comment that Glass and two comrades had been sent from the fort to the camp of Johnson Gardner, some eighteen miles down the Yellowstone, to notify him that Beckwourth had arrived. Beckwourth's story described the three trappers' fight with the Arikara as an attempt by the Indians to burn the trappers out. Rather than submit to the savages, Glass, Rose and Menard blew themselves up with three kegs of gunpowder they were carrying. This circumstance caused the bodies of the three men to appear burned and blackened when they were recovered for burial.[74]

With the exception of Glass and two men having been killed on the Yellowstone River in the spring of 1833, the rest of Beckwourth's story failed to match any verifiable accounts from the period. Three other contemporary renditions all agree that Johnson Gardner was camped near the headwaters of the Powder River at the time Glass, Rose and Menard were killed. Moreover, it seems farfetched that these three men, if actually sent to notify Gardner that the "great" Beckwourth was now at Fort Cass, would be carrying three kegs of powder.

Beckwourth ended his version of the Glass story by describing the burial of the three trappers near Fort Cass and the Crow Indians' deep emotional reaction to the death of these veterans:

> *We returned together and buried the three men, amid the most terrible scenes that I had ever witnessed. The crying was truly appalling. The three men were well known, and highly esteemed by the Crows. When their bodies were lowered to their last resting-place, numberless fingers were voluntarily chopped off and thrown into the graves; hair and trinkets of every description were also contributed, and the graves were finally filled up.*[75]

There is no way to know if the Crows held any of these men in such high esteem that they would react to their deaths by cutting off fingers and tossing them into the graves. If Edward Rose was actually one of the trappers killed, the death of a longtime friend to the tribe could have elicited the response described. The only way to ascertain the veracity of this part of Beckwourth's story would be to locate the graves of the three mountain men and perform an archaeological excavation. Proof of Beckwourth's story would be the presence of "extra" finger bones.

Unanswered questions

The Arikara attack on the William Ashley party in June of 1823 had resulted in an all-out war against the tribe which concluded in the total destruction of the Arikara villages. This caused the tribe to relocate further up the Missouri River near the Mandan Indians. By 1833, the Arikara had worn out their welcome with the Mandans and were essentially homeless, forcing their various bands to roam the country between the Yellowstone and upper Missouri River.[76] Thus an underlying irony for Hugh Glass was that the 1823 Arikara fight, in which Glass participated and was wounded, had put into motion events culminating in an Arikara war party lying in wait near Fort Cass on the spring morning in 1833 when Glass, Rose and Menard crossed the frozen Yellowstone River.

While there are good reasons to question aspects of the various accounts of the death of Hugh Glass, the historical documents presented in this essay clearly substantiate that Hugh Glass, Colin Rose and Hilain Menard were killed by Arikara Indians near Fort Cass in the spring of 1833. However, the examination of the historical record surrounding this event has created other questions:

Was the Colin Rose listed in the records of the UMO actually the infamous Edward Rose?

If not, where and how did Edward Rose die?

Would a thorough search of items once belonging to Maximilian Prince of Wied locate Catlin's drawing of Hugh Glass?

What happened to James Archdale Hamilton's manuscript on the life of Hugh Glass?

Clay J. Landry is an avid researcher whose study and writing on the material culture items used by the men of the Rocky Mountain fur trade has resulted in numerous published essays and presentations at fur trade symposia. Landry served as wilderness technical advisor for the Academy Award winning movie, The Revenant *(2015).*

NOTES

1. John Myers Myers, *Pirate, Pawnee and Mountain Man: The Saga of Hugh Glass* (Boston, MA: Little, Brown and Company, 1963), now published as *The Saga of Hugh Glass, Pirate, Pawnee and Mountain Man* (Lincoln, NE: Bison Book Printing, 1976). While the Myers book is a comprehensive analysis of the historical origins of the Hugh Glass saga, the book is not annotated. His discussions of the differences and likenesses of the accounts include detailed attributions but the book does not include a bibliography.
2. Dale Morgan, *The West of William H. Ashley* (Denver, CO: Old West Publishing Company, 1964); Richard M. Clokey, *William H. Ashley, Enterprise and Politics in the Trans-Mississippi West*, (Norman, OK: University of Oklahoma Press, 1980).
3. Morgan, *West of William Ashley*, 30.
4. For an in-depth discussion of the Arikara battle, see William R. Nester, *The Arikara War, The First Plains Indian War, 1823* (Missoula, MT: Mountain Press Publishing Company, 2001).
5. For a delineation of these circumstances and decisions, see Morgan, *West of William Ashley*, 58, 63; Clokey, *William Ashley*, 113; and Letter, William Ashley to Colonel John O'Fallon, Fort Brassaux, July 19, 1823, published in Morgan, *West of William Ashley*, 47.
6. Charles L. Camp, ed., *James Clyman, Frontiersman: The Adventures of a Trapper and Covered Wagon Emigrant as Told in his Own Reminiscences and Diaries* (Portland, OR: The Champoeg Press, 1960), 18-19.
7. Myers, *Saga of Hugh Glass*, 111-124.
8. Ibid.
9. Letter of Daniel T. Potts to T. Cochlen, July 7, 1824, Yellowstone National Park Museum Collection, Albright Visitors Center, Mammoth, WY.
10. Myers, *Saga of Hugh Glass,* 185.
11. Ibid.
12. Only the version of the Glass story written by Edmund Flagg in 1839 provided the name of the younger man of the two left by Henry to care for the mauled Hugh Glass. Flagg named the younger man as "Bridges" and from this, many historians have concluded that the younger man could have been James Bridger. Edmund Flagg, "Adventures at the head-waters of the Missouri," *Louisville Literary News-Letter*, September 7, 1839, 1:326-327, reprinted in the *Illinois Weekly State Journal*, September 19, 1839.
13. The first version of the Glass story to be printed names neither of the two men left to

care for Glass. "The Missouri Trapper," *Port-Folio,* Philadelphia, PA, March 1825, 214-219, reprinted in the *Missouri Intelligencer,* June 18, 1825. First attributed to Alphonso Wetmore, the article was later shown to be written by James E. Hall, the *Port-Folio* editor. The second version published in 1830 stated that "A man named Fitzgerald and a youth of seventeen" accepted Henry's proposal to remain behind with Glass. Phillip St. George Cooke, "Scenes and Adventures in the Army," *St. Louis Beacon,* December 2-9, 1830, republished in the *Southern Literary Messenger* in 1842. Edmund Flagg's version first named the older man "Fitzpatrick," which changed later in the story to "Fitzgerald."

14 "The Missouri Trapper," *Port-Folio.*

15 www.genealogybank.com.

16 Charles L. Camp, ed., *George Yount and his Chronicles of the West, comprising extracts from his "memoirs" and from the Orange Clark "Narrative"* (Denver, Co: Old West Publishing Company, 1966), 205.

17 Joy L. Poole, ed., *Over the Santa Fe Trail to Mexico: The Travel Diaries and Autobiography of Dr. Rowland Willard* (Norman, OK: The Arthur H. Clark Company, 2015), 23, 28, 29, 39. Willard was born in 1794 and died in 1884.

18 Ibid., 42-43.

19 Rowland Willard's Journal, 1825-1827, Yale University Library, Beinecke Rare Book and Manuscript Library, WA MSS S-2512.

20 Poole, *Over the Santa Fe Trail to Mexico,* 45, 47, 52.

21 Ibid., 147.

22 Ibid., 148.

23 Ibid., 147-148.

24 From the time of the Lewis and Clark Expedition to the era of the mountain men, the grizzly bear was referred to as the "white bear."

25 Ibid., 149.

26 Ibid., 150.

27 Rufus Sage, *Scenes in the Rocky Mountains and in Oregon, California, New Mexico, Texas, And The Grand Prairies* (Philadelphia, PA: Carey & Hart, 1846), 117-118; George F. Ruxton, Esq., *Adventures in Mexico and the Rocky Mountains* (London: John Murray, Albemarle Street, 1847), 271-273.

28 Jon T. Coleman, *Here Lies Hugh Glass - A Mountain Man, A Bear, and The Rise Of The American Nation* (New York, NY: Hill and Wang, 2012), 127.

29 Ibid.

30 Edmund Flagg, "Adventures at the head-waters of the Missouri," *Illinois Weekly State Journal,* September 19, 1839.

31 Camp, *George Yount and his Chronicles of the West,* 205.

32 Ibid.

33 John S. Gray, "Young Fur Trapper, Phillip Covington Travels to the Rockies with William Sublette," *Colorado Heritage Magazine* 1 (1982): 11-25.

34 Hiram M. Chittenden, *The American Fur Trade of the Far West,* 2 vols. (1935; Lincoln, NE: University of Nebraska Press, 1986), 1:330. Free Trappers were not employees of any company, and were therefore not obligated to trap and trade with any particular fur company. For more detail on trappers' status see Washington Irving, *The Adventures of Captain Bonneville, U.S.A. in the Rocky Mountains and the Far West,* edited by Edgeley W. Todd, (Norman, OK: University of Oklahoma Press, 1986), 69.

35 Raymond Wood and Mike Casler, "A Revised History of Fort Floyd," *North Dakota History Journal of the Northern Plains* 80, no. 4 (Winter 2015): 3-13; Chittenden, *American Fur Trade,* 1:330. According to Morgan, *West of William Ashley,* 311n397, the letters on which Chittenden based these assertions are no longer extant.

36 For the movements of Etienne Provost during 1828 see Jack B. Tykal, *Etienne Provost - Man of the Mountains* (Liberty UT: Eagle's View Publishing, 1989), 84-85.

37 Fred R. Gowans, *Rocky Mountain Rendezvous* (Layton, UT: Gibbs M. Smith, Inc., 1985), 66.

38 Chittenden, *American Fur Trade,* 1:330.

39 Letter, Kenneth McKenzie to the Gentleman in Charge of Fort Tecumseh, May 5, 1830.

40 Ibid.

41 The Chouteau Collection, 1752-1925. Missouri History Museum, St. Louis, MO, Library and Archives. Reels 17 and 18.

42 Fur Company Ledgers and Account Books, 1802-1871, Ledger, American Fur Company, Western, Upper Missouri Outfit, 1831-1835, Reel 5, Book T, page 298, Missouri History Museum, St. Louis, MO.

43 Chittenden, *American Fur Trade,* 2:694.

44 Aubrey Haines, "Hugh Glass," in *Mountain Men and the Fur Trade of the Far West,* edited by Leroy R. Hafen, 10 vols. (Glendale, CA: The Arthur H. Clark Company, 1968), 6:168n15.

45 Dale Morgan, *Jedediah Smith and the Opening of the West* (Lincoln, NE: University of Nebraska Press, 1953), 148.

46 Chittenden, *American Fur Trade,* 1:336.

47 Ibid.; Letter from Kenneth McKenzie to Pierre Chouteau, December 11, 1831, is quoted by Chittenden in *American Fur Trade,* however this letter cannot be located.

48 Jim Hardee, *Obstinate Hope, The Western Expeditions of Nathaniel Wyeth, Volume One: 1832-1833* (Pinedale, WY: Sublette County Historical Society, 2013), 369.

49 Ledger, American Fur Company, Western, Upper Missouri Outfit, 1830-1834, Reel 5, Book T, page 298, Missouri History Museum, St. Louis, MO.

50 Myers, *Saga of Hugh Glass,* 224; Haines, "Hugh Glass," 168; Chittenden, *American Fur Trade,* 2:694.

51 Willis Blenkinsop, "Edward Rose," *Mountain Men and The Fur Trade of the Far West,* 9:336.

52 Reuben Holmes, "Five Scalps," first published in the *Weekly Reveille,* July 17 and 24, 1848, republished in Stella Drumm, ed., *Glimpses of the Past* 5 (1938).

53 Blenkinsop, "Edward Rose," 336-344.

54 Chittenden, *American Fur Trade,* 2:678-679. See also John C. Ewers, ed., *Adventures of Zenas Leonard Fur Trader,* (Norman, OK: University of Oklahoma Press, 1959) 51-52, 147-149.

55 Chittenden, *American Fur Trade,* 2:679.

56 Haines, "Hugh Glass," 168; Fred R. Gowans, *Mountain Man & Grizzly* (Orem, UT: Mountain Grizzly Productions, 1986), 194.

57 Ledger, American Fur Company, Western, Upper Missouri Outfit, 1830-1834, Reel 5, Book T, pages 250, 298; Ledger, American Fur Company, Western, Upper Missouri Outfit, 1831-1836, Reel 6, Book W, page 189, Missouri History Museum, St. Louis, MO. In the records of the AMFC retail store in St. Louis, a "Hylaine Menard" is listed as a member of the 1829 William Henry Vanderburg expedition.

58 Clay Landry, "Rolling A Stone Into The Garden: The History and Trade Ledgers of Fort Hall, 1834-1837," presented at the 1997 Fur Trade Symposium, Museum of the Mountain Man, Pinedale, WY.

59 Clay Landry, "John Reed's Journal: Clerk to the Overland Astorians," presented at the 2006 Fur Trade Symposium, Museum of the Fur Trade, Chadron, NE, and published in the *Museum of the Fur Trade Quarterly* 43, nos. 3, 4 (Fall/Winter 2007): 18; Manuel Lisa's Men – List and Accounts, May 2-6, 1812, Missouri History Museum, Fur Trade Collection, Box 1/3; Morgan, *West of William Ashley,* 52.

60 Thomas D. Bonner, ed., *The Life and Adventures of James P. Beckwourth,* (New York, NY: Harper & Brothers, 1856), 84, 259.

61 Letter, J. F. A. Sanford to William Clark, July 26, 1833, Records of the Department of the Interior, Office of Indian Affairs, Letters Received 1824-1881. Record Group 75. The original letter was attached to an official report forwarded to Washington on August 17, 1833, by William Clark.

62 Delivering or riding an "express" meant that a man was sent for the sole purpose of delivering a message and he was to travel as rapidly as possible. This was the fastest means of delivering messages that the fur companies could devise, and the men were paid extra for accomplishing the task. Clay Landry, "Rolling A Stone Into The Garden."

63 Stephen S. Witte and Marsha V. Gallagher, eds., *The North American Journals of Prince Maximilian of Wied,* 3 vols. (Norman, OK: University of Oklahoma Press, 2010), passim.

64 Ibid., 2:115.

65 Ibid., 3:301.

66 Ibid.

67 Ibid., 3:301-302.

68 Letter, J. F. A. Sanford to William Clark, July 26, 1833.

69 Witte and Gallagher, *Journals of Prince Maximilian,* 2:128.

70 Haines, "Hugh Glass," 169; Haines, "Johnson Gardner," 159; Myers, *Saga of Hugh Glass,* 225.

71 George Catlin, *North American Indians,* (Edinburgh: John Grant, 1903) 2:207.

72 Chittenden, *American Fur Trade,* 1:387. Hamilton was an Englishman seeking anonymity for some undisclosed offense in England. His real name was James Archdale Hamilton Palmer. See also Myers, *Saga of Hugh Glass,* 220-222.

73 George Catlin would not have been at Fort Union in October of 1833, so when and how he presented Maximilian with a drawing of Hugh Glass is not clear. Witte and Gallagher, *Journals of Prince Maximilian,* 3:6, 7.

74 Bonner, *James P. Beckwourth,* 253-258.

75 Ibid., 258.

76 Nester, *The Arikara War, The First Plains Indian War, 1823,* 210.

"This Outrageous Desease" – Charles Larpenteur's Observations of the 1837 Smallpox Epidemic

by Michael M. Casler

The smallpox epidemic of 1837 devastated the Indian tribes living along the Missouri River. The literature on the epidemic has mainly focused on the destruction of the Mandan Indians living near Fort Clark, with little information on its progress farther upriver at Forts Union and McKenzie. This article details the disease at those sites and the impact it had on nomadic tribes on the upper Missouri. Based on observations from Charles Larpenteur's *Original Journal* and other primary sources, this analysis uses "on scene" descriptions of the patients, examines the spread of the disease, and considers the medical treatments for smallpox used by fur traders 178 years ago.[1]

Extant first person accounts of fur traders on the upper Missouri River during the nineteenth century are few. Only five have seen print: those recorded by Francis A. Chardon, Charles Larpenteur, Rudolf F. Kurz, Henry Boller and James H. Chambers. Of the five, only Chardon and Larpenteur

The hand-colored aquatint *Fort Union on the Missouri*, based on a c.1834 painting by Karl Bodmer, shows the American Fur Company fort on the bank of the Missouri River as Native Americans encamp nearby to trade.
JOSLYN ART MUSEUM, OMAHA, NEBRASKA, GIFT OF THE ENRON ART FOUNDATION, 1986.49.517.28

were eyewitnesses to the devastation of the smallpox epidemic of 1837 on the upper Missouri. Chardon's day-to-day journal at Fort Clark charts the progression of the disease from the first death of a young Mandan man on July 14, 1837, through the last mention of a smallpox-related death in May 1838.[2] Charles Larpenteur's version of events he witnessed as a junior clerk at Fort Union was first published in his autobiography in 1898, twenty-six years after his death.[3]

Since its publication, Larpenteur's *Forty Years a Fur Trader* has been considered primary source material by historians of the upper Missouri fur trade. The book was edited by Elliot Coues, MD, whose main interest was medicine and ornithology. In 1893, he began editing and publishing journals of American western exploration, starting with the *Journals of Lewis and Clark*. However, Coues's editing of the Larpenteur manuscript has been questioned – a question unanswered until 2007 with the publication of *The Original Journal of Charles Larpenteur*.[4] Comparison with the original journal clarifies that Coues rewrote the story of smallpox at Fort Union, using only the barest of facts from Larpenteur, to sensationalize the story of the contagion. Larpenteur's original journal entries provide direct observations about the smallpox epidemic and its spread among the fort's personnel and the Assiniboine.

The steamboat *St. Ange* was sketched by Rudolf F. Kurz in 1851. Built in 1849 for swift travel on the Missouri River, this side-wheeler of 254 tons was similar to the *St. Peters* of 1837.
NATIONAL ARCHIVES NAA-2856-53

The invisible cargo

On April 17, 1837, the *St. Peters*, annual supply steamer of Pratte, Chouteau & Company (previously The Western Department of the American Fur Company), departed St. Louis for the journey up the Missouri River.[5] The hold of the *St. Peters* carried almost $45,000 in trade goods and supplies for several upriver company posts.[6] Also stowed onboard were the annual government annuities, in the form of supplies and merchandise, for the Omaha, Pawnee, Sioux and Arikara nations. Besides the trade goods and annuities, the boat also carried Joshua Pilcher and John Dougherty, agents for the Sioux and Omaha/Pawnee respectively, along with supercargo William N. Fulkerson, sub-agent for the upper Missouri tribes.[7]

Shortly before the steamboat had covered the 439 river miles from St. Louis to Fort Leavenworth, smallpox, the invisible cargo, broke out among the passengers and crew.[8] In a series of letters to William Clark, Joshua Pilcher would describe the outbreak almost neutrally, in the most general terms. His first letter, penned on June 10, 1837, stated, "the smallpox broke out on board the steamboat before she passed Leavenworth her trip from thence to my post was protracted to forty days."[9]

Writing to Clark again a few weeks later, Pilcher said only that

> *it is regretted that the apprehensions expressed in my letter of the 10th Ultimo respecting the smallpox have been partly realized & that from all information I have been able to get, the disease is rapidly spreading.*[10]

Ten months later, on February 5, 1838, Pilcher would mention that a "Mulatto" deck hand had been the first to fall ill.[11]

The steamboat next approached Joseph Robidoux's post at the Black Snake Hills, along the Missouri River near present-day Saint Joseph, Missouri. Pilcher wrote,

> *a gentleman of the Indian department suggested to the Capt. of the boat that it would be well to put the man ashore and leave him – the Capt. doubting the*

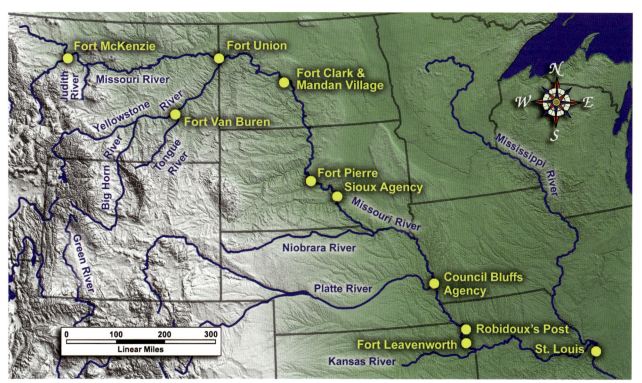

Missouri River forts exposed to smallpox carried by the steamboat *St. Peters* in the summer of 1837. Departing St. Louis on April 17, the boat traveled 1,766 river miles to Fort Union, arriving on June 24, 1837. Fort McKenzie was infected via keelboats from Fort Union. MAP BY CLINT GILCHRIST

[malady] and having use for the man declined doing so.[12]

By the time the *St. Peters* reached the Indian agency at Council Bluffs, approximately 222 river miles above Fort Leavenworth, several others on board had passed from the incubation period into the sometimes contagious "prodrome" stage of the disease. This early phase usually lasts two to four days, and is characterized by high fever of 101 to 104 degrees, malaise, prostration, cough, headache, backache, and for some, vomiting.[13] Here, Dougherty disembarked, taking the annuities for the agency. Three Arikara women who had been living with relatives among the Pawnee boarded the boat to return to their people upriver.[14]

After departing Council Bluffs, the boat struggled upstream due to low water in the Missouri River, and became stranded at the mouth of the Running Water, or Niobrara River. From here, on May 29, 1837, Captain Bernard Pratte, Jr., wrote to his cousin Pierre Chouteau, Jr., describing the river conditions, the problems he expected in delivering the cargo, and news that "as an added blessing I have small pox on board. We buried Vital Papin, and have 8 new cases, two since yesterday. I do not know where this will end."[15] Though Captain Pratte was aware of the seriousness of smallpox, he had no good choices for dealing with it.

The boat reached Pilcher's Sioux Agency near Fort Lookout on June 5, 1837.[16] By now the three Arikara women who had boarded at Council Bluffs, some 430 river miles below, had fallen ill. Pilcher wrote,

they all took the disease and were much afflicted with it when they passed my Agency and I was informed that they had not recovered from it when they reached the Mandan villages.[17]

WHAT WE KNOW TODAY ABOUT SMALLPOX
from the Center for Disease Control

Smallpox is an acute, contagious, and sometimes fatal disease caused by the *Variola* virus (an Orthopox virus), and marked by a fever and a distinctive progressive skin rash … There are four types of *Variola major* smallpox: **ordinary** (the most frequent type, accounting for 90 percent or more cases); **modified** (mild and occurring in previously vaccinated persons); **flat** and **hemorrhagic** (both rare and very severe). Historically, ordinary *Variola major* has an overall fatality rate of about 30 percent; however flat and hemorrhagic smallpox usually are fatal.[1]

The "flat" form of smallpox is associated with minute hemorrhagic spots on the skin called petechiae, and bleeding occurs from the front part of the eye, eyelids and mucous membranes, particularly in the nose. The blood maintains a high level of viruses in this type of smallpox as opposed to the other clinical forms of the disease. Following a shortened incubation period, symptoms may include high fever, severe headache, and abdominal pain.[2]

The Center for Disease Control currently estimates that for ordinary smallpox, with a fatality rate of 30 percent, one infected person can infect five others, and by the fifth generation of the disease, 3,125 people will be infected.[3] As true today as in 1837, there is no known cure or treatment for smallpox, but as of 1980, the World Health Organization declared smallpox eradicated in nature following a worldwide vaccination program. Reportedly, there are 2 labs in the world that still have the virus. One is the CDC in Atlanta and the other is in the Russian Federation.

1 Center for Disease Control, *Smallpox Fact Sheet*, 1, 3.
2 Center for Disease Control, *Overview of Smallpox, Clinical Presentations, and Medical Care of Smallpox Patients – Annex 1* found online at http://emergency.cdc.gov/agent/smallpox/medical-management, 5, 6 (accessed June 18, 2015).
3 Center for Disease Control, *Fact Sheet*, 11.

Twenty-five days after the *St. Peters* left the Sioux Agency, smallpox would erupt among the Sioux.[18]

The *St. Peters's* next destination was Fort Pierre, where it arrived on June 6, a day after leaving the Sioux Agency. While at the fort, the boat crew off-loaded a cargo of trade goods worth $21,366.[19] Boarding the boat here were Jacob Halsey, his pregnant mixed-blood wife, and their three-year-old son, en route to Fort Union to take over its management. Also embarking was fur trader Pierre D. Papin, and a Blood Indian man returning upriver to Fort McKenzie, above the mouth of the Marias.[20] The *St. Peters* left Fort Pierre on June 7, with Fort Clark as its next stop.

Eight mackinaws shuttling down to St. Louis, and loaded with the combined upriver fur returns from Fort Union, arrived at Fort Clark at 10 a.m. on June 16. The following day, Francis Chardon, Fort Clark's manager, boarded one of the mackinaws for a trip down the Missouri to intercept the *St. Peters* on its way upriver. The steamer carried his young son on a visit to his father. Chardon recorded his departure from Fort Clark on June 17, followed by the mackinaw's stranding "at the point of woods below the Square Hills" due to high winds.[21] On the 18th, he noted the crews had to unload one mackinaw due to its taking on water, wetting the cargo of packs.[22] On the same day, around 2 p.m., the *St. Peters* came into sight. Chardon boarded the steamer for his return back up to Fort Clark. If Chardon was anxious to see his son, he made no mention of the lad in his journal.[23] The *St. Peters* arrived at Fort Clark on Monday, June 19, at 3 p.m. The crew off-loaded $7,464 in trade goods, along with the passengers bound for this location.[24] Pierre Papin, who had boarded at Fort Pierre, went ashore along with the trio of Arikara women and the "wife and children of one of the headmen of the village."[25] As was common practice upon the arrival of the annual steamboat, a "frolick" took place that night among the boat crew, fort

The steamboat *St. Peters* docked at Fort Pierre on the Missouri River on June 6, 1837. Frederick Behman's 1854 watercolor *View of Fort Pierre* shows a bustling and well-appointed trading post. SOUTH DAKOTA STATE HISTORICAL SOCIETY

personnel and local Indians. The next morning, the steamboat headed for Fort Union, its final upriver stop.[26]

Curiously, Chardon did not mention the presence of smallpox on or before the boat's arrival at Fort Clark (see Arp article, this volume). If all of the affected passengers and crew had entered either the recovery or incubation stages of the disease upon arrival at Fort Clark, Chardon would have been unaware of any danger.[27]

Outbreak at Fort Union

It is at this juncture that Larpenteur's journal, in his own words rather than Elliot Coues's, sheds new light on his time at Fort Union and the spread of smallpox farther upriver:

On the way coming to this Post there were two individuals which dyed of this desase and several other cases ocoured before the arrival of the Boat at Fort Union with the exeption of Mr J Halsey a partener in the Company which came to take charge of the Post who some days previous to his arrival was taken by this outrageous Desease.[28]

Here Larpenteur proves what has been long suspected – a number of people were infectious while the boat was stopped at Fort Clark. Moreover, within a day or two of the *St. Peters* leaving Fort Clark, smallpox erupted onboard again, this time manifesting as the highly dangerous "flat" or "hemorrhagic" variety.[29]

Both Jacob Halsey and his unnamed pregnant wife became infected a couple of days after boarding the steamboat at Fort Pierre on June 7. Because the smallpox virus has a typical incubation period of

George Catlin's 1832 painting, *Distant View of the Mandan Village*, shows Fort Clark to the left of the Indian lodges. Catlin described the village site as "one of the most beautiful and pleasing that can be seen in the world." The steamboat *St. Peters* brought smallpox to Fort Clark on June 19, 1837. SMITHSONIAN AMERICAN ART MUSEUM #1985.66.379

twelve to fourteen days, they would have fallen ill within a day or two after departing Fort Clark, about June 21 or 22. Larpenteur did not say who fell ill first, but he described Mrs. Halsey's situation on the steamboat:

> It happened that a few days before her arrival [at Fort Union] she had had a lying in and Brought fourth a female child to the wourld and emmidiately was taken by the Small Pox During her agonies in her illness she fell out of her bed Broke one of her blood vessels and bled to death.[30]

Doctors now recognize that smallpox during pregnancy is more severe than in non-pregnant women or adult men. Fatalities for expectant mothers varied widely among outbreaks; estimates for an 1830 epidemic reached 81.5 percent.[31] It is thought that due to a suppressed immune system, pregnant women have a significantly greater chance that the infection will manifest in the more serious form of hemorrhagic smallpox.[32] Even more tragically, hemorrhagic cases usually result in either miscarriage or premature birth before the mother's death.[33]

The *St. Peters* arrived at Fort Union, the steamboat's final stop, on June 24, and would begin its downriver return trip to St. Louis before the end of the month.[34] The crew off-loaded close to $16,000 in trade goods at the fort.[35] Disembarking here were Jacob Halsey assuming his new job as manager, and his two children, besides other passengers who may have already been ill. Though it was known as early as 1813 that smallpox could be passed from mother to child during birth, Larpenteur did not say, and may not have known, whether Halsey's newborn was sick when she arrived at Fort Union.[36]

Jacob Halsey had been inoculated at some point in his life. When he arrived at Fort Union, he suffered from a "modified" form of smallpox.[37] According to Larpenteur,

> Mr Halsey was now at his worse but was not considered dangerous as it was the distinct small Pox. finely he recovered and hopes was entertained that there would be no more cases. he had kept himself confined to this room and no one to wait on him but those who had had it or that was well vaxinated and shoud good marks.[38]

Halsey's young son, however, was in the incubation stage of the disease when he disembarked at Fort Union. The youth probably became infected while confined to the family's cabin as both parents entered the symptomatic stage of the disease. By this point, the child already had prolonged face-to-face contact with his parents and they became the vector of his infection.

Five months later, Halsey would pen, "Fifteen days after I was taken sick a second case of this detestable pest made its appearance in the fort."[39] Larpenteur echoed this:

> unfortunately our joyful hopes were soon blighted by a new case which made its appearance on Mr Halseys son – and on

A portrait of Charles Larpenteur, clerk at Fort Union in 1837, appears on the 1898 frontispiece of *Forty Years a Fur Trader*, Elliot Coues's version of Larpenteur's story. SUBLETTE COUNTY HISTORICAL SOCIETY/MUSEUM OF THE MOUNTAIN MAN

> the same day Mr E. T. Denig a clerk of this Post was taken by a violent fever.[40]

Something about the child's symptoms panicked fort personnel and prompted the clerks to consult a medical text from the post library.

Modern Domestic Medicine was consulted during the epidemic at Forts Clark and McKenzie as well. The American Fur Company (AFC) stocked each of its posts with the 499-page 1829 edition costing $2.26 each. Robert Thomas was a New York physician who had compiled the medical manual for the use of laymen. The book documented accepted, regular treatments for a wide variety of medical problems, ranging from venereal disease to gunshot wounds.[41] Larpenteur recounted that

> Emmidiately after Mr Halseys sons case and fearful happrension of more Doctor [Thomas] Medical Book was braught

down from the Library and the treatment of small Pox vaxination noculation was read over and over and was informed that by noculation that the small Pox would be much lighter and [a] great deal less danger haprehended that by preparing the system well before the opperation that one case out of six hundread might prove fatal.[42]

Having read up on what to do, Larpenteur noted:

It was after this doctrine that wee all consented to noculation as to my self I do not pretend to say that I have more sence then those who I am under and am duty bound to serve and obey but I know I am no doctor nor fore tellar what as been done was intended for the good of the Company and the one of the Tribe.[43]

In 1837, Charles Larpenteur had been employed at Fort Union for only four years. Still a junior clerk in the fur trade hierarchy, he was compelled to follow orders. It was under these circumstances that he and the other clerks read the instructions, prior to inoculating Indian wives and mixed-blood *engagés* at the fort. According to Dr. Thomas:

The following circumstances are deserving of attention in inoculating for the Cow Pox, and substituting this mild and safe disease for the dangerous and pestilential one, the small pox.

That the matter with which we inoculate, be not taken later in the disease than the ninth day.

That the fluid be perfectly transparent, as it is not to be depended upon when it is in any degree opaque.

That the matter taken should be allowed to dry gradually and thoroughly before it is laid by for use, when not employed immediately, or in its fluid state.

That the punctures with the besmeared lancet be done as superficially as possible, and only one made in the same arm.

Here it may not be improper to remark, that the inoculation for this disease will not be likely to succeed well if there be any herpetic eruption on the skin ... It will be of the highest importance after vaccine inoculation to ascertain fully that the vesicle in the arm has not acted locally, but that it has effected the desired change in the constitution. With this view, it may be advisable to re-vaccinate at some after period, to test the security from any exposure hereafter to variolous infection.[44]

Having considered this expert advice, Larpenteur reported,

It was agreed that they all be noculated first their systems should be prepared great preparations for death next morning only behold the greates most skillful [physician] in the present wourld would not have ventured the like to give small Pox to seventeen persons whom were all obliged to [reside] within the Limits of about one hundred feet. they were noculated on the 12th [July] and on the 20th in the evening were all taken with the fever and that of the hottest kind Deceived much beyond all expectations by noculation which was to be of the mildest kind proved of the worse kind that of the confluent 4 [cases] and the Balance was the distinct and that so thick that it could scarcely be distinguished from the confluent.[45]

Probably due to a lack of any cowpox material, the clerks at Fort Union proceeded to inoculate people with live smallpox taken from Halsey. This method, known as variolation, had been the only practice known prior to the nineteenth century.[46]

Larpenteur's description of an eight-day incubation period, followed by an eruptive stage with immediate display of pustules, suggests that the matter used for inoculation, taken from Jacob Halsey, brought on not the ordinary variety of smallpox, but a more virulent form.[47] The seven women and ten men would have been extremely contagious, with sores inside the mouth as well as over the entire body. In this case, the rash would have given way rapidly to the hardened pustules most characteristic of smallpox. Intense itching and fever accompany this phase, which normally lasts about ten days.[48]

There is no specific treatment for smallpox except isolation and supportive care. Dr. Thomas recommended management of patients as follows:

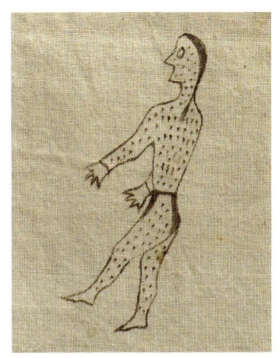

A detail from the Long Soldier Hunkpapa Lakota winter count for 1810-11 shows a man with smallpox. In 1837, smallpox spread to the Sioux along the Missouri River from the steamboat *St. Peters*. NATIONAL MUSEUM OF THE AMERICAN INDIAN/SMITHSONIAN INSTITUTION #NMAI 11/6720. PHOTO BY ERNEST AMOROSO.

> *To moderate and confine the fever within due bounds, it will be essentially necessary to keep the patient cool, by allowing a free admission of pure air into his chamber ... by frequently giving him cold diluting fluids to drink such as lemonade, imperial barley water or thin gruel acidulated with lemon or orange juice; and administering the saline draught joined with a few grains of nitre [saltpeter], every four or six hours. To keep the bowels open, and thereby diminish the febrile action a cooling laxative of the saline kind [Epsom salt] should be given occasionally.*
>
> *Should the throat be much affected, and there be great difficulty of swallowing, a blister may be applied to the neck, and gargles composed of an infusion of roses with diluted sulphuric acid be used frequently. When the eye-lids are much swelled, and the head is painful, we may apply a leech to each temple and afterwards if necessary a blister behind each ear.*[49]

Jacob Halsey's son and Edwin Denig had become ill around July 9. Soon, Larpenteur worried about how to protect the neighboring Assiniboine tribes from the disease:

> *Perhaps it was better to looze two squaws than to inflict this outrageous desease amongst the Tribe which probably might have been the case if my plan had been adopted although it was far beyond my haprehension for it was not likely that the desease was at this time in their system [as] I have mentioned before the desease had been kept much confined.*[50]

The clerk's strategy was to send the Assiniboine women in the fort out onto the prairie for nine days with instructions for how to treat any who fell ill. They were to be given provisions, and after this self-enforced quarantine, directions for a two-day march to the nearest Assiniboine encampment. Larpenteur had lived in the Indian country long enough to know "if an Indian dies amongst the whites no matter what care has been taken of him the whites will be blamed and pay must come to keep peace."[51] But before Larpenteur could present his plan, circumstances changed; despite increased security and limited exposure, the mother-in-law and brother of one of the Assiniboine wives left the fort around July 15 to return to their tribe.[52]

By July 20, 1837, Fort Union was under quarantine with the gates closed and locked; no Indians were allowed to enter.[53] On the west side, a 120 x 24' building, originally divided into six equal apartments in which clerks, hunters, and some skilled engagés lived with their wives and children, was partially converted into makeshift hospital.[54] Larpenteur lamented,

> therefor one cannot imagine what a pest was occasioned by those poor mortified boddies Laying like mortified [corpses] of whom several were soon expected to be. it became so unsuportible that it was impossible to enter the rooms without having a vile filed with camphor or some other essence ... continuously holding it up to the nose in the cool of the evening when was the shadow of the row of the dwelling houses was suffitient to extend to expose the sick to the cool air.[55]

As noted earlier, each fort in the Upper Missouri Outfit had a copy of *Modern Domestic Medicine*, as well as a kit stocked with remedies of the day. Fort Union's 1834 inventory included "10 kegs Epsom salts," "14 lbs salt petre," and "2¼ lbs blistering ointment."

Records from 1831-34 document the availability of gum opium, laudanum, camphor, leeches, and orange peels.[56] Though it appears that Fort Union stocked medicines called for in the treatment of smallpox patients as prescribed by Dr. Thomas, Larpenteur mentioned only keeping the sick cool as recommended for high fevers.

Above Fort Union

Meanwhile, the disease was transmitted to Fort Van Buren on the Yellowstone River via infected crewmen on the keelboat bringing up supplies from Fort Union. Halsey wrote, "At the Crow Post the disease was raging [among the fort personnel] but there were no Indians near." Perhaps hearing that smallpox was at Fort Van Buren, the Crow stayed away.[57]

Alexander Harvey's keelboat, sent from Fort Union to Fort McKenzie, fared no better. Three people on board broke out with smallpox. The sick were a young mixed-blood girl, related to the Deschamps and who had survived the massacre of her family the previous year; the Blood Indian man who had boarded the *St. Peters* at Fort Pierre; and a Creole cordeller by the name of LaDouck.[58]

Trader Harvey stopped the keelboat at the Judith River, approximately 430 river miles above Fort Union, and 73 miles below his destination. Harvey sent word to Alexander Culbertson at Fort McKenzie that they were now carrying the disease. Culbertson then instructed Harvey to remain at the Judith until the malady had run its course. Circumstances, however, were against the traders – 500 lodges of Blood and Piegan were camped around Fort McKenzie awaiting the arrival of new trade goods. Culbertson tried to explain to the Indians that the boat was carrying a deadly disease. Deeply suspicious, the Blackfeet could not believe a sickness could be as lethal as the head trader described, and threatened to fetch the boat

Fort McKenzie, at the mouth of the Marias River, sketched in watercolor and pencil on paper by Karl Bodmer in 1833. JOSLYN ART MUSEUM, OMAHA, NEBRASKA, GIFT OF THE ENRON ART FOUNDATION, 1986.49.211.A

themselves. By late July, Culbertson had little choice but to order the boat to the fort, but not before convincing the Indians to hold the traders blameless if the smallpox got among them.[59]

Culbertson dispatched six men in two canoes to help bring up the keelboat, but tragedy struck when one of the dugouts capsized and four men drowned.[60] When Harvey's keelboat finally arrived at Fort McKenzie, there were no new cases among the crew. The girl was recovering, but the Blood and Creole men were still very ill and both soon died.[61] Trade with the Blackfeet lasted five days, then the tribes departed.

Shortly after the Indians left, smallpox swept through the fort personnel. At its height, some fifty-one individuals were afflicted, including Alexander Culbertson.[62] As at Fort Union, they inoculated people using live smallpox virus, with the same disastrous results. By the time the epidemic burned its way through the fort, twenty-seven people, mostly Indian women, were dead. Ten days after leaving Fort McKenzie, smallpox broke out among the Blood and Piegan. No Indians came to trade at Fort McKenzie until late in the year, when the survivors reported the wholesale devastation the disease had wrought on the Blackfeet.[63]

Inoculation fails

Downriver at Fort Union, the first death among those inoculated was the Assiniboine wife of the tailor, sometime in late July.[64] Years later, Edwin Denig would write,

The disease was very virulent, most of the Indians dying through delirium and hemorrhage from the mouth and ears before any spots appeared.[65]

This must have been an understatement. Denig would have witnessed patients with the vesicular and pustular stages of smallpox hemorrhaging to the point of shock.[66] Extreme dehydration would also have come from fever, nausea and vomiting, decreased fluid intake due to discomfort in swallowing caused by pharyngeal lesions, and extensive skin peeling.[67] He might also have seen sufferers with large areas of abscessed skin, and bacterial super infections of the lesions resulting in toxemia or septicemia.[68] Death from smallpox generally results from profound toxemia that leads to respiratory and/or heart failure.[69]

The fur traders tried to keep the disease from spreading among the Assiniboine by conducting the trade away from the fort. Denig reported:

> When the disease first appeared in Fort Union we did everything in our power to prevent the Indians from coming to it, trading with them a considerable distance out in the prairie and representing to them the danger of going near the infection.[70]

In his November 2, 1837 letter to employer Pratte, Chouteau and Company, Halsey explained that

> During the prevalence of the malady the Assiniboines were continually coming in. I sent our interpreter to meet them on every occasion, who represented our situation to them and requested them to return immediately from whence they came, however all our endeavors proved fruitless.[71]

Larpenteur went into further detail in his journal:

> it is always the case that at all time when axcidint takes place others will soon follow it happened that during the most crittical [time] of this deasese when wee did not whish to see no one there was a band of about two hundred Indians [Assiniboine] came to trade and it was after a great deal of talk By one of the Best interpretter that the whole Missouri can afford that they would consent to trade out side the Fort.[72]

The interpreter referred to in the account above was Baptiste Contois, a *Métis* from the Red River area.[73] Trade negotiations such as those Contois coordinated were fairly structured affairs with the sharing of coffee and food, gift giving, speeches and eventually smoking the pipe once the agreement to trade was reached. While Contois, who spoke the Assiniboine language, would have been the main diplomat, he would have been accompanied by a trader or clerk during the prolonged face-to-face contact in the negotiations. Larpenteur kept on top of all the goings-on:

> the next day when the Trade was near over there were four or five indians got over the Picketts of the old fort mounted two of the best horses opened the door with the intention to take the whole band but they were to soon discovered they only succeeded in getting off with ... those two which they had mounted while in the Fort. not wistanding all this the Band was continuing towards the hills several of our activest men mounted the Emerican horses fast runners which were kept in the stables of the new Fort soon over took them and by the assistance of some good indians brought them back.[74]

Unfortunately, attempts to shield the Indians from the disease were futile. Larpenteur was astonished that

> the day after the indians Left us B Contois a half Breed from the red river who had taken an active part in getting Back

the Horses was taken [with] Dreadful Pain and fever and three days afterwards the confluent small Pox broke out on him.[75]

As it turns out, a person with smallpox can be contagious before a rash appears,

but the person would by then be symptomatic suffering from a fever and likely flu-like symptoms of body aches and headache. This period of time may last, on average, a couple of days.[76]

The Halsey and Larpenteur accounts differ in the number of people at the fort who became ill. Halsey put the number at twenty-seven, but Larpenteur counted only the seventeen who were inoculated on July 12. Ultimately, ignorance of the basic etiology of the smallpox virus and how it was spread served the pathogen well. Halsey thought it was in the air around the fort, claiming "the air was infected with it for a half mile without the pickets."[77] Denig lamented that:

It is hardly conceivable how the smallpox among the Indians could be cured by any physician. All remedies fail. The disease kills a greater part of them before any eruption appears. We have personally tried experiments on nearly 200 cases according to Thomas's Domestic Medicine, *varying the treatment in every possible form, but have always failed, or in the few instances of success the disease had assumed such a mild form that medicines were unnecessary.*[78]

For Charles Larpenteur, the cruelest blow arrived on August 4:

My squaw expired having two Days privious attacked by what worms which is said to prey on [the] human boddy after Death but to occur more Disagreable feelings on me this was to ocur before her Death.[79]

Besides suffering terribly from having no resistance whatsoever to smallpox, Larpenteur's wife had now contracted *Myiasis*, a parasitic infection caused when the green bottle fly (*Lucilia sericata*) lays eggs in untreated wounds. The larvae hatch and begin feeding. The fly would have been common around Fort Union, but such an infestation would have been rare in a living person at such northern latitudes.[80]

The last two deaths from smallpox that Larpenteur recorded at Fort Union came on August 12 and 16, 1837, respectively:

Poor Contois Was Put in to his earthly dwelling [and] *1 case more of the noculation small Pox proved fatal a squaw of one of the hands died and that of an indian family.*[81]

By the end of August, Edwin Denig had recovered enough from his illness to go buffalo hunting with Larpenteur:

August 29th This day two Buffalo Bulls were discovered about one mile from the Fort my self and Mr E T Denig went to try our luck in approaching them.[82]

Aftermath

At the beginning of October, Jacob Halsey was replaced at Fort Union by David D. Mitchell. Mitchell later reported to Pierre Chouteau, Jr., "A woeful picture of poor Halsey's conduct during the summer."[83] But it was Halsey who ordered a sally-port system of double gates installed at the front gate so that Indians could more safely enter the trade house. Only chiefs were allowed into the inner part of the fort through the second set of gates.[84]

Historians have singled out the captain of the *St. Peters*, Bernard Pratte, Jr., for not stopping the boat to let the disease burn itself out.⁸⁵ However, a number of mitigating factors pressed Captain Pratte upriver, among them the rigors of commerce, as well as ignorance of effective ways to deal with smallpox. The steamer was already struggling in the river's low water level. Waiting for the disease to run its course could have stranded the boat for the winter, leaving the trade goods and Indian annuities undelivered. The Indian agents on board would not have tolerated that. Government contracts for annuity deliveries were lucrative and were increasingly becoming part of the AFC's revenue stream.

The trade goods were a separate matter. A careful balancing act existed between the company suppliers and those in the field ordering goods from St. Louis, with some items needing two or three years to arrive. Company costs (including shipping, interest rates, supplies and other cash purchases) were to be repaid in furs, whose prices were subject to world-wide price fluctuations. The Financial Panic of 1837 already affected the AFC's St. Louis office, which was in crisis due to a flood of paper currency that hampered its ability to make payments to creditors. Waiting for the disease to abate would have lost an entire year's income for the company.⁸⁶

The fur traders on the upper Missouri have been faulted for standing by and watching as disease took the Indian tribes.⁸⁷ However, at least a few traders followed medical treatment procedures laid out by Dr. Robert Thomas in his medical manual. Francis Chardon was likely following Dr. Thomas's medical advice at Fort Clark when he noted in his journal on August 8, 1837: "to day I gave six pounds of Epsom salts in doses to Men, Women, and children." Dr. Thomas recommended using Epsom salts as "a cooling laxative" for controlling fevers.⁸⁸ At Fort McKenzie, Alexander Culbertson, desperate to combat the disease, employed the risky variation method to inoculate people, with the same poor results attested by Charles Larpenteur at Fort Union.

Charles Larpenteur has been treated shabbily for his role in the epidemic by fur trade historian Hiram M. Chittenden. Certainly, Elliot Coues's inaccurate story of smallpox at Fort Union, along with information from steamboat captain and fur trader Joseph LaBarge, a bitter personal enemy of Larpenteur, impacted Chittenden's opinion. Chittenden's reference to Larpenteur's "cynical coolness" in assuring the epidemic would not interfere with trade, and the "fiendish satisfaction" of an imaginary conversation between Larpenteur and another trader of the daily body count, can be laid squarely at the feet of Coues.⁸⁹

In 1837, Larpenteur, still a junior clerk at Fort Union, clearly stated that the decision to inoculate was "against my will[ing] consent that my squaw with the Balance come to get death put in to her [arm]."⁹⁰ He was then forced to watch helplessly as his wife died a horrible, tortured death with the final indignity of an infestation of maggots.

At Fort Clark on March 25, 1838, as the epidemic abated, Francis Chardon noted, "Mr. [Robert] Christy & Larpeter arrived from the Yellow Stone, on the way to St. Louis."⁹¹ Larpenteur was on his first leave of absence since arriving at his upper Missouri post in 1833. It would be the first time in ten years that Larpenteur would see his parents in Baltimore since leaving that city to venture west.⁹²

By the time the smallpox epidemic on the upper Missouri ended in the spring of 1838, Indian populations had been drastically reduced. Tribal societies were torn apart, and the balance of power on the Northern Plains was forever changed. Some tribes were driven to greater dependence on trading posts, while many of those unaffected by the disease moved into new hunting territories further west. Widely varying estimates of the death toll have been proposed over the years, but the simple truth is the number will never be known.

Michael M. Casler is an independent historical researcher, former National Park Service ranger, and retired EMT-B. He is the author of Steamboats of the Fort Union Fur Trade *(Fort Union Association, 1999) and editor of* The Original Journals of Charles Larpenteur *(Museum of the Fur Trade, 2007).*

NOTES

1. I am grateful to Dr. David J. Peck, author of *Or Perish in the Attempt: Wilderness Medicine in the Lewis and Clark Expedition* (Helena, MT: Far Country Press, 2000), for reading this article for accuracy and recommending changes that better describe the smallpox virus. Any remaining inaccuracies are my own.

2. Francis A. Chardon, *Chardon's Journal at Fort Clark, 1834-1839,* edited by Annie H. Abel (Freeport, NY: Books for Libraries Press, 1970), 121, 161.

3. Charles Larpenteur, *Forty Years a Fur Trader on the Upper Missouri,* edited by Elliot Coues, 2 vols. (New York, NY: Francis P. Harper, 1898).

4. Charles Larpenteur, *The Original Journal of Charles Larpenteur: My Travels to the Rocky Mountains Between 1833 and 1872,* edited by Michael M. Casler (Chadron, NE: The Museum Association of the American Frontier, 2007).

5. The *St. Peters* was built in Pittsburgh, PA, in 1836. She was a side-wheeler with the dimensions of 139 x 18.8 x 5.9' (119 tons). Michael M. Casler, *Steamboats of the Fort Union Fur Trade: An Illustrated Listing of Steamboats on the Upper Missouri River, 1831-1867* (Williston, ND: Fort Union Association, 1999), 35; James A. Hanson, "An Interesting Reference to the Upper Missouri Smallpox Epidemic of 1837," *Museum of the Fur Trade Quarterly* 47, no. 1 (Spring 2011): 2; Clyde D. Dollar, "The High Plains Smallpox Epidemic of 1837-38," *The Western Historical Quarterly* 8, no. 1 (January 1977): 18.

6. Michael M. Casler, "Drayage Included: Steamboat Operations of the American Fur Company at St. Louis," *Fur Trade Symposium 2000 Proceedings* (Williston, ND: Fort Union Association, 2001), 126.

7. Hanson, "An Interesting Reference," 2; Dollar, "Smallpox Epidemic of 1837," 18; Letter, Joshua Pilcher to William Clark, February 5, 1838, cited in Michael K. Trimble, "An Ethnohistorical Interpretation of the Spread of Smallpox in the Northern Plains Utilizing Concepts of Disease Ecology," *Reprints in Anthropology* (1979; Lincoln, NE: J & L Reprint Company, 1986), 33:68-69. The Pilcher letters cited in Trimble are found at the National Archives, Microfilm 234, Roll 884 (1836-1851).

8. River miles for this article are drawn from "Table of Distances, Missouri River – from its mouth to Three Forks, Montana," *Maps of the Missouri River* (Missouri River Commission, 1892-1895).

9. Letter, Joshua Pilcher to William Clark, June 10, 1837, cited in Trimble, "Spread of Smallpox," 64-65.

10. Ibid., 66. This letter is dated July 1, 1837.

11. Trimble, "Spread of Smallpox," 68.

12. Lesley Wischmann, *Frontier Diplomats: The Life and Times of Alexander Culbertson and Natoyist-Siksina* (Spokane, WA: The Arthur H. Clark Company, 2000), 67, 68; Dollar, "Smallpox Epidemic of 1837," 20.

13. "Prodrome" symptoms indicate the onset of disease. Center for Disease Control, *Small Pox Fact Sheet* 2014. Accessed June 18, 2015 from http://emergency.cdc.gov/agent/smallpox/overview/disease-facts.asp, 2.

14. Trimble, "Spread of Smallpox," 68-69; Dollar, "Smallpox Epidemic of 1837," 20.

15. Hanson, "An Interesting Reference," 2-5. It is possible that Vital Papin was the "Mulatto" deckhand who first contracted smallpox.

16. Stephen S. Witte and Marsha V. Gallagher, eds., *The North American Journals of Prince Maximilian of Wied,* 3 vols. (Norman, OK: University of Oklahoma Press, 2010), 2:138-139.

17. Trimble, "Spread of Smallpox," 70.

18. Ibid., 41; Dollar, "Smallpox Epidemic of 1837," 20.

19. Casler, "Drayage Included," 126.

20. Dollar, "Smallpox Epidemic of 1837," 21; Trimble, "Spread of Smallpox," 41; Larpenteur, *Original Journal,* 58; Chardon, *Journal at Fort Clark,* 394-395; John C. Ewers, *The Blackfeet: Raiders on the Northwestern Plains* (Norman, OK: University of Oklahoma Press, 1985), 65.

21. These are today's Square Buttes, north of Bismarck, ND, along the Missouri River. See John W. Hoganson and Edward C. Murphy, *Geology of the Lewis & Clark Trail in North Dakota* (Missoula, MT: Mountain Press Publishing Company, 2003), 89; Chardon, *Journal at Fort Clark,* 118, 315-316n478.

22. Ibid., 118. A mackinaw boat could carry up to 300 packs of buffalo robes (ten buffalo robes per pack). Casler, *Steamboats of Fort Union,* 4.

23. Ibid.

24. Casler, "Drayage Included," 126; Chardon, *Journal at Fort Clark,* 118; Dollar, "Smallpox

Epidemic of 1837," 21; Trimble, "Spread of Smallpox," 32.

25 Chardon, *Journal at Fort Clark*, 118-119; Trimble, "Spread of Smallpox," 69-70.

26 Chardon, *Journal at Fort Clark*, 118.

27 Chardon, *Journal at Fort Clark*, 118-119; Dollar, "Smallpox Epidemic of 1837," 21; Trimble, "Spread of Smallpox," 31-33.

28 Larpenteur, *Original Journal*, 58.

29 Dollar, "Smallpox Epidemic of 1837," 36; Trimble, "Spread of Smallpox," 43-44.

30 Larpenteur, *Original Journal*, 58.

31 Hiroshi Nishiura, MD, "Smallpox during Pregnancy and Maternal Outcomes," *Emerging Infectious Diseases* 12, no. 7 (July 2006): 1119.

32 The hemorrhagic form of the disease in pregnant women is thought to be a variation in the victim's immune system responding to the variola virus. So the virus does not change, the only difference is the victim's individual response to the disease.

33 Nishiura, "Smallpox during Pregnancy," 1120.

34 Steamboats did not travel upriver to Fort Benton until 1860. In 1837, Fort Union was the end of the line. The *St. Peters* carried smallpox back to St. Louis, where she was fumigated, and in 1838 she was dismantled. Casler, *Steamboats*, 35.

35 Casler, "Drayage Included," 126.

36 Robert Thomas, MD, *The Modern Practice of Physic* (London: Longman, Hurst, et al., 1813), 196-197. This Dr. Thomas is Scottish.

37 "Modified" smallpox is a milder form of the disease occurring in previously vaccinated persons, however these people may still be afflicted with the flat or hemorrhagic forms of the disease. CDC, *Overview of Smallpox*, 1.

38 Larpenteur, *Original Journal*, 58. Larpenteur's use of the word "distinct" is a medical term. Dr. Thomas's medical book only recognized two varieties of smallpox: "Distinct" and "Confluent," based on how the pustules present on the body of the patient. The confluent variety is the more virulent form of the disease. Robert Thomas, MD, *Modern Domestic Medicine* (New York, NY: Collins and Company, 1829), 113-115.

39 Letter, Jacob Halsey to Pratte, Chouteau & Co., November 2, 1837, cited in Chardon, *Journal at Fort Clark*, 394.

40 Larpenteur, *Original Journal*, 58. Larpenteur noted, "In refference to Mr E. T. Denig it appears that his fever was ocasioned by some other complaints for up to this date no small Pox as yet appeared."

41 James A. Hanson, "Bad Medicine: Medical Knowledge and Practice of the Upper Missouri Fur Trade," *Museum of the Fur Trade Quarterly* 40, no. 3 (Fall 2004): 4.

42 Larpenteur, *Original Journal,* 58n45.

43 Ibid., 59.

44 Thomas, *Modern Domestic Medicine*, 120-121.

45 Larpenteur, *Original Journal*, 59.

46 Correspondence with Dr. David J. Peck, February 4, 2016. Variolation, or use of the smallpox (variola) virus, was the inoculation method used prior to Edward Jenner's discovery of vaccination (cowpox or vaccinia virus from Latin *vacca,* cow) in 1798. Variolation, as noted by Dr. Thomas in his manual, is a much riskier procedure.

47 Based on a reading of *Modern Domestic Medicine*, it was decided to use fluid taken from Halsey's skin eruptions. This well-intended but dangerous step proved fatal to thousands. Dollar, "Smallpox Epidemic of 1837," 22.

48 The pharyngeal mucosa is the upper airway consisting of the mouth, tongue, nasal cavity, and throat. CDC, *Overview of Smallpox*, 4.

49 Thomas, *Modern Domestic Medicine*, 115-116.

50 Larpenteur, *Original Journal*, 59.

51 Ibid.

52 Ibid.

53 Letter, Halsey to Pratte, Chouteau & Co., November 2, 1837, cited in Chardon, *Journal at Fort Clark*, 394.

54 Erwin N. Thompson, *Fort Union Trading Post, Historic Structures Report, Part II* (Washington, DC: National Park Service, 1968), 197.

55 Larpenteur, *Original Journal*, 59.

56 Thompson, *Fort Union Trading Post*, 157-160. Thompson compiled a partial list of medicines kept on hand at Fort Union by examining the Chouteau Collections, Missouri History Museum, St. Louis, MO, for the years 1831-1834. Medicines for 1837 were not included.

57 Letter, Halsey to Pratte, Chouteau & Co., November 2, 1837, cited in Chardon, *Journal at Fort Clark*, 394; Bernard DeVoto, *Across the Wide Missouri* (1947; Boston, MA: Houghton, Mifflin and Company, 1975), 290.

58 Wischmann, *Frontier Diplomats,* 70; James H. Bradley, "Affairs at Fort Benton from 1831 to 1869," *Contributions to the Historical Society of Montana* (Helena, MT: State Publishing Company, 1900), 3:222; Larpenteur, *Original Journal*, 62; DeVoto, *Across the Wide Missouri,* 290.

59 Bradley, "Affairs at Fort Benton," 224-226; Wischmann, *Frontier Diplomats,* 71-72.

60 The rapids would later be named Drowned Man Rapids.

61 Bradley, "Affairs at Fort Benton," 223; Wischmann, *Frontier Diplomats,* 71-72.

62 Alexander Culbertson had been previously inoculated and thus had contracted a milder form of smallpox.

63 Bradley, "Affairs at Fort Benton," 224-226; Wischmann, *Frontier Diplomats,* 71-72.
64 Larpenteur, *Original Journal,* 59.
65 Edwin T. Denig, "Indian Tribes of the Upper Missouri," *Forty-Sixth Annual Report of the Bureau of American Ethnology* (Washington, DC: Government Printing Office, 1930), 399.
66 The vesicular/pustular stage exhibits raised blisters on the skin. These are filled with viral lymph fluid.
67 CDC, *Overview of Smallpox,* 11.
68 Ibid.
69 Ibid., 3.
70 Denig, "Indian Tribes," 399.
71 Letter, Halsey to Pratte, Chouteau & Co., November 2, 1837, cited in Chardon, *Journal at Fort Clark,* 394.
72 Larpenteur, *Original Journal,* 59-60.
73 Ibid., 49n8.
74 Larpenteur's "old fort" was Fort William, built in 1833 by Sublette and Campbell. It had been moved from its original location at the confluence to just east of Fort Union and was now being used to stable the company's horses. Larpenteur, *Original Journal,* 52n37, 60; Letter, Halsey to Pratte, Chouteau & Co., November 2, 1837, cited in Chardon, *Journal at Fort Clark,* 395.
75 Larpenteur, *Original Journal,* 60.
76 CDC, *Fact Sheet,* 12.
77 Letter, Halsey to Pratte, Chouteau & Co., November 2, 1837, cited in Chardon, *Journal at Fort Clark,* 394.
78 Denig, "Indian Tribes," 428.
79 Larpenteur, *Original Journal,* 60.
80 CDC, *Parasites–Myiasis* found online at http://www.cdc.gov/parasites/myiasis, (accessed June 20, 2015); Matthew Anderson and Phillip E. Kaufman, *Common Green Bottle Fly – Lucilia sericata (meigen)* University of Florida, Department of Entomology and Nematology, September 2011, found online at http://entnemdept.ufl.edu/creatures/livestock/flies/lucilia_sericata.htm, (accessed June 20, 2015). "*L. sericata* is the species of choice for 'maggot therapy,' a clinical procedure using living maggots to clean necrotic wounds." Email to the author from Dr. Roger Moon, University of Minnesota, Department of Entomology, May 18, 2015.
81 Larpenteur, *Original Journal,* 60.
82 Ibid., 66.
83 Thompson, *Fort Union Trading Post,* 62.
84 Letter, Halsey to Pratte, Chouteau & Co., November 2, 1837, cited in Chardon, *Journal at Fort Clark,* 395.
85 Bruce E. Johansen, *Silenced! : Academic Freedom, Scientific Inquiry, and the First Amendment under Siege in America* (Westport, CT: Praeger, 2007), 86; William E. Lass, *Navigating the Missouri: Steamboating on Nature's Highway, 1819-1935* (Norman, OK: The Arthur H. Clark Company, 2008), 102.
86 W. Raymond Wood, William J. Hunt, and Randy H. Williams, *Fort Clark and Its Indian Neighbors: A Trading Post on the Upper Missouri* (Norman, OK: University of Oklahoma Press, 2011), 160-161.
87 The *St. Peters* had hardly tied up at the St. Louis docks before efforts to assign blame for the disaster began. William N. Fulkerson, sub-agent for the upper Missouri tribes, did not help matters when he wrote to William Clark that a blanket stolen at the Mandan village was the source of the infection, thus starting the myth that "infected blankets" were intentionally given to the Indians. Clark himself later wrote of Fulkerson's statement that "he relates rather what he has heard, than that which came under his own observation." For 178 years Captain Bernard Pratte, Jr. and the traders along the Missouri River have served as easy targets for historians and academics casting the fur trade as responsible for this medical disaster. Trimble, "Spread of Smallpox," 67-73.
88 Chardon, *Journal at Fort Clark,* 126. Thomas, *Modern Domestic Medicine,* 116.
89 Hiram M. Chittenden, *The American Fur Trade of the Far West,* 2 vols. (Lincoln, NE: University of Nebraska Press, 1986), 2:615-617. By the time Dr. Washington Matthews provided Coues with the Larpenteur journal manuscript in November 1897, Larpenteur had been dead for 25 years. Larpenteur, *Original Journal,* i-x.
90 The woman who died of smallpox here was Charles Larpenteur's first Assiniboine wife; he later married another Assiniboine woman but never mentions either woman's name; Larpenteur, *Original Journal,* 59.
91 Chardon, *Journal at Fort Clark,* 154.
92 Ibid., 71-72.

The Rats at Fort Clark

by Don Arp, Jr.

From 1834 to 1843, Francis A. Chardon was in charge of a small fur trade post known as Fort Clark in what is now North Dakota. Chardon, an unhappy and volatile man, recorded details of his life in a journal from 1834 to 1839.[1] Apart from noting daily events and weather conditions, a key theme in the work was the fort's rat infestation. Transported to the fort via river boat, as smallpox would be soon after his arrival, rats had become such a problem that they routinely caused serious structural damage to post buildings. Almost immediately upon his arrival at the fort, Chardon began a crusade against the vermin. The last day's entry of every month included the monthly death toll and a running total of all the rats he had dispatched.

Though rarely noted, most forts along the Missouri River likely hosted a rat population. Chardon's unique set of data offers a window into outpost life that may prove useful to other researchers. This case study documents Fort Clark's fluctuating rat population, and chronicles events surrounding Chardon, the neighboring Mandan, and life at Fort Clark.

A post on the upper Missouri

Fort Clark was an American Fur Company (AFC) trading post established on the Missouri River adjacent to the Mitutanka Mandan village of Mit-tutta-hang-kush.[2] The temporal origins of the village and fort are in question. A trading structure called Tilton's Post had been built somewhere on the site by James Kipp sometime in 1822 or 1823. These dates coincide with the founding of Mit-tutta-hang-kush, but which came first is of some debate, with evidence existing for both sides. Between 1829 and 1831, Tilton's Post folded and the post known as Fort Clark was constructed by Kipp and fellow AFC trader David D. Mitchell. This post would operate until it burned in 1860.[3]

Fort Clark was strategically positioned, both geographically and culturally. The post was located near the river, affording a transport route for trade goods. Surrounding lands were an excellent source of bison (often called "cattle" by Chardon) and a variety of other commercially useful animals, such as wolf and deer. AFC personnel conducted business with the Mandan village located just outside

Norway or brown rats, Plate 54 of John James Audubon's *Quadrupeds of North America 1849-1854, Volume 2* (1851). COURTESY OF FOTOSTOCK

the gates, but also dealt with the Hidatsa, Crow, Yankton and Yanktonai.[4] The Mandan would abandon Mit-tutta-hang-kush after the 1837 smallpox epidemic struck; the Arikara moved into the village in 1838 and inhabited the site until 1861.

Fort Clark was not the last post to be built near the Mit-tutta-hang-kush village. In the latter half of the 1850s, a former employee of the AFC's Upper Missouri Outfit would found Primeau's Post.[5] After Fort Clark partially burned in 1860, the displaced personnel moved to the newer post, but Primeau's Post closed the next year when its economic base, the Indian village, was forever abandoned by the Arikara.[6] Deserted and in ruin, Fort Clark yet continued to serve passing steamboats as a source of wood for their boiler fires. Two steamboats, the *Effie Deans* and *St. Johns*, used wood from the fort in the spring of 1865.[7]

Luckily for archaeologists, the fort site and surrounding area was never tilled or farmed. The site, accompanying remains of Primeau's Post, and the Mandan (and later Arikara) village site are now part of the Fort Clark State Historic Site in Mercer County, North Dakota. The site was listed on the National Register of Historic Places in 1986.[8]

The bourgeois of Fort Clark

Francis Chardon, born c. 1795 and possibly named François Auguste Chardon, was a Philadelphian of French descent.[9] Though documentation is lacking, Chardon may have served under Andrew Jackson at the Battle of New Orleans.[10] Soon after the War of 1812, he appears to have moved to the West and learned the Siouan Osage language.[11] From 1827 to 1833, Chardon bounced around the upper Missouri region, working for the American Fur Company at places like Fort Union and Fort Jackson.[12] The AFC sent Chardon to Fort Clark in 1834 to serve as the post manager or *bourgeois*, a position he would hold until 1843.

chardon's journal

"As I keep a dayly a/c of Rats Killed at the Fort, since my arrival I must announce the Death of ninety seven."
Sunday, August 31, 1834

His time at the post would be one of depression, violence, death, and loss. Life at Fort Clark must have been partially responsible for Chardon's sometimes strange moods and even stranger actions.

Depending on the contemporary source consulted, Chardon was either an ill-tempered drunk, or an excellent host who possessed great business sense. Others, perhaps more accurately, have combined the two, describing him as "an able but unscrupulous man, and something of a desperate character when his evil nature was aroused."[13] AFC headman Pierre Chouteau, Jr., described Chardon as "too notorious to inspire confidence."[14] Part of Chardon's problem was his drinking. Fellow fur trader Charles Larpenteur gave a vivid account of just how much Chardon loved liquor:

> *Mr. F. A. Chardon, who was then in charge, and a very singular kind of man, entertained us in the best manner. Mr. Christy had a two-gallon keg of good whiskey, of which Mr. Chardon was so fond that he helped himself about every fifteen minutes, saying he had "a great many worms in his throat" – to the sorrow of Mr. Christy, who found his keg so nearly empty that he concluded to make Mr. Chardon a present of what was left.*[15]

Chardon's propensity to say what was on his mind, particularly about events and people around him, led to several written accounts describing him as hospitable but odd, crude, and sometimes contemptible.

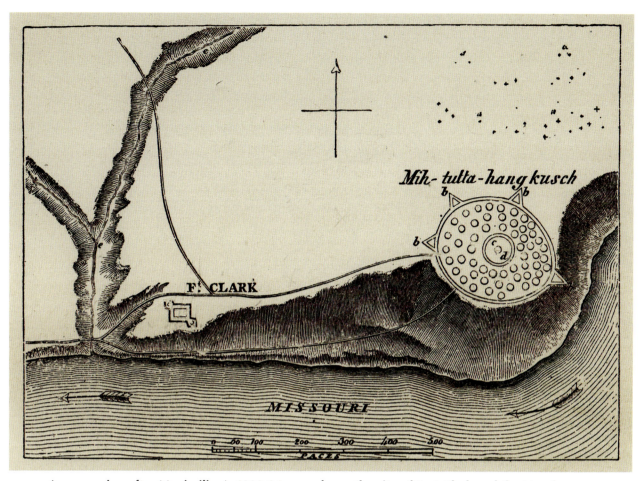

An engraving after Maximilian's 1833-34 map shows the site of Fort Clark and the Mandan village of Mit-tutta-hang-kush. Dots in upper right denote scaffolds for the dead. Letter "b" marks the village boundary. "C" marks the open space at the center of the village, where "d" is the sacred shrine. Scale at the bottom measures distance in "paces." STATE HISTORICAL SOCIETY OF NORTH DAKOTA (SHSND)

The personal journal he kept during his first years at Fort Clark is telling of his character, mindset, and opinions. There are few high points; most entries note daily hunting and post activities, unless the twin muses of alcohol and depression fueled Chardon's hand. The pervasive gloominess of entries that reveal his private feelings may explain why Chardon's journal entries ceased after 1839, five years into his nine-year appointment. The journal entry for Wednesday, January 27, 1836, about two years into his stint as post manager, is typical:

Wednesday 27th – Weather moderated very much since Yesterday – Made preparations to go out in search of cattle tomorrow. No news from any quarter – lonesome

One Single word lonesome - would suffice to express our feelings any day throughout the Year - We might add – discontented - but this would include the fate of all Mankind. It is a Melancholy reflection when we look forward into futurity – and know that the remnant of our days must be spent in toilsome and unavailing pursuits of happiness. And that sooner or later we must sink into the grave without ever being able to attain the object for which we have toiled and suffered so much. If we turn with discontent from this ideal picture, and take a retrospective glance at the past, the scene is no less gloomy. It is like a dreary expansive waste – without one green verdant spot on which Memory loves to linger. The day dreams in which we used to indulge during our halcyon days of Youth have long since proved as baseless as Visions ever are. The little experience that time has given only teaches us to Know,

That Man was Made to Mourn[16]

Why Chardon felt compelled to record the exact number of rats he killed is debatable. His tortured, petty personality could be ascribed to a reliance on alcohol, mixed with a surly attitude, boredom, and depression. This, coupled with his lack of respect for the Native Americans with whom he conducted business, led to tense incidents. What motivated his professional dislike of Native Americans is not fully understood. He would refer to the Arikara as "The Horrid Tribe" and in 1839 recorded in his journal the "splendid sight" of the Mandan village burning to the ground.[17] At Fort McKenzie in 1843, Chardon would blame the Piegan Blackfeet for the murder of his black servant. He attacked a group of Piegans coming to the fort to trade, and killed between four and nine after they entered the post. This act destroyed his trading relationship with the tribe.[18]

Such dislike for his customer base is strange, considering he was fluent in at least one native language, and throughout his career had an almost continual line of Native American wives and concubines, with whom he had at least three sons. Indeed, Chardon deeply cared for his sons and life partners.[19] He lost his Sioux wife, Tchon-su-mons-ka, before the outbreak of smallpox and was forced to watch his son, Andrew Jackson Chardon, fall to the disease during the summer of 1837.[20] What motivated his professional dislike of Native Americans is not fully understood. What is known is that Chardon's aversion to his native customers was situational, growing more serious over time, and was not limited to just one tribe.

Chardon's adversary: *Rattus norvegicus*

Prince Maximilian noted the rats' arrival on the upper Missouri with the Atkinson/O'Fallon Yellowstone Expedition of 1825.[21] The vermin, traveling upriver via keelboat, and later by steamboat, would have infested the Mandan village and Tilton's Post, and Fort Clark shortly thereafter. Beginning in 1834, Chardon was tireless in his efforts to kill the pests at the fort and tally his monthly death toll.

But regardless how many rats Chardon and his cronies killed, they at no time succeeded in abating the infestation. At one point, rats were being killed at the fort's meat rack, and on March 15, 1839, Chardon formed a work detail to repair one of the fort's palisade walls that had fallen down due to rat gnawing.[22]

What Chardon and his men faced at Fort Clark was the perfect opportunist – a species of rat called *Rattus norvegicus* (also known as the brown or Norway rat) seemingly designed for rapid spread and infestation. The species originated in China and Siberia.[23] Although sometimes referred to as the "Norway rat," the brown rat did not originate from that nation and in fact was not found there until 1762.[24]

The brown rat has a blunt muzzle, small ears, and grayish brown fur, although some specimens may actually be black in color. Globally, their 12-ounce-weight is fairly consistent, although there is variation in individual length due to climate; rats in the tropics have longer tails than those in colder environs.[25] Generally, the body of this species, from nose to buttock, measures from 10 to 12 inches, with its tail an additional 10 to 12 inches in length.[26] The brown rat produces litters of 8-10 young per birthing and, if provided with space and adequate nutrient base, can produce 12 litters a year. Said one expert, "The strong point about rats is that they are not great performers in any one sphere but are competent performers in most."[27]

As true as this may be, one factor is of greater significance than any other in the success of this species: food. The brown rat is voracious, exceedingly adaptable in its food habits, and far less fickle about its meals than the black rat (*Rattus rattus*).[28] A brown rat's diet is based on availability but when presented with a variety of food choices, the animal will sample all items available and work them into its diet if deemed acceptable.[29] Such dietary versatility is beneficial for the brown rat, but is also the main reason it is labeled as a pest.[30]

It should not be assumed that the brown rat is a dedicated scavenger. Stories of leverets (a young hare, usually less than one year of age) being killed and skunks being severely wounded by rats are widely cited.[31] Some sources note brown rats also attacking rabbits and ducks.[32] The amount of food that can be consumed by a colony of rats is impressive. Prince Maximilian, visiting Fort Clark in 1833, reported rats consuming five bushels of Indian corn (250 pounds) per day.[33] At a French slaughterhouse in 1840, *it was stated that the carcasses of the slaughtered horses, which sometimes amounted to thirty-five a day, were cleared to the bone by rats in the course of the following night.*[34]

The spread of the brown rat was explosive. Moving out of China and Siberia, the species had spread from Persia to England via English ships by 1720, and to America by 1775.[35] Europe and the Americas were already inhabited by the black rat. Although each species prefers slightly different habitats, the aggression and territoriality of the brown rat led it to nearly exterminate the black rat whenever the two had overlapping territories.

In America, the brown rat's spread was not as systematic as it had been in Europe. It appears that the species moved into the western United States from both the East and West coasts. The major issue that prevented rapid colonization in the western United States was the lack of population density, with a major exception being the posts and settlements along major trade routes like the Missouri River.[36]

The brown rat is predominantly associated with people and rarely develops wild populations, preferring to invade the wilderness on the coattails of human encroachment or to dwell in the urban jungle. In

An unknown artist sketched Fort Clark on July 14, 1860. The fort would burn down later that year. Note the earth lodge at far right. KANSAS STATE HISTORICAL SOCIETY

chardon's journal

"Eat a Rat this evening for supper."
Monday, May 4, 1835

---

either situation, the vast amounts of refuse, ground cover, and general filthiness associated with human life provide the rat with its habitat. Rats have increased their numbers and ranges notoriously by adapting to synanthropic niches – survival strategies and life-ways based upon the activity of and habitats created by *Homo sapiens*.[37] Brown rats in these niches carry contagions such as tularaemia and salmonella, which can be spread to humans by contact with foodstuffs, bites, or other modes of body-fluid transmittal.[38] Unlike the black rat, the brown rat is seldom associated with outbreaks of bubonic plague.

The conditions at Fort Clark were an ideal habitat for a colony of brown rats. Due to its function as a fur trade post, the fort had a large amount of meat, hide, and miscellaneous carcass items present. These items would provide necessary caloric intake to sustain a colony. With cover provided by the fort, village, surrounding fields, and burrows, the population could reproduce and grow.[39] The role of the Mandan village in providing the rats with food and cover cannot be discounted. For example, Native farmers provided the fort with 600 to 800 bushels of corn, which was constantly preyed upon by rats.[40]

The population of the rat colony could be controlled through food availability, predation, and extermination measures such as those conducted by Chardon and his men. The environment played a more important role in the success of rural rat populations than those of more populated urban centers. Rural rats "must adapt to changing sources of food, home, and seasons" to survive, whereas city rats take advantage of human dwellings that are designed to provide a consistent environment, and a population density that produces tons of edible refuse.[41] While Fort Clark would not provide resources at the levels encountered in an urban setting, it still supported infestation beyond modern belief, with relatively abundant food sources and the only controls on the population being the hostile North Dakota winters and Chardon's swift hand.

Chardon's body count

Chardon's battle with the Fort Clark rats, although not epically important, allows insight into not only the dynamics of the rodent population, but also events that affected both rats and humans living in or near the post. He may not have done so intentionally, but Chardon must be given credit for preserving this glimpse into the past.

Chardon never elucidated the methods he employed to kill rats. Maximilian noted that Karl Bodmer used fine birdshot to shoot large rats running along the roofs, and that Fort Clark's engagés sometimes shot the pests that invaded their rooms.[42] We do not know how he did it, but Chardon killed a staggering 5,021 rats between 1834 and 1839, equating to an average of nearly 70 rats per month. Consider October 1836, when Chardon recorded 294 rats killed in the fort – an average of more than nine rats per day.

An irregular series of archaeological investigations conducted on various portions of the Fort Clark site (1973-74, 1986, 2000, and 2001) produced corroborating evidence for Chardon's accounts of the rat infestation.[43] Samples taken from both Fort Clark and Primeau's Post show the brown rat accounted for 54 percent of micromammal bones recovered from the site, a significant percentage.[44] Also interesting is the longevity and progress of the rats' infestation. Primeau's Post, as previously noted, was established in the late 1850s, more than twenty years after Chardon arrived at Fort

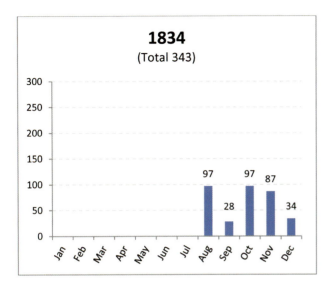
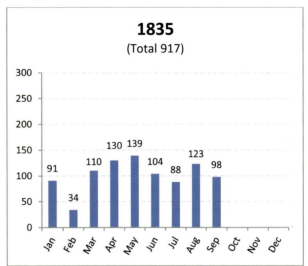
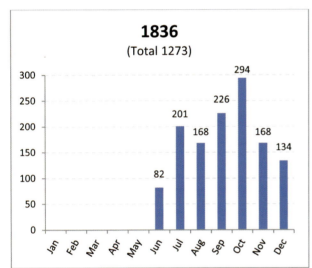
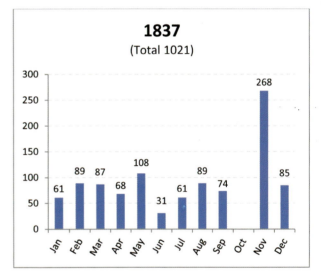
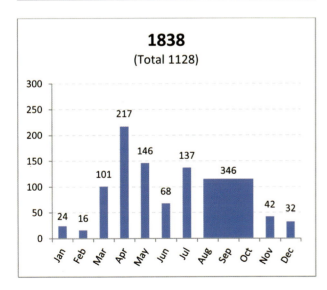
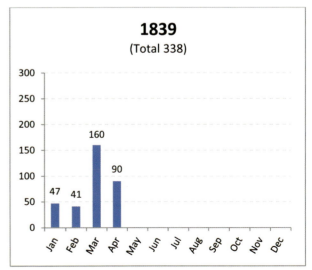

Grand total: 5,021

Rat kills counted by Francis A. Chardon at Fort Clark, 1834-39. CHARTS BY CLINT GILCHRIST

chardon's journal

"Some days since some of the Indians stole a rat trap."
Sunday, September 30, 1835

Clark and a decade or so after he departed. The presence of rats at Primeau's Post, established through the archaeological evidence, shows that the vermin, probably with large colonies established in Mit-tutta-hang-kush as well as in Fort Clark, had a sufficient nutritional base and population size to expand when new structures were built.[45]

It is archaeological conjecture at best, but it would seem that the village site, if ever sampled, would produce results similar to, if not greater than, those from Primeau's Post and Fort Clark. The Mandan population at Mit-tutta-hang-kush was estimated at 1,600 people. This is several times larger than the handful of persons occupying Fort Clark. It may be suggested, based on human population numbers, that after introduction of the brown rat, the village would have become the location of the main rat colony, with Fort Clark a lesser satellite colony. These colonies, as will soon be seen, were not necessarily independent and isolated from one another. Events occurring at the fort and village would illustrate the dynamic influence of resources upon the rat population.

Interpreting the data

Chardon's data begins when he arrived in 1834 and leaves off when he abandons the journal in 1839. Thus it is not a complete picture of rat infestation or extermination through Chardon's tenure at Fort Clark.

There are other reasons why Chardon's tally of the rats he killed cannot serve as an accurate basis from which to infer the living population of rats at the post. Accuracy issues arise when considering the erratic habits of the person recording. Several theories could be advanced for why more rats were killed in certain months or years than in others. Variables include the amount of time Chardon spent indoors and his temperament. The most obvious bias affecting the data was Chardon's mental state and whether this instigated a fixation on killing rats. No doubt he was also motivated by a desire to safeguard furs and the fort's infrastructure, but varying degrees of depression and alcoholism could have either hampered or aided his efforts to combat rats.

Although the weather in North Dakota can be harsh and the winters brutal, comparing the numbers of rats killed against seasonal patterns showed little correlation. Some winter months like January showed as few as 24 or as many as 91 rats killed. Warmer months like July showed as few as 61 or as many as 201 eradicated. Further, birthing could occur whenever conditions such as access to food and shelter supported pregnancy. To best understand the dynamics of Fort Clark's rodent inhabitants, each year must be examined to find correlation between data patterns and historical events.

The methodology used in searching for trends was rudimentary and involved graphing each year's monthly totals, then correlating rises and falls in the number of deaths to known significant environmental or human historical events. A major issue in analysis of these trends is the quality of the data itself. Examination is limited by the possibility of biases in recording and the paucity of data for some years. But, making do with the data available, some understanding of the interplay of human history, ecology, and one synanthropic species can be achieved.

The data for 1834-35 presented no real pattern. The irregularity in these years may have been a simple function of inconsistent eradication efforts, or a harsh environment. The hardiness of the brown rat is partially responsible for the numbers remaining fairly high, albeit with great fluctuation. At no point does the rat colony appear to be near extinction. The pattern found in 1836 does vary significantly, between 82 and 294. Perhaps the rats found a new food source and this discovery either caused or coincided with a birthing. The spike to 294 kills in October is impressive, suggesting either a related population growth or increased hunting by Chardon.

The strongest correlation of rat population to human activity, and not just to Chardon's recording bias, occurs in 1837 in conjunction with the arrival of smallpox in July. The number of rats killed remains fairly consistent until November when there is a large spike, which closely follows the pattern of the previous year. The cause of this surge in the fall is unknown, but could be explained by lower temperatures driving rats as well as men indoors or simply more time spent inside the fort by Chardon and his men. Another possible cause for this pattern, however, could have been the smallpox epidemic. The dynamics and ramifications of this outbreak are addressed and discussed in more detail below.

The data for 1838 is the most complete record of rat killings and may be the best representation of a rat population at Fort Clark. There is a spike in rat deaths from February to April, then the usual decline to June. From June until the August-October period, there is an increased kill rate, though graphically exaggerated due to Chardon's lumping three months together. Then, the usual drop in December. Upsurges may represent the presence of matured individuals from birthings that could have happened in a previous month. No adverse or positive documented event occurred to hinder or aid the population.

The data set for 1839 is by far the smallest, possibly due to a fire on January 9 that destroyed Mit-tutta-hang-kush.[46] The January to February period seems quite similar to the same period in 1838. With the fire, the number of rats killed in the fort would

chardon's journal

"Employed the Men arranging the Pickets of the Fort, as they are eat off at the foundation by Rats, and in a fair way to tumble down."
Friday, March 15, 1839

---

be expected to jump immediately, because rats fleeing the village would have moved into the fort, increasing the rat population inside its walls. The spike does come, but not until March. It is doubtful that large numbers of rats died in the fire, because they have an amazing survival instinct and could escape faster than humans. It could coincide with a matured birthing, new food source, increased hunting by Chardon, or all of the above. The set is too small to detect a pattern.

The response to smallpox

On June 19, 1837, the steamboat *St. Peters* arrived at Fort Clark [see Casler article, this volume].[47] Although it was transporting supplies for the post, the ship was also a chariot of death, delivering smallpox to the Mandan village and Fort Clark. As the steamboat progressed upriver toward Fort Union, it spread its lethal cargo to any group it encountered. The location of villages and trading posts along the river facilitated the proliferation of the virus within dense populations that possessed no resistance to it. From 1836-40, smallpox was a pandemic among Native Americans, infecting tribes from the Missouri River to the Pacific Coast and from the Rio Grande River north to Canada and Alaska.[48]

The first smallpox death at Mit-tutta-hang-kush struck on July 14, 1837. By summer's end, the disease's mortality rate had reached 93.75 per cent, leaving only 100 survivors out of a total Mandan population of 1,600.[49] Those still alive abandoned the village of dead and dying people, for whom proper funeral rites were impossible.[50] This event ties in with what can only be termed an explosion of rats. The number of rats killed in 1837 prior to the outbreak are relatively low, especially compared to 1835 and 1836. That fall, the number of killed rats jumped from 74 in September to 268 in November.

The dead rat count, corresponding to a population boom, rose dramatically because of an expanded food source: the dead villagers. When Mit-tutta-hang-kush was abandoned, those near death were left behind and hundreds of bodies were left unburied. Rats, as scavengers, are quick to find dead carcasses. Within a day or two, rats can discover a corpse, scavenge the soft tissues, then gnaw on exposed bones. A typical cadaver would have provided the rats with about 1,200 calories per pound.[51] This larger source of nutrients fueled at least one birthing episode. Once the village was scavenged to the extent possible, the well-fed vermin turned to the fort. When the Arikara moved into the village the following year, bringing their stored foodstuffs and refuse, the rats would find a renewed supply of nutrients, and a restored habitat, at the village.

Conclusion

Humans introduced rats to ideal synanthropic niches at both the Fort Clark site and the nearby Mandan village, causing myriad problems for the human inhabitants. Later, smallpox was likewise introduced, killing off most of the native and some of the non-native humans, and creating a bigger infestation of rats due to an increased source of nutrients. The rats did not directly compete with the human inhabitants of the village or the post except for items like stored food, but they certainly took advantage of the opportunities provided to them.

Chardon's idiosyncratic record, though incomplete, suggests that rats were likely a significant problem at all settlements along the Missouri River.

Don Arp, Jr., holds an MA in anthropology (specializing in archaeology) from the University of Nebraska-Lincoln. His research has been cited in several textbooks and a New York Times bestseller. Arp has published in numerous journals, including the Journal of Forensic Identification, Journal of Pidgin and Creole Languages, *and* Group Practice Journal.

NOTES

1. Francis A. Chardon, *Chardon's Journal at Fort Clark, 1834-1839,* edited by Annie H. Abel (1932; Lincoln, NE: University of Nebraska Press, 1997).
2. W. Raymond Wood, "Integrating Ethnohistory and Archaeology at Fort Clark State Historic Site, North Dakota," *American Antiquity* 58, no. 3 (1993): 544.
3. Tom Thiessen, "Historic Trading Posts Near the Mouth of the Knife River," in Tom Thiessen, ed., *Ethnohistorical Studies*; "The Phase I Archeological Research Program for the Knife River Indian Villages National Historic Site, Part 2," *Occasional Studies in Anthropology* 27 (Lincoln, NE: Midwest Archeological Center, 1993), 62-63; Wood, "Integrating Ethnohistory," 545.
4. Wood, "Integrating Ethnohistory," 545.
5. Ibid.
6. Ibid.
7. James E. Moss, ed., "Ho! For the Gold Mines of Montana: Up the Missouri in 1865, Part 1," *Missouri Historical Review* 57 (1963): 179.
8. Wood, "Integrating Ethnohistory," 545. Information about the Fort Clark Historic Site is available at http://www.history.nd.gov/historicsites/clark/index.html.
9. Chardon, *Journal at Fort Clark*, xli.
10. Ibid.
11. William Swagerty, "Introduction," Chardon, *Journal at Fort Clark*, xviii.
12. Ray H. Mattison, "Francis A. Chardon," in Leroy R. Hafen, ed., *Fur Traders, Trappers and Mountain Men of the Upper Missouri* (Lincoln, NE: University of Nebraska Press, 1995), 61.
13. Hiram M. Chittenden, *The American Fur Trade of the Far West* (New York, NY: The Press of the Pioneers, Inc., 1935), 372.
14. Mattison, "Francis A. Chardon," 61-63.
15. Charles Larpenteur, *Forty Years a Fur Trader on the Upper Missouri,* edited by Elliot Coues (New York, NY: Francis P. Harper, 1898), 144.

16 Chardon, *Journal at Fort Clark*, 55.
17 Ibid., 103, 129, 133, 144, 181, 188, 190, 191.
18 Larpenteur, *Forty Years,* 218-219.
19 Chardon, *Journal at Fort Clark*, xxi.
20 Ibid., xix.
21 Elizabeth A. Fenn, *Encounters at the Heart of the World; A History of the Mandan People* (New York, NY: Hill and Wang, 2014), 290.
22 Chardon, *Journal at Fort Clark,* 188, 192.
23 Graham Twigg, *The Brown Rat* (London: David & Charles, 1975), 19.
24 Ibid., 22.
25 Ibid., 17.
26 Phillip Whitfield, ed., *A MacMillian Illustrated Encyclopedia of Animals* (New York, NY: MacMillian Library Reference, 1999), 61.
27 Twigg, *Brown Rat*, 29.
28 Ibid., 44.
29 Ibid., 29; Samuel A. Barnett, *The Rat: A Study in Behaviour* (Chicago, IL: Aldine Publishing Company, 1963).
30 Barnett, *The Rat,* 44.
31 Twigg, *Brown Rat*, 36, 37.
32 Fritz Steiniger, "Soziologie der wanderratte," *Zeitschrift für Tierpsychologie* 7 (1950): 356-379. Twigg, *Brown Rat*, 36.
33 Stephen S. Witte and Marsha V. Gallagher, eds., *The North American Journals of Prince Maximilian of Weid* 3 vols. (Norman, OK: University of Oklahoma Press, 2012), 3:53, 53nM1.
34 Twigg, *Brown Rat,* 74-75.
35 Ibid., 22. Alfred Henry Miles, *Natural History in Anecdote* (New York, NY: Dodd, Mead & Company, 1895), 227.
36 Twigg, *Brown Rat*, 22, 25.
37 Dena Dincauze, *Environmental Archaeology* (Cambridge, MA: Cambridge University Press, 2000), 473.
38 Whitfield, *Encyclopedia of Animals*, 61.
39 Twigg, *Brown Rat*, 78.
40 Witte and Gallagher, *Journals of Prince Maximilian*, 3:53.
41 Twigg, *Brown Rat*, 76.
42 Witte and Gallagher, *Journals of Prince Maximilian*, 3:95, 271.
43 For a discussion of previous fieldwork, see W. R. Wood, "Integrating Ethnohistory and Archaeology at Fort Clark State Historic Site, North Dakota," *American Antiquity* 58, no. 3 (1993); also W. R. Wood, W. J. Hunt, R.H. Williams, *Fort Clark and Its Indian Neighbors: A Trading Post on the Upper Missouri* (Norman, OK: University of Oklahoma Press, 2013).
44 Dr. William J. Hunt, e-mail message to author, June 18, 2003; W. J. Hunt, "Fort Clark Site, Central North Dakota, Early Historic Trade Along the Missouri River," in *Archaeology in America: An Encyclopedia,* edited by L. S. Cordell, K. Lightfoot, F. McManamon and G. Milner (Santa Barbara, CA: ABC-CLIO, 2008), 266-268.
45 H. A. Boller, *Among the Indians: Eight Years in the Far West: 1858-1866* (Philadelphia, PA: T. E. Zell, 1868), 33; W. J. Hunt, ed., *Archaeological Investigations at Fort Clark State Historic Site, North Dakota, 1973 through 2003: Studies at the Fort Clark and Primeau Trading Posts* (Flagstaff, AZ: PaleoCultural Research Group, 2003), 199, 225.
46 Wood, "Integrating Ethnohistory," 551.
47 Clyde D. Dollar, "The High Plains Smallpox Epidemic of 1837-38," *Western Historical Quarterly* 8, no. 1 (January 1977): 21.
48 Frank Fenner, Donald Henderson, Isao Arita, Jezek Zednek, and Ivan Ladnyi, *Smallpox and its Eradication* (Geneva: World Health Organization, 1988), 240.
49 Robert Beaglehole, Ruth Bonita, and Tord Kjellstrom, *Basic Epidemiology* (Geneva: World Health Organization, 1993), 21.
50 Wood, "Integrating Ethnohistory," 544.
51 William Haglund, "Rodents and Human Remains," in *Forensic Taphonomy: The Postmortem Fate of Human Remains,* edited by William Haglund and Marcella Sorg (Boca Raton, FL: CRC Press, 1997).

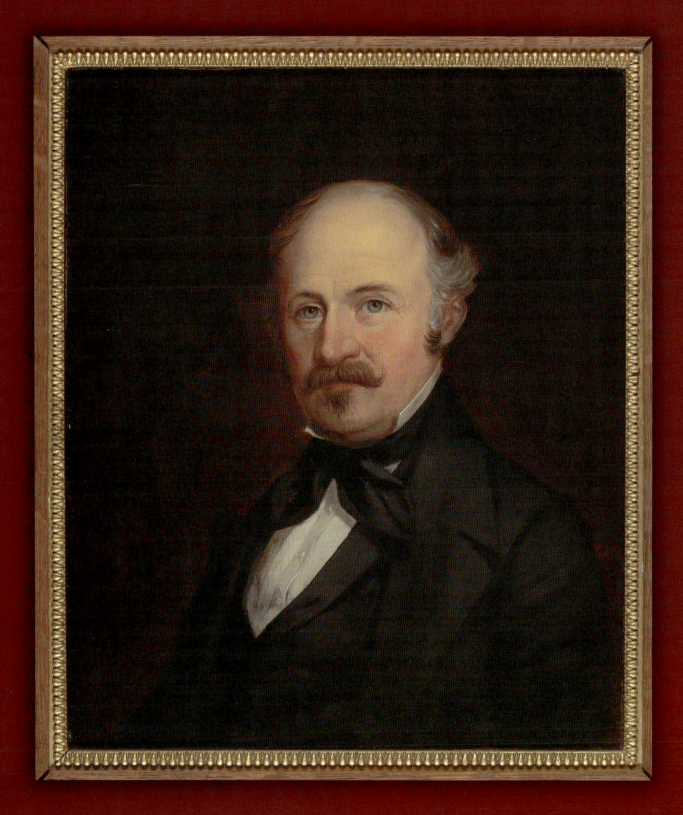

John Augustus Sutter (1803-1880), was painted by Stephen William Shaw in 1851, as Sutter's California fortune stumbled toward bankruptcy. Interestingly, the artist was engaged to Sutter's daughter Eliza for a short time after this portrait was completed. THE BANCROFT LIBRARY, UNIVERSITY OF CALIFORNIA, BERKELEY, BRK00001315 20A.TIF

The Influence of the Fur Trade on John Sutter

by Jim Hardee

Johann Augustus Sutter was a familiar name to settlers on the Overland Trails, and later it was at Sutter's sawmill that gold would be discovered, setting off the '49ers' rush to stake their claims. Sutter's Fort, dubbed New Helvetia (New Switzerland) by Sutter himself, is now surrounded by Sacramento, California, but it was an important rest and resupply station, or even a final destination for many following the California Trail into the Sacramento Valley. Early emigrant diaries cite Sutter's hospitality as a much-needed balm after the arduous journey to the Golden State. Yet it was Sutter's prior interactions with fur traders and mountain men that led him to place his post at that particular site in the northern region of Alta California. Without their influence, Sutter might easily have established his enterprise in the Los Angeles Basin, instead.[1]

Many of Sutter's entrepreneurial methods in California can be attributed to his six-month westward journey with Rocky Mountain fur traders in 1838. As he created his empire, Sutter would implement what he had learned: trapping as a means of income; employing low-paid, unskilled indigenous people as laborers; and extending credit to keep customers obligated.

Born in Germany to Swiss parents in 1803, Sutter married Annette Dubled in 1826. His mother-in-law set him up in the dry goods business in Burgdorf, Switzerland which failed after four struggling years, leaving him badly in debt. At age thirty-one, Sutter found himself with a wife and five children but no job. To escape debtor's prison, Sutter abandoned his family and left the country to seek opportunity in America.[2] He would not see them again until 1850.

Sutter reached New York in 1834 and joined other German emigrants bound for St. Louis, where several German-speaking colonies thrived along the Missouri River. He tried several ventures there, including farming and merchandising. He dabbled in the Indian trade among the displaced Delaware (Lenni Lenape), who had been driven from the eastern states to a reservation near Westport. By spring of 1835, Sutter had taken up as a Santa Fe merchant. About that time, he began using the title "Captain Sutter," though he had served only during his youth in Switzerland, and rose only to first underlieutenant in the reserve infantry of the Canton of Berne.[3]

In Taos, New Mexico, Sutter met "Mr. Popian," the town alcalde, or magistrate, describing him as an educated Canadian who had studied for the clergy but never taken orders.[4] This was Charles H. Beaubien, who had left his birthplace in Quebec at about twenty-one years of age, arriving in New Mexico in the spring of 1824.[5] In his initial years in the region, Beaubien worked as a trapper, including an 1827 expedition under Sylvestre Pratte.[6] By 1829, he had put away the traps, settled in Taos, and begun running a store.[7] He soon married Maria Paula Lobato, with whom he started a family. In 1829, Beaubien was granted naturalization as a Mexican citizen, and changed his name from Charles to Carlos. His business prospered, he got involved in local politics, and by the time Sutter arrived, Señor Beaubien had been named the first alcalde of Taos.[8]

California dreamin'

Sutter reported that as a trapper, Beaubien

had been in the southern part of California and gave me much information about this country. He said that it was a beautiful region with a fine climate and perpetual summer.[9]

Glorious tales of California's wonders were rife throughout Santa Fe and Taos. Few details of Beaubien's California journey are known, but the alcalde's enthusiasm was contagious, and Sutter decided to try his luck farther west. Sutter was probably aware that Beaubien had successfully negotiated a large land grant from the Mexican government, and he would have tucked that notion away for later use.[10]

A dashing young Sutter, illustrated wearing his Swiss militia uniform, is identified as "founder of the Territory New Helvetia on the Sacramento ... Upper California" on the frontispiece of Bruno Schmolder's *Neuer praktischer Wegweiser für Auswanderer nach Nord-Amerika* (Mainz, Germany: 1849). Schmolder visited Sutter in California in **1843.** NATIONAL LIBRARY OF THE NETHERLANDS

Unfortunately, Sutter's capacity for getting into debt caught up to him before he could hit the trail. After acquiring horses from the Apaches in New Mexico, Sutter drove them to Missouri for quick sale, and by spring of 1837 was investing the funds in real estate around the growing river town of Westport.[11] Triggered by a summons from the Jackson County sheriff ordering him to appear in court to answer charges from a creditor, the over-leveraged Sutter packed his bags and left Westport on April 1, 1838 – the day before his date with the judge. It was perhaps his first attempt in America to establish "a small empire on credit," a habit he would never break.[12] Joining Sutter on a short ride west to the Delaware Indian reservation, just across the Missouri River, were Pablo Gutierrez, a Mexican whom Sutter had hired in Santa Fe and who would work for him the rest of his life, and a German known only as Wetler.[13]

Sutter had stated he intended to reach California via Sonora. This meant he would have to return to Santa Fe, and on the strength of charity, legitimate loans, and forged drafts, work his way westward over old Spanish routes that would later become the Gila Trail, terminating in today's Los Angeles Basin.[14] Wagon trains bound for New Mexico had a choice of routes, but a heavily used road led out of Westport, passed over a high ridge, and was free from major stream crossings for at least eighty miles. Sapling Grove and several other creekside campsites were popular stopping points on the first or second night out of Westport.[15] It is likely that Sutter arrived at Sapling Grove after leaving Westport, planning to join a caravan heading west for Santa Fe.

Sapling Grove was a common rendezvous point for all parties aiming for either the rendezvous country of the Rocky Mountains, or the Southwest and California. The respective trails would split just a few miles beyond Sapling Grove. Sutter would also have found any of the campsites a good place to sign on a few more hands. These spots were popular with Santa Fe traders, missionaries, and mountain men. Later, soldiers, Oregon and California emigrants, and '49ers would join the throng. Wagon trains routinely passed through the Delaware reservation, often crossing the Kansas (or Kaw) River near modern Muncie, Kansas, a ford known as Delaware Crossing or Grinter's Ferry.[16]

American Fur Company influence

While Sutter was thus biding his time at Sapling Grove, a supply train was being organized in Westport by the Western Department of the American Fur Company (AFC) to take merchandise to the annual summer rendezvous in the Rocky Mountains.[17] The expedition was directed by an experienced fur trader, the Irish-born Andrew Drips, or "Tripps" as Sutter would call him.[18] Second in command of the caravan was Moses "Black" Harris, another veteran mountain man.[19]

Also accompanying the AFC convoy was Scottish nobleman Sir William Drummond Stewart, who had been traveling in the West since 1833, mostly for the love of adventure.[20] His companion was the *Metis* Antoine Clement, a proficient hunter and seasoned trapper.

Drips and his "train of empty carts" left Westport on April 22, 1838, headed for the Kansas River crossing, where they would be met by a Company flatboat bringing the rendezvous-bound goods upriver.[21] The AFC cavalcade consisted of around sixty men and about two dozen Red River carts, two-wheeled vehicles often called *charrettes*. Other freight vehicles consisted of a pair of four-wheeled wagons, together with about 200 horses and mules. Completing the caravan was a throng of "ten or fifteen Indian women and children," the wives and offspring of some of the hired hands.[22] On this trip, Stewart had one wagon of equipment that was pulled by four mules. A second private wagon was owned by George Rogers

Charles "Carlos" H. Beaubien (1800-1864), photographed in the early 1860s. THE MUSEUM OF NEW MEXICO, PALACE OF THE GOVERNORS PHOTO ARCHIVES (NMHM/DCA) #008799

Hancock Clark, son of renowned explorer William Clark.[23]

The day Drips motioned the cavalcade forward was a Sunday, thus a contingent of four missionary couples set to go west with the Company, all of whom were newlyweds, opted to delay for a day in order to observe the Sabbath [See Jill R. Ottman, "1836 and 1838: When White Girls Crashed the Party," *RMFTJ* 8]. William Gray had wed Mary Augustus Dix about two months earlier, having proposed on the same day they met. The other recently-married twosomes were Elkanah and Mary Richardson Walker, Cushing and Myra Fairbanks Eells, and Asa and Sarah White Smith. Cornelius Rogers, a twenty-two-year-old bachelor, completed the delegation that had volunteered to reinforce the evangelistic efforts Marcus Whitman had established earlier in Oregon territory. As it turned out, the contentious natures of these individuals, who were still getting to know one another, did not mesh well with each other or with the mountain men they were joining.

In 1836, William Gray had accompanied the Whitman-Spalding party to the Pacific Northwest, where they constructed a mission. Gray had returned East the following spring to recruit more helpers and, with luck, to find a wife. En route, Gray stopped at the 1837 trapper rendezvous and met Drips. Gray made arrangements for Drips to escort the fresh crop of westbound missionaries to the mountains with the AFC caravan in the spring of 1838.[24]

Now, instead of departing Westport with Drips, the missionary party began its overland trek the following day, on Monday, April 23, planning to catch up with the AFC pack train as soon as possible. The couples brought twenty-five horses and mules, nine yearling heifers, four fresh milk cows, and a dog named King. They hired mountain man John Stevens to help with the livestock and their single wagon.[25] Paul Richardson, a hunter and former employee of fur trader Nathaniel Wyeth, also joined their ranks.[26]

Meanwhile, Black Harris had led the AFC brigade to Sapling Grove, eight miles from Westport, and called a halt for the first day. As mentioned earlier, John Sutter was likely waiting here to join a suitable caravan to Santa Fe, and would have first encountered Drips's supply train at this camp. The fortuitous meeting would be a turning point not only in Sutter's life, but in the history of the West.[27]

Sutter indicated he had "engaged six men, all experienced mountaineers, and a Mexican servant; three of my men were Germans, two Yankees, and one was a Belgian."[28] Sutter's hiring practices, engaging men without the money to pay them, would have been as common then as it is now.

Adventurer Frederick Wislizenus would describe the convivial atmosphere of the Sapling Grove camp a year later:

The different parties who were to join the expedition met for their first night camp at Sapling Grove ... Our caravan was small. It consisted of only twenty-seven persons. Nine of them were in the service of the Fur Company of St. Louis (Chouteau, Pratte & Co.), and were to bring the merchandise to the yearly rendezvous on the Green River. Their leader was Mr. Harris, a mountaineer without special education, but with five sound senses, that he well knew how to use. All the rest joined the expedition as individuals ... Some others spoke of a permanent settlement on the Columbia; again, others intended to go to California, and so on. Almost all, however, were actuated by some commercial motive. The majority of the party were Americans; the rest consisted of French Canadians, a few Germans, and a Dane ... Our first camp, Sapling Grove, was in a little hickory wood, with fresh spring water ... After we had attended to our animals, and had eaten our supper, we sprawled around a fire, and whiled away the evening with chatting and smoking.[29]

During such an evening around the campfire in 1838, Sutter chatted with William Stewart, who had much to share about his life and adventures among the mountaineers of the West. Sutter wrote:

Sir William Drummond Stewart, a Scotchman, advised me to take the route over Fort Hall, a station of the Hudson's Bay Company on the road to Oregon. Stewart had been buffalo hunting several times in the Rocky Mountains ... He told me that this route was shorter and easier, and that at Fort Hall I should be able to find men who would be willing to accompany me to California. On account of the warlike Indians, I could not think of going directly to California.[30]

Thus, Sutter took the "Scotchman's" learned advice, changing his plan from the southern route over the Gila Trail to a trek along what would become the Overland Trail to Oregon and California. It would be much safer for Sutter's small party to travel in a group of well-armed men who knew the dusty road to the Rockies. Fort Laramie, a point of resupply, was also on the route. And, should he decide to go as far west as Fort Vancouver on the Columbia River, that Hudson's Bay Company (HBC) post would provide a jumping off point from which to travel south into California.

The next morning, the AFC supply train continued on its way, following a section of the Santa Fe Trail up the south bank of the Kansas River. By April 27, Harris had guided it to a point of timber near modern Manhattan, Kansas, where the Company flatboat would soon arrive with the supplies, and the river would be crossed.[31] The missionaries trooped into the AFC encampment late on the morning of April 28. Other than Gray, none of the Oregon-bound party were known to the fur brigade leaders, so while waiting for the crossing, Drips and Stewart paid a social call on the reverend and his companions.[32] None of the missionary diaries mention Sutter, but perhaps, with over seventy men in camp, they had yet to make his acquaintance.[33]

The Company boat, cordelled (pulled by ropes) upstream, arrived in time to effect the crossing on April 29, a Sabbath in name only, as Mary Walker bemoaned. It was quite a spectacle and everyone who lived anywhere close came to watch. Indians from a nearby village lined the bank. The livestock swam across the current while the flatboat made repeated trips ferrying people and baggage. Once everything was safely on the north bank, camp was reset among cottonwoods.[34]

Finally, the loaded caravan was set to move. Parting from the Santa Fe Trail, it rolled west along the Sublette Trace, which would become a portion of the Oregon Trail sometimes known as the Kansas Route.[35] Pulling out on April 30, Harris took the lead, riding a "large and distinguishably white mule," that would be easy for those coming behind to keep in sight. Following the guide was Stewart's wagon, then Drips in his cart hauled by three mules harnessed in single file. Next in order were the tarp-covered carts carrying the rendezvous supplies, trailed by Clark's wagon, then the loaded pack animals of the mission band. Their cattle brought up the rear of the nearly half-mile-long cavalcade. The ladies often road at the back of the line, a dusty position. Still, they were admonished not to fall too far behind.[36]

Apart from his own account, the first evidence of Sutter's presence among the missionaries may appear in their wives' diaries after two weeks on the trail. On May 15, Mary Walker reported she

fell in company with a gentleman from New Orleans who has traveled in Europe, Africa, &c., who has entertained us with descriptions of Switzerland, Italy, etc. Gave an account of Swiss dogs digging men out who are buried in the snow.[37]

Another possibility is that Mrs. Walker was referring in this passage to Sir William Drummond Stewart, who had wintered in New Orleans and was known to have traveled in the places mentioned. However, she had met Stewart earlier in the trip and would have presumably named him in this diary entry, rather than calling him "a gentleman."

Mary Walker would mention Sutter by name on July 27, describing an instance when "Sutor" was unable to keep up with the main part of the caravan, thus she and the Swiss man brought up the rear together.[38]

Following the north side of the Kansas River soon brought the caravan to the Big Blue. Turning up that river took the

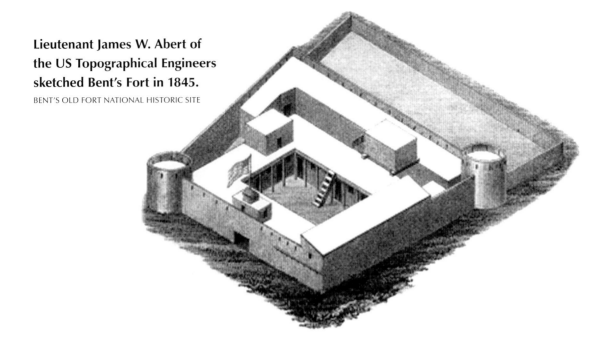

Lieutenant James W. Abert of the US Topographical Engineers sketched Bent's Fort in 1845.
BENT'S OLD FORT NATIONAL HISTORIC SITE

supply train to the Platte, where Drips continued along its north fork. Soon, they had passed several landmarks; Sutter got a look at Courthouse and Chimney rocks, among others. On May 21, 1838, Sutter met John B. Sarpy, a trader among Indian tribes along the Platte and also in the service of the American Fur Company.[39] By May 30, the caravan had reached Fort William, just beginning to be called Fort Laramie.[40]

In charge at the post was Lucien Fontenelle, an experienced mountaineer who had been involved with the fur trade since at least 1819, working for one company or another. Like Sutter, he had earned a reputation as a hard drinking man; possibly the two men got along well.[41] Artist Alfred Jacob Miller had met Fontenelle the year before and spoke kindly of the post commander. Miller also painted several images of the log-stockaded trading post, describing Fort Laramie as

a quadrangle form, with bastions at the diagonal corners to sweep the fronts in case of attack; over the ground entrance is a large blockhouse, or tower, in which is placed a cannon. The interior is possibly 150 feet square, a range of houses built against the palisades entirely surround it, each apartment having a door and window overlooking the interior court.[42]

This was not the first wilderness trading post Sutter had visited. While involved in the Santa Fe trade, he had stopped at Bent's Fort on the Arkansas River.[43] Sutter had likely examined those fortifications, making mental notes for future use, as he would now have done at Fort Laramie. Though Sutter's opinion of Fort Laramie was not recorded, Myra Eells wrote in her diary that "it compares well with the walls of the Conn. State Prison."[44]

The ensuing days were spent resting, washing and mending clothes, and allowing the livestock to recuperate. The ladies prepared a meal and invited several of the AFC officers to join them for dinner. Though Sutter was not named, he might have been a part of this special supper.[45]

Before departing Fort Laramie, the missionary contingent left its wagon at the fort, along with a few cattle too worn out to continue. Gray may have remembered Marcus Whitman's difficulty getting a Dearborn carriage over the road two years earlier.[46]

On June 2, 1838, Drips signaled the supply train westward, now joined by Fontenelle, who planned to attend the rendezvous and then take an AFC brigade out to trap. A man was sent ahead, probably Moses Harris, to alert trappers throughout the mountains to the approaching supplies, and to a change in the rendezvous location. Originally slated to occur on the Green River site, the gathering was moved to the Popo Agie River on the east side of the Continental Divide. The courier posted a sign at the original location.[47] HBC field captain Francis Ermatinger would find the note, and thus be able to fulfill the agreement he had made the year before with missionary William Gray. Ermatinger was to help bring the new crop of missionaries from the trapper rendezvous to Oregon. His guide to the Popo Agie country was identified by historian Clifford Drury as Baptiste Dorion.[48]

Proceeding up the North Platte, the landscape began to change as the trail entered the Black Hills, known today as the Laramie Mountains. The caravan soon crossed the Platte, the route then ascending the Sweetwater. Ten days out of Fort Laramie, Sutter caught his first glimpse of the snow-capped Wind River Range of the Rocky Mountains. Two days later, the supply train reached Independence Rock, where many earlier overland voyagers had etched their names in its granite surface. The young Clark made his mark, "Geo. R. H. Clark 37," but if Sutter inscribed his name, it has not survived the elements over time.[49]

1838 Popo Agie Rendezvous

On June 17, some of Joseph Walker's men, preceding their leader to the trapper gathering, came to the AFC camp.[50] Some of these trappers may have been with Walker on his expedition to California in 1833.[51] Of the dozens in Walker's California brigade, only a few names are known. Walker's clerk, Zenas Leonard,

Francis Ermatinger, Hudson's Bay Company trader, photographed in about 1850.
THE ROYAL BC MUSEUM AND ARCHIVES #A-01308

kept a personal journal of the trip. Those he named were William Craig, Bill Williams, Levin Mitchell, George Nidever, Powell (Pauline) Weaver, and the Meek brothers, Joe and Stephen.[52] At least six of Walker's men had stayed in California, but how many of the remainder were still trapping in the Rockies and would have attended the 1838 rendezvous is impossible to determine.[53] Crossing the Popo Agie River, the caravan pulled into rendezvous on June 23.

On his trip west, Sutter was increasingly surrounded by people with fur trade experience. We have no record that Sutter ever interviewed any of the mountain men to glean what lay ahead. What we do have are Sutter's recollections of the journey, and the record of his activity after reaching California. As will be seen, his choices mirrored many practices in the fur trade canon.

An experienced merchant familiar with civilized commerce, Sutter confined his description of rendezvous to *a few block houses and stores where hunters and trappers bought their supplies. Every year the traders and trappers would meet here for a few weeks to make their barters. It was only a temporary trading post.*[54]

On June 25, Joe Walker himself arrived. Walker and his large company had spent the spring in the Southwest and possibly California, collecting and driving hundreds of horses that they hoped to sell, if not at the rendezvous, then at the trading posts springing up in the mountains.[55] Walker would have represented a rich storehouse of information for Sutter – if the two ever conversed – about the road to California, how to cross the Great Basin, and surmounting the Sierra Nevada Mountains.

If Sutter camped near the argumentative missionaries, he was likely aware of visits by William Craig, a veteran of Walker's California brigade whose insights Sutter would have found valuable.[56] Myra Eells periodically extended dinner invitations to Craig, Walker, Drips and their wives, and wrote of making dresses for these ladies.[57] If Sutter also attended those evening soirees, he would have learned much from these mountaineers.

With the fur trade on the decline, rumors were spreading that no rendezvous was planned for the summer of 1839.[58] Some trappers were already looking for new opportunities, and Sutter found them anxious to sign on with him for a trip to the Pacific coast. At the same time, Walker's horse herd, thought to have been stolen from California ranches, may have spurred trapper ambitions.[59] To Sutter's chagrin, he

could find enough men here to accompany me to California, but I was wise enough not to accept them. They wanted to organize a band of robbers under my leadership in order to steal cattle and rob missions and settlements.[60]

Sutter did hire a couple of mountain men, a German named Niklaus Allgeier, and the Austrian Sebastian Keyser; both would work for Sutter for several years to come.[61]

Another trapper with California experience appeared at this rendezvous. Christopher "Kit" Carson had gone from New Mexico via the Sonoran route to the Pacific shores in 1829, as a member of Ewing Young's party. Having traveled north to the Sacramento Valley, Carson remembered plenty of pasturage for horses and lots of beaver in surrounding streams. If Sutter spoke with Carson, the conversation would likely have made the storekeeper ponder not only alternate routes, but also the Sacramento River area. It was probably not the first time one of Sutter's informants had mentioned this major waterway. Carson's autobiography mentioned the missionaries and Sir William, but did not record Sutter's presence.[62]

Sutter, however, did mention Carson in connection with a slave purchase:

The young Indian I had bought from Bill Brown at the Rendezvous, who in turn had bought him from Kit Carson. I paid for him with a beaver order of one hundred dollars on the Hudson's Bay Company. Since these beaver orders were worth more than their equivalent in American money, the boy really cost me one hundred and thirty dollars. This was rather a high price, but the Indian was very useful to me because he could speak English.[63]

It is not clear if the transaction between Brown and Carson happened while camped on the Popo Agie, or if the exchange had occurred in the more distant past.[64] Many mountain men accepted Indian slavery as a method of increasing productivity. Among tribes that frequented summer rendezvous, the Utes had learned early on that Indian children could be traded for horses, particularly in Mexican provinces. A substantial trade in slaves extended from the southwest into Canada. Indeed, Native servants accompanied HBC men on expeditions throughout the Rockies.⁶⁵ In any case, Sutter's purchase of the boy was yet another transaction made on credit, a practice that was a cornerstone of his business ventures.⁶⁶ Whether or not Sutter had been accustomed to servants in his previous life, he would take full advantage of Indian slaves in his California empire.

At rendezvous, Sutter likely noticed many of the men's near-servitude. Those who had spent the prior year trapping beaver usually needed more supplies than the number of beaver credited to their accounts would allow them to purchase. But this lack of resources seldom slowed the trapper. As Benjamin Bonneville explained, debt was the order of the day:

> *For a free mountaineer to pause at a paltry consideration of dollars and cents ... would stamp him with the mark of the beast in the estimation of his comrades. For a trader to refuse one of these free and flourishing blades a credit, whatever unpaid scores might stare him in the face, would be a flagrant affront scarcely to be forgiven.*⁶⁷

Here was yet another example to Sutter of how to keep a workforce on the job under the heavy thumb of debt from which it could hardly escape.

Unable to find a satisfactory escort, Sutter knew that he "could not think of going directly to California" with only the handful of men under his command.⁶⁸ Besides, Stewart had recommended a route via Fort Hall, not across the Sierra, and Sutter still hoped to recruit men at that post. Thus, on July 8, when a group of fourteen HBC men arrived from Fort Hall to conduct the missionaries to the Columbia River, Sutter opted to gather his small band of recruits and go with them.⁶⁹

This was the party guided by Dorion and led by Francis Ermatinger, whom Sutter referred to as Franz.⁷⁰ Born in Portugal, Ermatinger had worked for Hudson's Bay since 1818 and had traveled throughout HBC's Columbia Department for the past dozen years, becoming quite familiar with the territory.⁷¹ Ermatinger's HBC assignment had been to spend the winter at Fort Hall. He had made the trip to rendezvous purely for the benefit of the missionaries.⁷²

Sway of the Hudson's Bay Company

After less than three weeks at the 1838 Rocky Mountain rendezvous, the greenhorns had had their fill. Waiting for them at Fort Hall were longed-for fresh horses and supplies, including flour, rice, and meal, sent from the Oregon mission. Thus, Ermatinger and his charges set out for that destination on July 12.⁷³ The party crossed South Pass on the 15th, camping on a stream that flowed to the Pacific. Mary Eells felt her unborn baby kick for the first time that evening.⁷⁴

Trapper Joe Meek had left his AFC brigade at rendezvous to travel with his Nez Perce wife and family, who were accompanying Ermatinger's group to visit relatives in the Northwest.⁷⁵ As mentioned earlier, Meek had been to California with Walker's brigade in 1833 – another potential source of information for Sutter. Ermatinger led the party on to the Bear River, camping at Soda Springs on July 25. While there, the ladies used the effervescent fountains to mix dough, then baked biscuits in their tin reflector oven. "The bread is as light as any prepared with yeast," reported Sarah Smith.⁷⁶ Joe Meek "obtained a taste of the coveted luxury, bread – of which, during nine years in the mountains he had not eaten."⁷⁷

Two days later, Sutter rode with Meek, Ermatinger's HBC escort, and the missionaries into Fort Hall, an HBC post originally established by the American Nathaniel Wyeth in 1834 near modern Pocatello, Idaho. This was the day Mary Walker first named Sutter in her diary. Walker was not feeling

Fort Hall, illustrated in 1849, was originally built as a log stockade by Nathaniel Wyeth in 1834. The post was purchased by the Hudson's Bay Company in 1836 and would become a major stopover for overland travelers. IDAHO STATE HISTORICAL SOCIETY, #1893-B

well, and noted that Sutter also lagged. He was good enough to accompany her:

> Set out as usual with Dr. G & wife, but Ermatinger & Batiste came on & they set off with them & left me behind. Capt. Sutor happened to be with me, and not having on his spurs was unable to keep up. So he & I were left alone without guide.[78]

The pair was the last of the party to reach the fort, but they were happy to find a breakfast set with boiled ham, bread, and salted buffalo tongue. For the first time since leaving the Missouri frontier, the emigrants sat on stools at a table to eat a meal.[79]

Here, Sutter had the opportunity to examine another fur trade post on this journey. Mrs. Walker described Fort Hall as

> built of doughbees which are clay made in form of brick two feet long, six inches deep. The wall is double & the room as cool as a cellar almost.[80]

No doubt Sutter compared these adobes along the Snake River with the ones he had seen at Bent's Fort on the Arkansas.

At the post, Sutter met Thomas McKay, an experienced HBC trader and brigade leader who had come to the Rockies with John Astor's Pacific Fur Company in 1811.[81] Likely more interesting to Sutter, McKay had been with Alexander McLeod's expedition to California in 1829-30. McLeod had begun the journey from Fort Vancouver and traveled overland as far south as modern Stockton, California. McKay might have related to Sutter the bitter, snowy winter his brigade faced in the mountains of northeastern California. All of the horses died, the traps and heavy equipment were lost, and the brigade's furs had to be cached for later retrieval.[82] Still, here was another route to California for Sutter to consider.

According to Sutter, Ermatinger provided him an Indian guide, informing the native that Sutter was "a King George man," not a "Boston."[83] This would protect Sutter's

Fort Boise in about 1849. The Hudson's Bay Company instituted many improvements to the post's structure as greater numbers of emigrants stopped by on their way west. IDAHO STATE HISTORICAL SOCIETY, #1254-D

status, because the British HBC maintained a lengthier, somewhat more stable relationship with tribes of the Northwest than did many Americans. Though Ermatinger had Swiss heritage, the record provides no indication that this common thread created a strong bond between the two men, or that Ermatinger treated Sutter with more kindness than he did other travelers.[84]

On July 31, leaving its cattle at Fort Hall, the missionary delegation continued its journey, accompanied by Sutter. Men from Fort Hall, deployed as escorts, led the way to Fort Boise on the east bank of the Snake River, near the mouth of the Boise. Two full weeks of traveling along the south side of the Snake brought them to the post on Wednesday, August 15, 1838.[85]

In charge at Fort Boise was Francois Payette, a forty-five-year-old Canadian fur trader.[86] This HBC outpost was not as well appointed as others. Reverend Gray described it several years later as "a miserable pen of a place":

It consisted of cottonwood poles and crooked sticks set in a trench, and pretended to be fastened near the top. The houses or quarters were also of poles, open; in fact, the whole concern could hardly be called a passable corral, or pen for horses and cattle, I think, from appearances, the fort had been used to corral or catch horses in.[87]

Payette welcomed his guests with a feast of milk, butter, salmon, turnips and pumpkins. Mrs. Walker created a boiled pudding and a turnip sauce to accompany their fish entrée. Sturgeon was offered at another meal. While at Fort Boise, Payette and Sutter joined the missionaries for tea; Sarah Smith baked a pie and some biscuits for the occasion.[88] Sutter went so far as to say, "How glad we were to come to a resting place where we could get something decent to eat!"[89]

The following Monday, Sutter's band and the missionary couples packed up and took the trail once more. Two Indians were assigned to guide them to the site of Whitman's work among the natives. Riding predominantly north, they struck the Powder River, soon crossed the Grand Ronde Valley, and entered the Blue Mountains. At about 2 p.m. on August 30, they at last reached the Whitman Mission at Waiilatpu, on the Walla Walla River seven miles west of present Walla Walla, Washington. The weary travelers were cordially welcomed by Marcus Whitman, Henry Spalding and their wives. Sutter and the newcomers were provided with melons, pumpkin pies and milk for a late lunch. Mrs. Walker wrote that

Towards night we partook of a fine dinner of vegetables, salt salmon, bread, butter, cream &c. Thus our long toilsome journey at length came to a close.[90]

Yet Sutter still had miles to go. As a goodwill parting gesture, Sutter gave his leather-bound French and English pocket dictionary to Elkanah Walker. The flyleaf reads "Elkanah Walker Presented by Capt. Sutor," in Mary's handwriting.[91]

From Waiilatpu, Sutter planned to travel to Fort Walla Walla, twenty-five miles west at the confluence of the Columbia River, with the further goal of reaching Fort Vancouver. Payette's Indian guide brought the Swiss and his men as far as Walla Walla, where Pierre Pambrun received them kindly. Sutter described "Tambrun" as "an educated man who had served as an officer in the British Army," recognizing the common bond of a military background.[92] Pambrun had been appointed Fort Walla Walla's chief clerk in March 1832. Fort Walla Walla produced mediocre fur returns, but its proximity to the Cayuse and Nez Perce tribes, famous for vast herds of prime horses, was integral to keeping HBC supplied with mounts and pack animals. The fort was also an important jumping-off point for the interior, particularly the Snake River country.

Consequently, many travelers became acquainted with Pambrun, including fur trade notables Nathaniel Wyeth, Benjamin Bonneville, Joe Meek, Robert Newell, William Craig and numerous Americans traveling the Oregon Trail.[93]

Copious amounts of horse meat were eaten by the employees of this post. In addition to imported provisions and the few consumables grown in fort gardens, 700 head had been slaughtered to feed eleven men over a three-year period.[94] Sutter was somewhat taken aback at Pambrun's food staple, maintaining that

Since I was not accustomed to horse meat, it struck me as quite singular when the commander said at our departure: "I am sorry you are going now, I have just killed a fat mare."[95]

After a few days at Fort Walla Walla, Sutter was ready to continue his journey to Fort Vancouver, some 200 miles beyond. He procured yet another guide to steer him down the Columbia River to The Dalles, a large rapid that HBC's Ross Cox referred to as a three-mile "succession of boiling whirlpools."[96] A Methodist mission, named Wascopam after the local population, had just recently been established at this location.[97] According to Sutter's diary,

The Dalles was a model settlement for that early date, combining a Methodist mission with a trading establishment, both in charge of H. K. W. Perkins and Daniel Lee. When I asked for a guide to the Willamette Valley, Mr. Lee told me that he himself would bring me there. He intended to exchange horses, which he had purchased from the Indians, for cattle in the Willamette Valley.[98]

Missionary Daniel Lee took a convoluted overland course westward toward the Willamette River, paralleling the Columbia, causing delays that did not set well with Sutter's two experienced mountaineers, who soon rebelled. Sutter reported,

> As I myself was anxious to reach California before the end of the year, I finally gave in. So we struck out over the mountains through the wildest country which I had ever seen.[99]

Sutter's self-guided crew made it to the Willamette Valley eight days ahead of Lee, but it was not an easy trek. At several steep places, the horses had to be let down by ropes. Had it not been for his Mexican servant, Sutter's livestock would have all been carried away by the current during a stream crossing. Sutter's diary continued:

> One night we camped at the foot of Mount Hood. We had nothing to eat but dried fish, and there was no grass and no water for the animals. However, when we started the next morning, the mules and horses suddenly scented water, and then nothing could hold them. When we arrived in the Willamette Mission on the ninth of September, six days after our departure from the mission at The Dalles, people would not have believed us had I not carried with me a letter from Mr. Perkins.[100]

Sutter alleged that the Willamette Valley missionaries tried to persuade him to settle there, but he was determined to go on to Fort Vancouver, and ultimately, California.[101] After billeting his small team in the Willamette Valley, Sutter took to the Columbia via canoe, paddling downriver to the HBC headquarters, where he arrived in early October after six months of coaching by mountain men and fur traders.[102]

At Fort Vancouver, Sutter encountered James Douglas, Chief Trader for the Hudson's Bay Company and commander of the fort in the absence of Chief Factor John

Sir James Douglas served as HBC Chief Trader when Sutter knew him at Fort Vancouver. He was promoted to Chief Factor in 1839 and eventually became Governor of Vancouver Island, retiring in 1864.

McLoughlin, away on business.[103] Before leaving the trapper rendezvous, Sutter had thought ahead and acquired a letter of introduction from Sir William Drummond Stewart. Stewart knew Douglas from the winter the Scot had spent at Fort Vancouver in 1834-35. This personalized document, informing a fellow Brit of the Swiss gentleman's plans, noticeably smoothed Sutter's path:

> Hence I was made welcome and was invited by the Governor to spend the winter among the hospitable Britishers. If they just hadn't smoked so much tobacco! I could hardly get my breath in their smoking room.[104]

In his October report to HBC command in London, Douglas announced the arrival of "Captain Sutter, a Swiss gentleman ... The object of his visit, is not exactly known." Given that Sutter appears to have provided

Fort Vancouver, pictured here in a Gustav Sohon lithograph of 1854, was the grandest post operated by the HBC below the 49th Parallel. It was established on the bank of the Columbia River in 1825-1829. The post palisades enclosed forty buildings, with goods and services comparable to those of a large town in more civilized areas. FORT VANCOUVER NATIONAL HISTORIC SITE

different stories to different people, this is not surprising. Douglas explained that

> all that I can learn of his history is, that he derives his title from a commission formerly held in the French army, and has no connection whatever to the U.S. Government. He left Europe with a respectable fortune, invested it in business, and was unfortunate during the late commercial pressure in the United States, and at present proposes to drive Cattle from California to the Wallamate.[105]

Lee's mission log noted Sutter's "tarry" at Fort Vancouver, and described what he understood to be Sutter's plan: "Capt. Suter" was on

> his way to California intending to return with cattle, leave them here, go to Switzerland and return with his family and friends and found a Swiss settlement.[106]

Lee was not the only one who thought he understood Sutter. Numerous men in the Fort Vancouver area were willing to accompany Sutter in the ensuing spring to bring livestock back to their farms on the Columbia. But this would have meant spending the winter at Fort Vancouver to avoid the snow-packed passes barring the southern route – time Sutter was loathe to waste, so eager was he to get to California.

Sutter weighed several alternatives, from common trapper trails to sailing ships. Trapping expeditions to California had launched from Fort Vancouver every year since 1826. Michel Laframboise, who allegedly had a wife of high rank in every important Indian tribe along the route, led the first HBC party to the Sacramento River in 1832.[107] Thus, while at the HBC post, Sutter would have had access to several trappers familiar with the Sacramento Valley, even though he had evidently given serious consideration to heading south on the overland route that was becoming known as the Siskiyou Trail.[108]

Douglas suggested sailing to Hawaii, then boarding a ship bound for San Francisco or Monterey, a relatively common itinerary. It had worked nicely in 1834 for naturalist Thomas Nuttall, who had sailed to Oahu from Fort Vancouver, then to Monterey, and eventually all the way home to Boston.[109] Sutter liked the notion, and "since there was a vessel about to sail for the Sandwich Islands ... decided to follow Governor Douglas's advice."[110] The vessel was the HBC bark *Columbia*, loaded with 60,000 board feet of lumber for Hawaii and the season's fur packs bound for London. Sutter paid £15 for his cabin and £6 for accommodations in the forecastle with the ship's crew, taking only two men with him: his German companion Wetler, and the bilingual Indian boy. Sutter's plan was for the others "to follow by the [Siskiyou Trail] as soon as I had settled in California." Three from this group are known to have reunited with Sutter in California by this or another means: Allgeier, Keyser, and Gutierrez.[111]

Sutter sold the horses and mules he had acquired to settlers around Fort Vancouver, then embarked for Hawaii when the *Columbia* sailed on November 11, 1838. Twenty-eight stormy days later, the Swiss gentleman disembarked at Honolulu with a pocket full of introductory letters, including a new one penned by Chief Trader James Douglas to accompany those written by the head officers of every post he had visited along the way, and from the mission directors as well.[112]

Having thought to save five months by sailing to Hawaii, rather than waiting for good weather to cross the mountains, Sutter spent eight months negotiating the last leg of his westward journey:

As a Vessel of the Compy was ready to sail for the Sandwich Islands, I took a passage in her, in hopes to get Soon a Passage from there to California, but 5 long Months I had to wait to find an Opportunity to leave, but not direct to California, except far out of my Way to the Russian American Colonies on the North West Coast, to Sitka ... I remained one Month there and delivered the Cargo of the Brig Clementine, *as I had Charge of the Vessel, and then sailed down the Coast in heavy Gales, and entered in Distress in the Port of San Francisco, on the 2d of July 1839 ... In Monterey I arranged my affairs with the Custom House, and presented myself to Govr. Alvarado, and told him ... that I intend to Settle in the interior on the banks of the river Sacramento.*[113]

Putting to use the lessons learned

By the time he reached California on July 2, 1839, Johann Augustus Sutter possessed a template for success gleaned from a wide range of sources. He had visited seven fur trading posts: Bent's Fort, New Archangel, and forts Laramie, Hall, Boise, Walla Walla, and Vancouver. These were the most important frontier enterprises in the Southwest, the Rocky Mountains, the American and British shared regions of the Pacific Northwest, and Russian Alaska. From discussions with some of the foremost traders in the business, Sutter had learned how the industry was conducted. He had received numerous opportunities to discuss California's potential with many men who had been in that land of plenty.

While in Santa Fe and Taos, Sutter had probably learned the benefits of Mexican land grants from fur trader Carlos Beaubien. Sutter put Beaubien's example to good use in California when, in 1841, he obtained title to nearly 50,000 acres from Governor Juan Alvarado. After the required one-year residence in Alta California, Sutter appeared

VIEW OF CAPTAIN SUTTER'S FORT, NEAR SACRAMENTO CITY, CALIFORNIA, NOW MANNED BY U. S. TROOPS.

An 1846 engraving of Sutter's Fort notes that it is "now manned by U.S. troops," a reference to the Mexican-American War. CALIFORNIA STATE PARKS, SUTTER'S FORT SHP: #5487

before Alvarado. He received citizenship and requested a land grant of eleven square leagues (more than 48,000 acres). Sutter convinced Alvarado that the New Helvetia grant would be a place for American emigrants to settle, thus colonizing the region's north for Mexico.[114]

The land grant would effectively provide a buffer to Mexican settlements in the south, protecting those residents from marauding Indians, hunters, and trappers who might visit the valley.[115]

Sutter must have selected his New Helvetia location carefully. Most of the trading posts he had visited were located at the confluence of two rivers, and Fort Vancouver's access to the Pacific gave it a special advantage. He had probably made up his mind when he left Alaska that his colony would be at the confluence of the American and Sacramento rivers, with navigable access to ocean trade routes.[116] In choosing that site for Sutter's Fort, he combined a frontier outpost with an idea of maritime trade in a location fur trappers already frequented on their way to and from Oregon Country. And it was also, as it turned out, where Americans would naturally gather after crossing the Sierra Nevada Mountains.[117]

Further, Sutter designed his New Helvetia to physically resemble successful settlements like Bent's Fort and Fort Vancouver.[118] Compare Sutter's own description of his fort on the Sacramento (built predominantly by Indian labor using the model practiced at the California missions):

I built a one-story building of adobe. This house was about forty feet long and contained a blacksmith shop, a kitchen, and a room for myself ... I built a large house near the first adobe building ...

surrounded with walls eighteen feet high, enclosing altogether seventy-five thousand square feet. The walls were made of adobe bricks and were about two and a half feet thick. At two corners I built bastions with walls five feet thick ... Within the enclosure I erected other buildings; barracks for the soldiers, workshops and dwellings, a bakery, a mill, and a blanket factory. The tannery was built on the spot where I had first landed ... There were several outhouses for vaqueros and other employees.[119]

How did Sutter know what supplies to stock at his fort? During visits to fur trading posts and while at the rendezvous, Sutter learned what items were traded and what merchandise was wanted in return. Having done business in Santa Fe and with the Delaware people outside of Westport, Sutter saw the goods that were necessary for a frontier lifestyle. Now, in the Sacramento Valley, Sutter traded with Indians, hired trappers, and bought and sold beaver pelts as well as other valuable skins. In short, from 1839 on, he too relied on the fur trade for what cash resources it could bring. Beaver became Sutter's initial medium of exchange:

From the Hudsons Bay Company I received likewise great supplies, and particularly Powder, lead, and Shot, Beaver Trapps and Clothing (on Credit, to be paid for in Beaver and Otter Skins). They would not have done this to everyone; but as I has been highly recommended to these gentlemen from England and personally acquainted, they have done so.

There were plenty of beaver and otter skins, the former being worth four dollars and the latter three dollars a pound, as well as elk and deer skins.[120]

How did Sutter acquire and control employees? From observing how conglomerate fur companies operated, he learned that access to, and control over, a labor force was essential, particularly using Native peoples as low-paid, unskilled workers. The success or failure of his venture depended in large measure on the skill with which he handled these often unpredictable charges. Fortunately, he had some experience with the Indian trade and had been in close contact with numerous Indian peoples during his travels through the Rocky Mountains and in the Northwest, all of which proved helpful in his dealings with tribes in the Sacramento Valley. Sutter used Indian labor much as he had seen fur traders do, but he modified mountain practices to suit his needs.[121] He also extended credit to workers, creating a debtor class obligated to bring its furs and to engage in menial jobs under its creditors.

Sutter learned by observing company traders that manipulating prices for goods sold and received was essential to sustaining his operation. Sutter realized that frontier enterprise was less about competition and free markets, and more about control, manipulation of workers and monopoly. From time spent among the beaver men, Sutter could see how sharp business practices drove out rivals.[122]

Sutter's hospitable treatment at the hands of British fur traders may have molded his pattern of caring for immigrants and passersby. During his journey west, every HBC post he visited had freely offered food and comfort, assisting weary travelers with everything at their disposal. Sarah Smith noted, "I often think this company outdo the Americans in kindness & hospitality."[123] Sutter's reputation for generosity was frequently cited in the diaries of early travelers to the Golden State, many extolling Sutter's Fort as a much needed Mecca of recovery after a long, arduous journey across the continent. John Bidwell, for example, wrote in 1841,

> *Sutter received us with open arms and in a princely fashion, for he was a man of the most polite address and the most courteous manners, a man who could shine in [any] society ... Nearly everybody who came to California made it a point to reach Sutter's Fort. Sutter was one of the most liberal and hospitable of men. Everybody was welcome – one man or a hundred, it was all the same.*[124]

By contrast, Sutter also learned from HBC alliances with Native Americans and AFC price wars at rendezvous – to give just two examples – how to treat competitors.

HBC trappers who worked California streams a few years later met Sutter's hostility and contempt. In the spring of 1842, with his fort "protected by a body of runaway sailors, vagabond trappers from the United States, & other desperadoes," Sutter repeatedly threatened Francis Ermatinger, leader of HBC's southern trapping party working along the Sacramento River that year, in an effort to drive him from California. Hearing of Sutter's threats against Ermatinger and HBC brigades, HBC Governor George Simpson expressed regret at having loaned Sutter between three and four thousand dollars to aid his settling in California.[125] Gratitude for past favors was soon forgotten.

In less than ten years, Sutter would find himself at the receiving end of such disregard. After gold was discovered on January 24, 1848, the Gold Rush enveloped California. His workmen quit their jobs to hunt for gold, and tens of thousands of new arrivals ignored the law and helped themselves to Sutter's land, crops and livestock. Sutter took on merchant partners hoping to supply the miners, but his partners cheated him, and before long he was ruined, with creditors hounding him.

In 1849, an attorney was hired to sort out Sutter's finances. He began by selling lots in Sacramento City, a new town developed from Sutter's land grant. Enough money was raised to pay off much of Sutter's old debt, including $7,000 to HBC. James Douglas came to collect the payment in person.[126]

Sutter lost the fort to his creditors and moved to a small farm fifty miles north. Between January 1851 and December 1852, he mortgaged his farm at least six times and finally went bankrupt. In 1879 he lamented,

> *the discovery of the gold has destroyed all my enterprises and plans[,] and bad designing men and thieves and even the courts treated me very badly & unjust.*[127]

John Sutter died impoverished in a Pennsylvania hotel room in 1880.

By establishing a fortified settlement in Mexican California's Sacramento Valley in 1839, Johann Augustus Sutter attracted overland emigrants from the United States. In the right place at the right time, Sutter aided grateful Americans who subsequently enshrined the Swiss émigré as a western hero of American expansion.[128] His role as alcalde in the less populous north assisted the Mexican government, but also gave him the freedom to deepen American influence in the region. Had Sutter instead carried out his original intent to reach California via the Sonoran Route, his New Helvetia settlement may well have remained in the south, where it would have seen more competition from other American merchants, been less useful to the Mexican government, and allowed the British presence in the north to become more entrenched.[129] The fur trade, its trappers, and traders exerted more influence on the subsequent settlement of the American West than has been noted by historians.

Jim Hardee has served as the director of the Fur Trade Research Center since 1998 and has been the editor of the Rocky Mountain Fur Trade Journal *since 2009. He has researched, written and presented extensively on the Rocky Mountain fur trade. In 2016, Hardee received the Idaho Historical Society's "Esto Perpetua" Award.*

NOTES

1. This paper was presented by the author at the Oregon-California Trails Association's 33rd Annual Convention, held at Stateline, Nevada, in September 2015. For examples of Sutter's hospitality mentioned by California emigrants, see diaries written by John Bidwell and Henry W. Bigler. Both diaries can be found online at: http://www.over-land.com/diaries.html (accessed 3-12-16).

2. For details on Sutter's early life see, James Peter Zollinger, "John Augustus Sutter's European Background," in *California Historical Society Quarterly* 14, no. 1 (March 1935): 28-46.

3. Albert L. Hurtado, *John Sutter, A Life on the North American Frontier* (Norman, OK: University of Oklahoma Press, 2006), 12, 20-22, 24-27; Zollinger, "Sutter's European Background," 35-37; James Peter Zollinger, *Sutter, the Man and His Empire* (1935; Gloucester, MA: Peter Smith, 1967), 20, 28.

4. Erwin G. Gudde, *Sutter's Own Story: The Life of General John Augustus Sutter and the History of New Helvetia in the Sacramento Valley* (New York, NY: G. P. Putnam's Sons, 1936), 9. An alcalde served as the municipal magistrate, somewhat like a sheriff with powers akin to a modern justice of the peace.

5. Beaubien is listed on a permit issued by Superintendent of Indian Affairs William Clark on December 29, 1823, allowing sixteen men to enter the Indian country. Lawrence R. Murphy, "Charles H. Beaubien," in Leroy R. Hafen, ed., *The Mountain Men and the Fur Trade of the Far West*, 10 vols. (Glendale, CA: The Arthur H. Clark Company, 1965-1972), 6:23-25, 25n10.

6. David J. Weber, "Sylvestre S. Pratte," Hafen, *Mountain Men and the Fur Trade*, 6:367.

7. In his Mexican citizenship petition, Beaubien stated he left Canada in 1821 and arrived in Mexico two years later but made no explanation of the intervening years. If he went to California during this period, it was not recorded. Murphy, "Charles H. Beaubien," 25n10.

8. Ibid., 26-28. Maria Paula's maiden name is sometimes spelled "Lovato."

9. Gudde, *Sutter's Own Story*, 9-10; see also Hurtado, *John Sutter*, 21; Richard Dillon, *Fool's Gold, The Decline and Fall of Captain John Sutter in California* (New York, NY: Coward-McCann, Inc., 1967), 42.

10. Murphy, "Charles H. Beaubien," 29-31.

11. Hurtado, *John Sutter*, 27-28; Zollinger, *Sutter, the Man and His Empire*, 35.

12. Ibid.

13. Ibid., 30-32; Dillon, *Fool's Gold*, 45. In 1829 the Delaware in southwestern Missouri had been relocated to a "permanent" reservation consisting of the lands within the fork of the Kansas and Missouri rivers. Louise Barry, *The Beginning of the West: Annals of the Kansas Gateway to the American West, 1540-1854* (Topeka, KS: Kansas State Historical Society, 1972), 175-179, 302.

14. Dillon, *Fool's Gold*, 46; Gudde, *Sutter's Own Story*, 11; Hurtado, *John Sutter*, 31-32. Sutter's other options included going by ship around South America or taking what would become the Oregon-California Trail.

15. Will Bagley, *So Rugged and Mountainous: Blazing Trails to Oregon and California, 1812-1848* (Norman, OK: University of Oklahoma Press, 2010), 7. "Elm Grove Campground," found online at http://www.santafetrailresearch.com (accessed 8-15-15).

16. Harry E. Hanson, comp., "A Historical Outline of Grinter Place from 1825 to 1878," *Historic American Buildings Survey* (Philadelphia, PA: National Park Service, undated), 11, 23-24, 29.

17. The Western Department of the American Fur Company was bought from John Jacob Astor in 1834 by Pratte, Chouteau & Company, though in the West, it was still generally referred to as AFC. Fred R. Gowans, *Rocky Mountain Rendezvous* (Layton, UT: Gibbs M. Smith, Inc., 1985), 103.

18. Sutter referred to Andrew Drips as "Tripps" in both his diary and his reminiscences. Kenneth N. Owens, ed., "General Sutter's Diary," in *John Sutter & a Wider West* (Lincoln, NE: University of Nebraska Press, 1994), 3; Gudde, *Sutter's Own Story*, 12. For more on Drips, see Harvey L. Carter, "Andrew Drips," Hafen, *Mountain Men and the Fur Trade*, 8:144-151.

19. For more on Harris, see Jerome Peltier, "Moses 'Black' Harris," Hafen, *Mountain Men and the Fur Trade*, 4:103-117.

20. This would be Stewart's last adventure to the Rockies. The recent death of his older brother left the responsibilities of Murthly Castle and the family estate in Perthshire on his shoulders. Stewart was a legitimate army officer, having fought in the Napoleonic Wars. James C. Auld, "Murthly, A Castle of the Rocky Mountain Fur

Trade," *The Rocky Mountain Fur Trade Journal* 7 (2013): 106-107.

21 Cushing Eells, "Reminiscences of Cushing Eells," in Clifford M. Drury, ed., *First White Women Over The Rockies*, 3 vols., (Glendale, CA: The Arthur H. Clark Company, 1966), 3:295. The boat that brought supplies upriver was never adequately described but was variously called flatboat, pirogue, and keelboat.

22 Drips had two Indian wives with him: Macompemy, an Otoe he had been with for about fifteen years, and a second, younger woman whose name and tribal affiliation were unidentified; Carter, "Andrew Drips," 144. Drury, *First White Women Over The Rockies*, 3:84-85.

23 George Rogers Hancock Clark, his brother, William Preston Clark, and their step-brother, John D. Radford, traveled with the AFC caravan. After William Clark's first wife Julia Hancock died, he married Harriet Kennerly Radford, who brought three children into the relationship. The missionary diaries of the 1838 trip west mention only two sons of William Clark but it is clear from the Kennerly letter that three boys from the Clark family went to the mountains. Conceivably, the stepson was not identified as a Clark since his last name was Radford. William had an alcohol problem and after finishing that year at college, it was thought a western adventure might do him good, notwithstanding the wanton nature of the trapper gathering to which they traveled. Sadly, the boys had not returned from the West at the time of their father's death on September 1, 1838. Letter, James Kennerly to Jefferson Clark and Clark Kennerly, June 22, 1838, reproduced in William Clark Kennerly, *Persimmon Hill, A Narrative of Old St. Louis and the Far West* (Norman, OK: University of Oklahoma Press, 1948), 88; Eells, "Reminiscences of Cushing Eells," 3:302-303; and William E. Foley, *Wilderness Journey, The Life of William Clark* (Columbia, MO: University of Missouri Press, 2004), 263.

24 For Gray's attendance at the 1838 rendezvous, see William H. Gray, *Journal of his Journey East, 1836-1837* (Fairfield, WA: Ye Galleon Press, 1980), 56-63. Gray was already in Westport when the other missionary couples got to town. Gowans, *Rocky Mountain Rendezvous*, 130, 153-154; Letter, Asa Smith to John Smith, April 22, 1838, in Drury, *First White Women Over The Rockies*, 3:139.

25 Hurtado, *John Sutter*, 32-34; Drury, *First White Women Over The Rockies*, 2:58, 3:73, 144n12. The missionary diaries identify the packer only as Stevens. The first name, John, comes from Barry, *Beginning of the West*, 346.

26 Hurtado, *John Sutter*, 32-34; Drury, *First White Women Over The Rockies*, 2:58, 3:73, 144n12. For more on Richardson, see Nathaniel Wyeth, "The Correspondence and Journals of Nathaniel J. Wyeth, 1831-6," F. G. Young, ed., *Sources of the History of Oregon* (Eugene, OR: University Press, 1899), 147-148, 235, 241, 246, 250; John K. Townsend, "Narrative of a Journey Across the Rocky Mountains," *Early Western Travels, 1748-1846*, edited by Reuben G. Thwaites, 32 vols. (New York, NY: AMS Press, 1966), 21:166-169, 185, 211-214, 237-238, 245, 264.

27 Gudde, *Sutter's Own Story*, 12. Although Sutter's published account would state that he left Sapling Grove for the Rocky Mountains on April 11, 1838, that is clearly incorrect. It is conceivable that Sutter's handwritten 22 was mistakenly transcribed as 11, or that Sutter meant his speedy April 1 departure from Westport to elude creditors.

28 Ibid.

29 Frederick A. Wislizenus, *A Journey to the Rocky Mountains in the Year 1839* (1840; St. Louis, MO: Missouri Historical Society, 1912), 27-29.

30 Gudde, *Sutter's Own Story*, 11-12.

31 Barry, *Beginning of the West*, 344-345, 347.

32 Drury, *First White Women Over The Rockies*, 2:73-74.

33 Ibid., 2:73, 3:72-73. The ladies carried a "tin baker," the latest technology in reflector ovens that allowed them to bake breads and pies when time on the trail allowed. Drury, *First White Women Over The Rockies*, 3:143, 143n11.

34 Barry, *Beginning of the West*, 347; Drury, *First White Women Over The Rockies*, 2:74, 3:73, 242.

35 The Sublette Trace was named for fur trader William Sublette, an early traveler on this route to the Rockies. See Barry, *Beginning of the West*, 262-264. Moses Harris had accompanied Sublette on this trail in 1827, headed from the mountains to St. Louis.

36 Drury, *First White Women Over The Rockies*, 2:75, 3:297.

37 Ibid., 2:80.

38 Ibid., 2:108; Dillon, *Fool's Gold*, 51.

39 Drury, *First White Women Over The Rockies*, 3:244; Hiram M. Chittenden, *The American Fur Trade of the Far West*, 2 vols. (Stanford, CA: Academic Reprints, 1954), 1:390. Fort William, on the Laramie River, would soon be renamed Fort John though that title was short-lived. The fort was already being called Fort Laramie. That Sutter met Sarpy is evidenced by a letter he wrote while in Hawaii. Dillon, *Fool's Gold*, 71.

40 This trading post was constructed in 1834 under the direction of William Sublette and Robert Campbell. It was purchased by Pratte, Chouteau & Company in 1836. Gowans, *Rocky Mountain Rendezvous*, 105, 143.

41 Alan C. Trottman, "Lucien Fontenelle," Hafen, *Mountain Men and the Fur Trade*, 5:99. One of Sutter's early companions in America was John Laufkotter, who claimed Sutter was a heavy drinker. Alcohol was prominent in the earliest accounts of his business on the Santa Fe Trail and later in California. "His earliest manifestation of alcoholic behavior – hard drinking among convivial companions – was scarcely remarkable in antebellum America. Still, among a group of enthusiastic drinkers, Sutter led the way, Laufkotter recalled." Hurtado, *John Sutter*, 24, 30.

42 Marvin C. Ross, *The West of Alfred Jacob Miller (1837)* (Norman, OK: University of Oklahoma, 1968), Plate 49.

43 B. D. Wilson and Doyce B. Nunis, Jr., "A Mysterious Chapter in the Life of John A. Sutter," *California Historical Society Quarterly* 38, no. 4 (December 1959): 323.

44 Drury, *First White Women Over The Rockies*, 2:88.

45 Ibid., 2:88, 3:82.

46 Ibid., 2:88; E. Rick Williams, "Wheels to Rendezvous," *RMFTJ* 4 (2010).

47 For a discussion of the change of the rendezvous location, see Gowans, *Rocky Mountain Rendezvous*, 180-184. The quote is from Cushing Eells, found in Drury, *First White Women Over The Rockies*, 2:101n25.

48 Lois Halliday McDonald, *The Fur Trade Letters of Francis Ermatinger* (Glendale, CA: The Arthur H. Clark Company, 1980), 195, 206, 213. McDonald implies that Ermatinger was fulfilling a promise he had made to Gray the previous year. If McDonald is correct, the promise had something to do with Gray having taken Ermatinger's young son, Lawrence, to Buffalo, NY, then to family in St. Thomas, Ontario. Gray mentions having the boy along on the eastbound trip and delivering him in St. Thomas in October 1837, an eight-day trip out of his way. Thus, Ermatinger may have been returning a favor by similarly going out of his way to escort the missionaries as far as Fort Hall. See also Gray, *Journal of his Journey East*, 49, 75. For Dorion as Ermatinger's guide, see J. Nielson Berry, "Madame Dorion of the Astorians," *Oregon Historical Quarterly* 30, no. 3 (September 1929): 272-278. Baptiste's father, Pierre Dorion, Jr., had served for a short time in 1804 as an interpreter for the Lewis and Clark Expedition. His mother, Marie, had accompanied his father who joined the Wilson Price Hunt party traveling overland to Astoria in 1811. The infant Baptiste and his three-year-old brother were with their parents on this expedition. It should be noted that Pierre Dorion, Sr. was also an interpreter for Lewis and Clark.

49 Drury, *First White Women Over The Rockies*, 2:89-93, 3:82-88. For Clark's inscription, see Matthew C. Field, *Prairie and Mountain Sketches* (Norman, OK: University of Oklahoma Press, 1957), 175.

50 Drury, *First White Women Over The Rockies*, 2:93.

51 For a detailed account of Walker's California expedition, see Bil Gilbert, *Westering Man: The Life of Joseph Walker, Master of the Frontier* (New York, NY: Atheneum, 1983), 122-147.

52 Ibid., 123-124.

53 Zenas Leonard, *Narrative of the Adventures of Zenas Leonard*, edited by Milo M. Quaife (Chicago, IL: R. R. Donnelley & Sons Co., 1934), 196.

54 Gudde, *Sutter's Own Story*, 12.

55 Drury, *First White Women Over The Rockies*, 2:97; Gilbert, *Westering Man*, 169-172. George Ruxton reported Walker and a band of men had received fifty horses from the Navaho. If the story is true, additional stock may have come from trading or rustling in and around Santa Fe. George F. Ruxton, *Life in the Far West*, edited by Leroy R. Hafen (Norman, OK: University of Oklahoma Press, 1951), 92-93.

56 Frederick A. Mark, "William Craig," Hafen, *Mountain Men and the Fur Trade*, 2:106-107.

57 Drury, *First White Women Over The Rockies*, 2:98-99.

58 Osborne Russell, *Journal of a Trapper*, edited by Aubrey L. Haines (Portland, OR: Champoeg Press, 1955), 90-91.

59 Bernard De Voto, *Across the Wide Missouri* (Boston, MA: Houghton, Mifflin and Company, 1947), 343.

60 Gudde, *Sutter's Own Story*, 12-13.

61 Hurtado, *John Sutter*, 39. Another Sutter biographer clarified that Allgeier was Bavarian, and that Keyser was from Tyrol, a region in present-day southern Austria and northern Italy. Zollinger, *Sutter: The Man and His Empire*, 41.

62 Harvey Lewis Carter, *"Dear Old Kit," The Historical Christopher Carson* (Norman, OK: University of Oklahoma Press, 1968), 44-49, 71; Charles L. Camp, "Kit Carson in California: With Extracts from His Own Story," *California Historical Society Quarterly* 1, no. 2 (October 1922): 111-151.

63 Gudde, *Sutter's Own Story*, 17.

64 Tom Dunlay, *Kit Carson & The Indians* (Lincoln, NE: University of Nebraska Press, 2000), 76-77, 105-106. In 1844, Carson would buy another Indian boy, a Piute captive between twelve and fourteen years old, for $40, claiming he would train the lad to steal horses. Some historians think Sutter's Indian boy's second language was Spanish. See, for example, Caroline Higley,

"The Rise and Fall of Sutter's Golden Empire," *Montana: The Magazine of Western History* 14, no. 3 (Summer 1964): 30.

65 Dunlay, *Kit Carson*, 76. For an extensive examination of the Indian slave trade, see Leroy R. Hafen, *The Old Spanish Trail* (Glendale, CA: The Arthur H. Clark Company, 1954), 259-283.

66 Hurtado, *John Sutter*, 12.

67 Washington Irving, *The Adventures of Captain Bonneville, U.S.A. in the Rocky Mountains and the Far West*, edited by Edgeley W. Todd, (Norman OK: University of Oklahoma Press, 1986), 136.

68 Gudde, *Sutter's Own Story*, 12.

69 Drury, *First White Women Over The Rockies*, 3:94-95.

70 Gudde, *Sutter's Own Story*, 13.

71 Harriet D. Munnick, "The Ermatinger Brothers, Edward and Francis," Hafen, *Mountain Men and the Fur Trade,* 8:157-160.

72 McDonald, *Letters of Francis Ermatinger*, 195, 206, 213; Gray, *Journal of his Journey East*, 49, 75.

73 Drury, *First White Women Over The Rockies*, 3:95.

74 Ibid., 2:97. Sarah Smith recorded the date of crossing of Continental Divide as the 16th.

75 Francis Fuller Victor, *The River of the West* (Hartford, CT: R. W. Bliss & Co., 1870), 239-242. Victor dated these events as occurring in 1837 but specifically named missionaries Gray and Smith, thus she is mistaken in her chronology.

76 Drury, *First White Women Over The Rockies*, 3:99.

77 Victor, *River of the West*, 241-243.

78 Drury, *First White Women Over The Rockies*, 3:100.

79 Ibid.

80 Ibid., 2:109n22. This description comes from a lengthy letter Mary Walker wrote on July 27 while at Fort Hall. Wyeth had originally built a log stockade, but sometime after HBC bought the post from Wyeth in 1837, the Company replaced the pickets with adobe.

81 For more on McKay, see Annie Laurie Bird, *Thomas McKay* (Caldwell, ID: The Caxton Printers, Ltd., 1972), 13, 17, 22, 49-51.

82 Doyce B. Nunis, ed., *The Hudson's Bay Company's First Fur Brigade to the Sacramento Valley: Alexander McLeod's 1829 Hunt* (Fair Oaks, CA: Lawton & Kennedy, 1968), 15, 39-42.

83 Gudde, *Sutter's Own Story*, 13. Native peoples in the Northwest differentiated between Anglo Hudson's Bay Company employees in their midst ("British" or "King George Men") and Anglo American trappers, explorers and missionaries ("Bostons"), despite their common language, similar physical appearance and style of dress. See Alexandra Harmon, *Indians in the Making: Ethnic Relations and Indian Identities Around Puget Sound* (Berkeley, CA: University of California Press, 1998), 80.

84 McDonald, *Letters of Francis Ermatinger*, 208.

85 Drury, *First White Women Over The Rockies*, 2:110-113, 3:102-105.

86 Payette first arrived at the mouth of the Columbia in John Astor's second Pacific Fur Company ship, the *Beaver*, in May 1812. Payette later hired on with North West Company and is believed to have been the first Euro-American to enter the Payette River region of modern Idaho as a member of Donald McKenzie's 1818 brigade. Kenneth L. Holmes, "Francois Payette," Hafen, *Mountain Men and the Fur Trade*, 6:325-352.

87 William H. Gray, *A History of Oregon, 1792-1849* (1870; New York, NY: Arno Press, 1973), 140.

88 Drury, *First White Women Over The Rockies*, 2:113-114, 3:105.

89 Gudde, *Sutter's Own Story*, 13.

90 Drury, *First White Women Over The Rockies*, 2:106-108, 114-116.

91 Clifford M. Drury, *Elkanah and Mary Walker, Pioneers among the Spokanes* (Caldwell, ID: The Caxton Printers, Ltd., 1940), 94. This token having been meant for Mary Walker was posited in Dillon, *Fool's Gold*, 63. In a later work, Drury indicated that this small volume had been given to him by the Walker's youngest son, Samuel, in 1938. Drury, in turn, presented it to the Whitman National Monument. Drury, *First White Women Over The Rockies*, 2:116.

92 Gudde, *Sutter's Own Story*, 13.

93 Frederick Merk, *Fur Trade and Empire, George Simpson's Journal, 1824-25* (Cambridge, MA: The Belknap Press of Harvard University Press, 1968), 54-55; Elizabeth B. Losey, *Let Them Be Remembered, The Story of the Fur Trade Forts* (New York, NY: Vantage Press, Inc., 1999), 466-473.

94 Merk, *Fur Trade and Empire*, 128.

95 Gudde, *Sutter's Own Story*, 13.

96 James R. Gibson, *The Lifeline of the Oregon Country: The Fraser-Columbia Brigade System, 1811-47* (Vancouver, BC: University of British Columbia, 1997), 125-128.

97 Robert Boyd, *People of The Dalles, The Indians of the Wascopam Mission* (Lincoln, NE: University of Nebraska Press, 1996), 9, 12.

98 Gudde, *Sutter's Own Story*, 14.

99 Ibid., 14-15.

100 Ibid., 15.

101 For a brief history of Fort Vancouver, see R. G. Robertson, *Competitive Struggle, America's*

Western Fur Trade Posts, 1746-1865 (Boise, ID: Tamarack Books, Inc., 1999), 241-242.

102 Gudde, *Sutter's Own Story*, 16.

103 Margaret A. Ormsby, "Sir James Douglas," in *Dictionary of Canadian Biography*, University of Toronto, 2015, found online at: http://www.biographi.ca/en/bio/douglas_james_10E.html (accessed September 3, 2015).

104 Gudde, *Sutter's Own Story*, 16.

105 Letter, James Douglas to the Governor Deputy Governor and Committee Hon. Hudsons Bay Comy., October 18, 1838, in John McLoughlin, *The Letters of John McLoughlin from Fort Vancouver to the Governor and Committee, First Series, 1825-38*, edited by E. E. Rich (London: The Hudson's Bay Record Society, 1941), 256.

106 Charles Henry Carey, ed., "The Mission Record Book of the Methodist Episcopal Church, Willamette Station, Oregon Territory, North America, Commenced 1834," in *The Quarterly of the Oregon Historical Society* 23, no. 3 (September 1922): 263. Sutter's family finally reached California in January 1850, paying their own way with money provided by John Sutter, Jr., the eldest son, who had joined his father on his own initiative in the fall of 1848. Iris H. W. Engstrand, "John Sutter: A Biographical Examination," in Owens, *John Sutter & a Wider West*, 81.

107 Doyce B. Nunis, "Michel Laframboise," Hafen, *Mountain Men and the Fur Trade*, 5:151-153. The 1832 brigade was actually the fourth HBC party to enter California. However, it was the 1832 Laframboise expedition that kindled an HBC interest in trapping the Sacramento Valley.

108 Richard Dillon, *Siskiyou Trail, The Hudson's Bay Fur Company Route to California* (New York, NY: McGraw-Hill Book Company, 1975), 265.

109 Jeannette E. Graustein, *Thomas Nuttall, Naturalist: Explorations in America, 1808-1841* (Cambridge, MA: Harvard University Press, 1967), 313, 315-317.

110 Gudde, *Sutter's Own Story*, 16.

111 Letter, James Douglas to the Governor Deputy Governor and Committee Hon. Hudsons Bay Comy., October 18, 1838, in McLoughlin, *Letters*, 256; Gudde, *Sutter's Own Story*, 17; Hurtado, *John Sutter*, 41, 78, 121.

112 Hurtado, *John Sutter*, 41.

113 Owens, *John Sutter & a Wider West*, 4.

114 Zollinger, *Sutter: The Man and His Empire*, 79-82.

115 Samuel Nelson, *The Sutter Case*, United States Reports, 69 U.S. 562 (2 Wall.). For labor practices borrowed from California missions, see James A. Sandos, "Between Crucifix and Lance: Indians and White Relations in California, 1769-1848," *California History* 76, no. 2/3 (Summer - Fall, 1997): 218.

116 Howard R. Lamar, "John Augustus Sutter, Wilderness Entrepreneur," in Owens, *John Sutter & a Wider West*, 32-33.

117 Ibid., 27, 30-31, 33.

118 Gudde, *Sutter's Own Story*, 48, 65-66.

119 Owens, *John Sutter & a Wider West*, 10-11; Gudde, *Sutter's Own Story*, 46. For a discussion of Sutter's interaction with HBC once he was settled in California, see Alice B. Maloney, "Hudson's Bay Company in California," *Oregon Historical Quarterly* 37, no. 1 (March 1936): 9-23.

120 Oscar Lewis, *Sutter's Fort, Gateway to the Gold Fields* (Englewood Cliffs, NJ: Prentice-Hall, Inc., 1966), 24-27; Albert L. Hurtado, *Indian Survival on the California Frontier* (New Haven, CT: Yale University Press, 1988), 55.

121 These concepts are pointed out by Hurtado, *John Sutter*, 50.

122 Gudde, *Sutter's Own Story*, 21-22. According to Gudde, site selection may have been solidified in June 1839, about the time Sutter left Sitka. While in the Russian colony, Sutter's attention was certainly called to the report of Otto von Kotzebue, who had sailed the Sacramento River up to the mouth of the American River in November of 1824. Sutter also had a copy of Sir Edward Belcher's account of the exploration of the Sacramento River in the fall of 1837, which stressed the beauty and fertility of the interior valley of California.

123 Drury, *First White Women Over The Rockies*, 3:105.

124 John Bidwell, "Life in California Before the Gold Rush," *The Century Magazine* 41, no. 2 (December 1890), also found online at: http://www.sfmuseum.org/hist2/bidwell1.html (accessed September 2, 2015).

125 Letter, George Simpson to Governor and Committee of HBC, March 1, 1842, in John McLoughlin, *The Letters of John McLoughlin from Fort Vancouver to the Governor and Committee: Second Series, 1839-44*, edited by E. E. Rich (London: The Hudson's Bay Record Society, 1943), 240-241n1.

126 Hurtado, *John Sutter*, 242-244; Zollinger, *Sutter: The Man and His Empire*, 275.

127 Letter, John Sutter to Smith Rudd, December 26, 1879, Rudd Manuscripts, Lilly Library, Indiana University, Bloomington, Indiana.

128 Albert L. Hurtado, "Empires, Frontiers, Filibusters, and Pioneers: The Transnational World of John Sutter," *Pacific Historical Review* 77, no. 1 (February 2008): 19.

129 American entreprenuers living in southern California in 1838 included William Wolfskill, J. J. Warner, Isaac Williams, William Workman, George Yount and Jacob P. Lease. See pertinent entries in Donovan Lewis, *Pioneers of California* (San Francisco, CA: Scottwall Associates, 1993).

Amorpha nana, or dwarf false indigo, was first described for science in 1813 by English naturalist Thomas Nuttall, who collected North American plants during the Astor Expedition of 1811-12. Illustration from *The Curtis Botanical Magazine* 47 (1819-1820), plate 2147.

BIODIVERSITY HERITAGE LIBRARY, DIGITIZED BY MISSOURI BOTANICAL GARDEN

Naturalists in the Rocky Mountain Fur Trade Era: "They are a Perfect Nuisance"

by Carol Kuhn

The trappers and traders of the Rocky Mountain fur trade era, and the naturalists who journeyed with them, seem unlikely traveling companions. But with the golden age of the Rocky Mountain fur trade coinciding with the golden age of western North American botanical exploration, these joint ventures were inevitable. Naturalists also accompanied military and government expeditions of the era (see Appendix B, page 92, for a comprehensive list of fur trade and government expeditions accompanied by naturalists).

By attaching themselves to parties that were already planned, guided, and largely supplied by others, the botanists were able to travel more safely and economically than if they had attempted to mount a purely botanical expedition. Funding for such piggy-backed studies frequently came from wealthy private speculators and powerful institutions, such as Kew Royal Botanical Gardens in England, and their upstart American versions such as the Philadelphia Academy and New York City's Elgin Botanical Garden. Like fur trappers, botanists were collecting and distributing a raw natural product, but unlike furs, trade in plants remained sustainable.

This paper investigates the botanical explorers of the trans-Mississippi West fur trade era, and their primary reasons for venturing into the Rocky Mountains. While these early naturalists may have appeared to their traveling companions as bona-fide dandies looking for adventure in places where they had no business, there was a method to their perceived madness.

The naturalists collected plants to increase scientific knowledge and to gain compensation through sales. The beauty of the burgeoning commercial botany trade lay in the fact that thousands of plants could be germinated from seeds collected in the North American wilds, then grown in nurseries to be sold to hungry arboretums, botanical gardens, and research institutes in England, mainland Europe, and the developing eastern seaboard of the United States. Comparable to the fur trade, botanical exploration was a business from which a savvy collector and his benefactors could reap a handsome profit.

The nineteenth century naturalists

Much like other contemporary explorers, naturalists in the early nineteenth century were usually entrepreneurial jacks-of-all-trades. Many explorers, leaders, and businessmen known to historians are also recognized in the sciences as botanists, ornithologists, mammalogists, or geologists. All are referred to as "collectors," and most were as resourceful at cobbling together the method and means for exploration as they were at combining their areas of expertise. They might, for instance, graft scientific goals onto fur trade expeditions.

Nathaniel J. Wyeth is known in the botanical world as having collected some of the first plant specimens for scientific purposes in the trans-Mississippi West, while pursuing his own independent fur trade venture.[1] After English botanist Thomas Nuttall's solo botanical excursion to the British Northwest was curtailed due to increasingly poor relations between Britain and the United States, he fortuitously connected with Wilson Price Hunt and the Astorians, or, as contemporary botanist Elias Durand

Thomas Nuttall (1786-1859). ATTRIBUTED TO J. WHITFIELD. HARVARD UNIVERSITY PORTRAIT COLLECTION, GIFT OF PROFESSOR EDWARD TUCKERMAN TO ASA GRAY FOR THE UNIVERSITY, 1865, H185

described them, an unidentified "party of traders and hunters."[2]

Government or military journeys could also serve the naturalists, especially when in positions of authority themselves, or backed by influential supporters. John Eatton LeConte, botanist and entomologist, was also Captain LeConte, Assistant US Army Topographical Engineer.[3] Botanist Frederick A. Wislizenus was a surgeon assigned to the Doniphan Expedition's return journey from New Mexico, 1846-1847. Some botanists received a special military invitation. Charles Andreas Geyer, for example, accompanied the US Army-sanctioned expedition of Joseph Nicollet to map the land between the Missouri River and the source of the Mississippi.[4]

John Torrey, known to the military world as an assistant surgeon, US Army at West Point in 1824, is known in the botanical world as one of the greatest minds of the nineteenth century. He was recruited to join the 1819 Stephen H. Long Expedition as mineralogist (not, as commonly reported, as botanist).[5] Upon learning that there would be no monetary compensation, and even worse, that all collected materials, including journals and notes, would be considered government property, Torrey declined the offer.[6] William Baldwin, US Navy surgeon, is known today chiefly for his brief assignment as botanist for the Long Expedition.

A well-placed acquaintance in the field could make all the difference. Dr. William Darlington, prominent Philadelphia botanist of the early 1800s, wrote,

> *I had informed Dr. [William Baldwin] that I had written to the Secretary of War [John C. Calhoun], in behalf of his appointment as Botanist, in the proposed [Stephen H. Long] expedition.*[7]

Edwin James was then pressed into service by Stephen H. Long personally, after the unfortunate death of Dr. William Baldwin during the expedition.[8] Still other naturalists traveled at the behest of wealthy benefactors who purchased "subscriptions" to help defray costs and provide a stipend. The subscribers were promised a percentage of the botanical collections based upon the amount of money they invested.

Equipment

The naturalists did not travel lightly. They needed proper equipment to collect seeds, press plants for scientific specimens, and nurture live plants intended for replanting at distant commercial nurseries and private gardens. The tools of their trade were several. First, there must be a collecting implement. This was normally a digging and cutting device, though botanist Thomas Nuttall reportedly chose to use his rifle's barrel as a digging tool, and Scottish-born

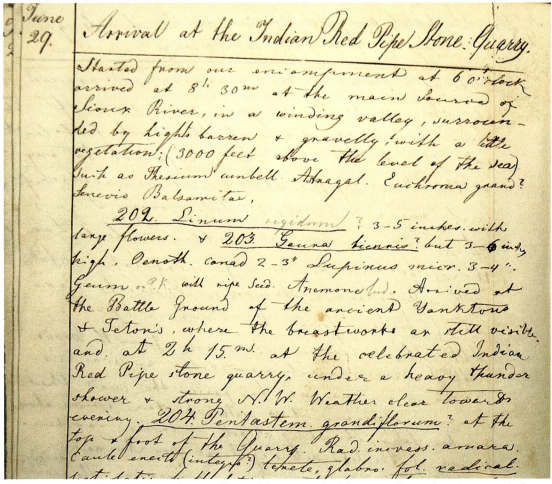

Page 36 of Charles A. Geyer's botany journal is covered with notes about the plants and places he observed. AMANDA RUBASCH AND KATE HUBER IMAGES. JOURNAL HOUSED AT SMITHSONIAN ARCHIVES, WASHINGTON, DC.

David Douglas (for whom the Douglas fir is named) used his firearm to shoot pine cones out of the ancient evergreens of the Pacific Northwest.[9] The most important collecting tool was the vasculum, a metal or treated leather carrying tube, wherein plants were placed for safekeeping. Once back at base camp, the samples were hurriedly prepared for live transport or placed in a plant press to create dried specimens.[10]

The plant press, or folio, was the botanists' portable, one-man version of the fur trappers' beaver pelt press. The folio required a large amount of paper to press and dry collected plants. English botanist John Bradbury described carrying a "large inflexible port-folio containing several quires of paper, for the purpose of laying down specimens of plants."[11] Also critical to the collector was a field journal for record keeping. Collectors' journals proved to be a significant source of information for historians and biographers as well as for contemporary botanists.

Some specimens, particularly small animals, were preserved in alcohol. Prince Maximilian made note of collecting a rattlesnake and preserving it in brandy "as a live creature of this kind is not the most agreeable traveling companion."[12] Plants preserved in this manner would be useful only as scientific specimens, as the alcohol would pickle seeds or live roots, rendering them nonviable. Drying and pressing specimens would have been a far more common method of preserving and transporting plant specimens for scientific research.

William Baldwin's calling card was graced by this lithograph, based on a portrait by the famed painter Charles Willson Peale. THE LUESTER T. MERTZ LIBRARY OF THE NEW YORK BOTANICAL GARDEN.

Travel accommodation

Historian William Stanton observed that, despite the possibility of encountering army officers who lacked respect for science, "the field investigator prized the opportunity to join the [Corps of Topographic Engineers] expeditions into the West, even as 'scientific hitchhikers.'"[13] However, a perusal of journals, letters, and books written by these field investigators reveals significant frustration and jealousy. The increasingly intolerant Astorian voyageurs viewed fellow traveler Nuttall as mad. Henry Marie Brackenridge, traveling with Manuel Lisa's 1811 party up the Missouri, was witness to this, noting in his journal for Monday June 3, 1811:

> *To the ignorant Canadian boatmen, who are unable to appreciate the science, [Nuttall] affords a subject of merriment; le fou, the fool, is the name by which he is commonly known.*[14]

The greatest source of friction between the naturalists and their fellow journeymen involved the lack of opportunities for the collectors to actually *collect* their treasured specimens. Bradbury, after departing Fort Osage on April 10, 1811, with the Astorians, bemoaned that "we had a fair wind and employed our sail, wherefore I could not go ashore without danger of being left behind."[15]

There was clearly no love lost between John Bradbury and fur trader Manuel Lisa, who sent his flotilla, with Bradbury and the aforementioned Brackenridge aboard, on a break-neck descent of the Missouri River back to St. Louis, apparently reneging on a promise to allow time for Bradbury's botanical excursions. Bradbury complained,

> *I lost the opportunity of collecting a great number of new plants on my return, through the breach of faith towards me by Mr. Lisa, who agreed that his boats should land me at different places; which promise he neither did, nor intended to perform.*[16]

Canadian fur companies could be just as harsh. Thomas Nuttall's December 1820 geology paper, read before the Academy of Natural Sciences, Philadelphia, groused, "The coast of Lake Superior I was then prevented from examining, by the sinister regulations of the company of the north-western fur-traders," referring to the North West Fur Company.[17]

Botanist J. H. Redfield, describing the death of William Baldwin from tuberculosis early in Long's 1819-1820 expedition to the Rocky Mountains, suggested that frustration may have hastened Baldwin's demise. Redfield asserted that as the *Western Engineer* made her way slowly up the Mississippi and Missouri rivers, Baldwin "chafed under the restrictions, both of military rule and of increasing weakness, and in his desire to make the most of the few opportunities

David Douglas (1798-1834), at age 30.
ROYAL HORTICULTURAL SOCIETY, LINDLEY LIBRARY

allowed him for collecting, he doubtless exhausted his little remaining strength."[18] Indeed, from his deathbed, Baldwin penned his colleague, Pennsylvania botanist William Darlington, his assessment of river expeditions and the needs of naturalists:

> *a steam boat is not calculated for exploring ... little opportunity has been afforded to the Naturalists to do any thing ... In short, not one moment has been granted to the Naturalists, to explore, that could be avoided; and the most productive situations have all been passed by ... This steamboat scheme has been too hastily adopted. No mode of travelling is so poorly calculated for Naturalists.*[19]

This scalding critique refutes Secretary of War John C. Calhoun's earlier letter to Darlington, asserting the government's high esteem for exploring naturalists accompanying expeditions into the West.[20]

Time did not improve the situation for traveling naturalists. Eight years after Baldwin's final letter to Darlington, famed botanical collector David Douglas, accompanying a Hudson's Bay Company fur venture by boat, commented in a May 1827 journal entry: "Finding this mode of travelling very irksome ... I began to think this sort of travelling ill adapted for botanising."[21]

Botanical explorer Thomas Drummond (no relation to William Drummond Stewart) established an apparently acceptable means of botanizing during his travels across Canada via canoe with the Hudson's Bay Company in 1825-27:

> *When the boats stopped to breakfast, I immediately went on shore with my vasculum, proceeding along the banks of the river, and making short excursions into the interior, taking care ... to join the boats ... at their encampment for the night. After supper, I commenced laying down the plants gathered in the day's excursion, changed and dried the papers of those collected previously – till daybreak, when the boats started. I then went on board and slept till the breakfast hour, when I landed and proceeded as before.*[22]

But Drummond was not so lucky in early 1831, when he arrived in St. Louis on his way to the western United States. His July 19 letter to sponsor Sir William Jackson Hooker of Kew Gardens, London, summarized his travel options:

> *Unfortunately, owing to the lateness of my arrival at St. Louis, it was impossible for me to proceed up the Missouri, the fur traders, whom I wished to have accompanied, generally leaving their head-quarters on the first of May, or even sooner. I delivered my letters of introduction, however, and received most liberal offers of assistance, with a view to forward my objects. There are here two companies; 1st, The American*

Overland travel was not necessarily better for scientists. Ornithologist John Kirk Townsend, while traveling with Thomas Nuttall and Nathaniel Wyeth near Scotts Bluff (current Nebraska), noted in his journal on May 31, 1834:

> *I had been daily scanning the great extent of the desert for some little oasis such as I had now found; ... and yet the caravan would not halt for me; I must turn my back upon ... my fond anticipations, and hurry forward over the dreary wilderness which lay beyond. What valuable and highly interesting accessions to science might not be made by a party, composed exclusively of naturalists, on a journey through this rich and unexplored region!*[25]

John Kirk Townsend (1809-1851).

OREGON HISTORICAL SOCIETY, #BA019649

> *Fur Company, of which Mr. Chiato [Chouteau] is the acting agent. They generally go out by the route of Santa Fe, assembling at a small village ... called Toas [Taos], from whence they proceed to the mountains. The 2d company was under the direction of General Ashley, and he still retains a considerable interest in it. Their hunting ground is near the source of the Missouri. In short, there will be no difficulty in getting to the mountains.*[23]

Drummond apparently traveled at least a portion of that journey via steamboat. In a December 14, 1831, letter to Hooker, he expressed frustration that travelling by steamboat,

> *you have very few opportunities for collecting. The only time is when they stop to take in wood, which, being usually kept in flat boats in readiness, is very short indeed.*[24]

On occasion the naturalists had opportunity to go ashore due to the misfortunes of the crew. While procuring passage on a boat headed for Fort Vancouver in 1825, David Douglas happily noted that

> *The current at this season of year being exceedingly powerful from the melting of the snow in the mountains, the boats made but little way ... so that I botanised along the banks.*[26]

Collector Charles Andreas Geyer botanized from Missouri to Vancouver during an 1843-44 excursion organized by famed botanist Dr. George Engelmann of St. Louis, collecting 10,000 specimens along the way. The American Fur Company denied Geyer transportation upriver from St. Louis. Geyer was incensed by his rejected requests for transport:

> *I failed to get passage up the Missouri to the Yellowstone River ... could not prevail on the Amer. Fur Company to grant me a passage in their steamboat by claims to friendship and obligation even it was*

> *indirectly rejected. The reason is plain to those who know their illegal dealing with intoxicating liquors, to which they of course, want as few witnesses as possible.*[27]

Geyer's contractual obligations with Engelmann were ultimately fulfilled, thanks in part to the generosity of Sir William Drummond Stewart, who by coincidence was in St. Louis organizing his 1843 invitation-only, privately catered "rendezvous" of rich young fur-trapper-wannabes. Finding that Geyer was not welcomed on the AFC's annual journey up the Missouri, Stewart invited Geyer to join his caravan. While it is tempting to read this as Stewart's kindness toward a fellow explorer in need, Sir William did not provide this service completely free of charge. At the outset, the two men struck a deal whereby Geyer would receive transportation in return for choice selections from his live collections, to be shipped to Stewart's recently inherited Murthly Castle in Scotland. Geyer, writing to Sir William Hooker on May 16, 1845, made note of having an extensive collection of seeds "which are not all destined for Sir Stewart."[28]

Clash of cultures

Peter Skene Ogden, a chief trader for Hudson's Bay Company, apparently was not a connoisseur of the natural sciences, or at least not of naturalists, as evidenced in his February 25, 1837, letter to fellow HBC trader John McLeod:

> *Here are also five more Gent. as follows 2 in quest of Flowers 2 killing all the Birds in the Columbia & 1 in quest of rocks and stones all these bucks came with letters from the President of the U. States and you know it would not be good policy not to treat them politely they are a perfect nuisance.*[29]

Nuisance or not, the HBC was fully aware that supporting "ostensibly disinterested scientific activity was one way in which the company created a positive corporate image in Great Britain."[30]

Conversely, some naturalists were not connoisseurs of the wild orgy known as rendezvous. While confined by illness to his tent at the 1834 rendezvous, John Kirk Townsend made note of the "perfect bedlam," remarking that he was

> *compelled all day to listen to the hiccoughing jargon of drunken traders ... and the swearing and screaming of our own men, who are scarcely less savage than the rest, being heated by the detestable liquor which circulates freely among them.*[31]

After leaving that rendezvous, Townsend experienced additional bedlam during July 4th celebrations, wherein "we who were not *happy* had to lie flat upon the ground to avoid the bullets which were careening through the camp." Townsend, waxing philosophical in retrospect, would recall that

> *amid all the mental sterility, and absence of moral rectitude, which is so deplorably prevalent, there yet lingers some kindliness of heart, some sentiments which are not wholly depraved.*[32]

Unfortunately for their fellow travelers, the naturalists were at times unprepared for the rigors of the wilderness. David Douglas wrote on October 16, 1826, "Mr. [Alexander R.] McLeod was kind enough to give me part of his bedding" after a "dull, foggy and raw" morning's travel, suggesting that Douglas had broken one of the primary rules of survival: he had not procured appropriate equipment for his own self-sufficiency.[33] Upon beginning a 270-mile trek in the Pacific Northwest, Douglas wrote on April 19, 1827, that "Mr. [John] Work presented me with ... a pair of inferior snowshoes called bear's paws."[34] Ten days later, Douglas lamented,

Obliged to put on my bears' paws; path rough ... ascending two steps and sometimes sliding back three, the snowshoes twisting and throwing the weary traveller down ... so feeble that lie I must among the snow, like a broken-down waggon-horse entangled in his harnessing, weltering to rescue myself.[35]

Hard-won plant specimens were sometimes, by necessity, converted to food during particularly difficult journeys. In a cold rainy slog back from an unsuccessful attempt to reach the headwaters of River Cheecheeler, David Douglas on October 24, 1825, bemoaned that for sustenance,

We used all the berries I had collected on this journey, and Mr. [Alexander] McKenzie suffered some inconvenience from having eaten a few roots of a species of Narthecium.[36]

As alluded to earlier, the fluid used for preservation of priceless scientific specimens was on occasion re-purposed by individuals interested in more immediate gratification. Townsend, describing the loss of his pickled specimens' preserving liquid, wrote:

During the journey across the country I constantly carried a two-gallon bottle of whiskey, in which I deposited various kinds of lizards and serpents and when we arrived in Columbia the vessel was almost full of these crawling creatures. I left the bottle on board the brig when I paid my first visit to the Wallammet falls, and on my return found that Thornburg had decanted the liquor from the precious reptiles which I had destined for immortality and he and one of his pot companions had been <u>happy</u> upon it for a whole day.[37]

The specimen at left, *Inula graminifolia*, was collected by Dr. Edwin James on Long's 1819 expedition to the Rockies. THE LUESTER T. MERTZ LIBRARY OF THE NEW YORK BOTANICAL GARDEN

In 1819, Thomas Nuttall became the first botanist to explore Arkansas. During this expedition, he described the Osage orange and gave the tree its scientific name, *Maclura aurantiaca*. Named after William Maclure (1763-1840), a philanthropist, printer, and co-founder of the Philadelphia Academy of Natural Science, this tree supplied the native tribes with tough wood for their bows. French trappers, the first to encounter the tree, named it *bois d'arc*. ARCHIVES OF THE GRAY HERBARIUM HARVARD UNIVERSITY, CAMBRIDGE, MASSACHUSETTS, USA

A specimen collected by David Douglas in the American West, 1824-25: *Quercus garryana* (Oregon white oak). Douglas named the plant after Nicholas Garry, secretary of the Hudson's Bay Company.

©THE BOARD OF TRUSTEES OF THE ROYAL BOTANIC GARDENS, KEW, REPRODUCED WITH THE CONSENT OF THE ROYAL BOTANIC GARDENS, KEW

The bounty of the land

Botanical collectors harvested western North American plants as either live samples for transplant, seeds for investors to purchase and germinate through their own devices, or as pressed, dried specimens to be glued to sheets of paper and used as permanent records. Dried plant specimens were sold, often in packs of 100 sheets, to eager collectors: universities, herbariums, researchers, or amateur collectors.[38] Many of these preserved plants still exist today, silent relics of the actual place, the actual day, of recorded events in the fur trade era. They are tangible artifacts with notes attached, identifying when and where they were collected, and by whom.

Today, people can look at a plant that Nathaniel Wyeth collected at "Little Goddin River Sources of the Columbia June 9th." By reviewing Wyeth's journal, it is clear that Wyeth collected that plant on the same day that "a [buffalo] bull was run into camp which I shot at my lodge door," the same day that Francis Ermatinger dressed the wound of an Indian who had been gored by a bull.[39] One can view that preserved plant online, or in person at the great repository of so many plant specimens of that bygone North American era, the Kew Botanical Garden herbarium in London.[40]

This is the unrealized historical importance of botanical collections, the only extant, authentic artifacts of specific dates and locations of the fur trade. The fur trade saw no need to preserve and identify a specific beaver pelt for posterity.

Yet the naturalists, too, sought to generate income. Live plants, bulkier and harder to maintain and transport than dead pressed specimens, nevertheless held potential for profit (see Appendix A, page 91, for a selection of botanical specimen sales in the 1840s). Live plants and seeds, advertised in journals and catalogues, were destined for sale to a wide range of customers and venues: wealthy European gentlemen horticulturalists and nouveau-riche Americans stocking their private gardens; botanical research institutions such as the famed Royal Botanical Gardens at Kew and Chiswick House in London; and burgeoning commercial nurseries, such as David Hosack's Elgin Gardens in New York City, and Stark Brothers in Louisiana, Missouri (founded in 1819 and still in business).

Prior to beginning his westward collecting journey from St. Louis in 1810, John Bradbury communicated a business plan to his English sponsors, the proprietors of the Botanic Garden at Liverpool, wherein he described a goal to "transmit to New Orleans whatever I may find which I deem not described," meaning plants that were new to science.[41] His sponsors would provide him £100 annually, slightly more than $7,500 today, for his "travel and subsistence." Bradbury's son would be stationed as gardener at New Orleans to "receive & send to Europe from time to time whatever is valuable – to propagate the plants and send them in quantities in a Mature State."[42]

Thomas Nuttall clearly intended to make money from the sale of plants and seeds. As early as 1815, Nuttall expressed a desire to bring more American species into the horticultural trade. He actively met with other botanists for advice on where to collect, and he "consulted with the [Philadelphia] nurseryman Bernard McMahon on what kinds of plants were popular."[43]

Nineteenth-century English botanist John C. Loudon tabulated approximately 1,350 tree species introduced into England in the 290 years between 1540 and 1830.[44] Nearly half were presented during the twenty-year period between 1811 and 1830, and the vast majority of those were from the North American West.

The most voracious of these live plant collectors was David Douglas, best known today as the botanist who introduced North American evergreen trees, including Douglas fir, lodgepole pine, and sugar pine, into the British and European landscape and timber industry. Less known is that Douglas also introduced hundreds of shrubs and herbaceous plants into English horticulture. In his 1836 eulogy of Douglas, Sir William Joseph Hooker proclaimed

> *our* Flora Boreali-Americana ... *will constitute a lasting memorial of Mr. Douglas' zeal and abilities; whilst not only in this country, but throughout Europe, and in the United States of America, there is scarcely a spot of ground deserving the name of a* <u>Garden</u>, *which does not owe many of its most powerful attractions to the living roots and seeds which have been sent by him to the Horticultural Society of London.*[45]

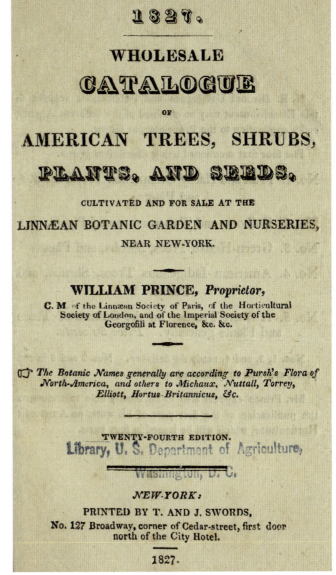

William Prince's 1825 catalogue offered nursery plants and seeds grown from specimens collected during the early naturalists' expeditions. Prince's Flushing, New York, nursery had sales agents in Britain, Russia, and throughout Europe.
BIODIVERSITY HERITAGE LIBRARY. DIGITIZED BY US DEPARTMENT OF AGRICULTURE, NATIONAL AGRICULTURAL LIBRARY.

Hooker listed the plants which David Douglas had introduced to England as live plants or seeds from his 1826-27 collecting expedition to the trans-Mississippi West – an astonishing 164 species, including ponderosa pine, Oregon maple, Oregon grape, and virgin's bower – all collected by Douglas during that one expedition.

Europe's passion for new plants was palpable, and the race of supply and demand was on. Thomas Nuttall collected *Ribes aureum* while traveling in western North America with Bradbury in 1811. Nuttall then quickly shipped seeds to England, where two short years later, in 1813, the species was already being sold in Chelsea, England. John Fraser, Jr.'s nursery advertised it as "collected in Upper Louisiana and principally on the River Missourie, North America."[46] John Loudon noted that in these early decades of the 1800s

> *by far the finest ornamental trees and shrubs are from North America. Our greatest hopes for future introductions are from the unpenetrated regions of North America ... American trees and shrubs, being rare, or newly introduced, bore enormously high prices.*[47]

Britain was eager not just for valuable timber species like acer, oak, elm, ash, and birch, but also sought American shrubs which would thrive in England's similar climate.[48]

Historian Savoie Lottinville commented that Nuttall needed some means of sustaining himself in his adopted home of Philadelphia:

> *Through seedmen such as Bernard McMahon, and in England, John Fraser, Jr., and James Dickson, Nuttall had learned about the steady, if modest, rewards to be had from selling seeds of new or little-known species.*[49]

Nuttall in this way was able to provide the American people with a flora, or treatise on native plants, in their own language, published and printed on North American soil. This awakened an intrinsic botanical curiosity, and created a wide new market for his plant and seed collections. By 1819, Nuttall was positioned to capitalize on his amassed botanical knowledge.[50]

The botanical marketplace

Thomas Drummond's main benefactor, Kew Gardens' director Sir William Jackson Hooker, had procured eager subscribers to help defray the costs of Drummond's 1831 exploration. In return, patrons would receive sets of pressed plants or seed packets collected during Drummond's journey. In 1834, Hooker, editor of the *Journal of Botany,* published a brief account of Drummond's excursion, along with advertisements announcing the availability for sale of exciting new plants.[51]

Botanical publications like Hooker's kept potential customers abreast of new collecting expeditions. His *Companion to the Botanical Magazine,* for example, featured the following consecutive announcements in 1836:

> *Mr. Nuttall is returned to the United States after a most interesting expedition across the Rocky Mountains to the shores of the Pacific at the mouth of the Columbia, and a voyage thence to the Sandwich Islands. We understand the journey has been a very successful one in point of botanical acquisitions, and the Rocky Mountains having been crossed considerably to the southward of Mr. Drummond's or Mr. Douglas' route, the character of the vegetation will be proportionably different, and we trust Mr. Nuttall is engaged in preparing an account of them for the press.*[52]

Below the announcement regarding Nuttall, Hooker advertised a recently proposed botanical expedition involving the botanist August Fendler, who remained unidentified in the announcement:

> *It gives us pleasure to be able to say that a botanical collector is about to proceed*

to Santa Fe, in North Mexico, under the auspices of Dr. Torrey of New York. He will accompany the Caravan, which leaves St. Louis (on the Missouri) about the end of May next, and will reach Santa Fe in about sixty-five days. The party will not return until October, thus affording the collector ample opportunities for drying plants, &c. His outfit is calculated at three hundred dollars currency [about $7,600 in current dollars]. Those, who contribute to this, will receive plants at the rate of one hundred specimens for every five dollars. To those who purchase specimens on the return of the collector, without having contributed to his outfit, the price will be seven dollars per hundred. Considering the highly interesting character of the country to be explored, and the difficulty of getting access to it (the whole journey to and from St. Louis having to be made on horseback), the terms are certainly extremely moderate.[53]

Printed matter of the early and mid-1800s teemed with advertisements and catalogues announcing the recent arrival of various sorts of plant specimens from North American expeditions, and the nursery stock germinated from seeds collected during those expeditions.[54] Moreover, the collectors' global community of fellow botanists communicated prodigiously through private letters. In an 1848 *London Journal of Botany*, Hooker republished part of George Engelmann's November 14, 1847, letter to Asa Gray, one of the giants of North American botany:

You would do me a favour ... if you would have a short notice published immediately here and in England, stating that Mr. A. Fendler has arrived in St. Louis with a rich botanical collection from near Santa Fe, and that he offers about 10 sets of something like four or five hundred (perhaps more) species ... most of them in the best possible state of preservation, and well selected ... that the price is ten dollars a hundred, transportation from St. Louis to be paid by the subscriber.[55]

Pressed plant specimens were being bought, sold, and traded among botanical hobbyists as well as by research botanists needing herbarium specimens to prepare their "Floras" – massive plant identification and classification books. These early collections were used to describe and name each species of plant. The many surviving herbarium specimens from that day are still an important part of today's botanical DNA research. As early as 1841, Gray emphasized:

It becomes necessary to refer to the herbaria where the original specimens are preserved. In this respect the collections of the early authors possess an importance far exceeding their intrinsic value.[56]

To prove his point, Gray referenced Hooker's herbarium at Glasgow, Scotland, which included

nearly complete sets of ... the collections of Drummond and Douglas in the Rocky Mountains, Oregon, and California, as well as those of ... numerous officers of the Hudson's Bay Company.[57]

Asa Gray advertised Geyer's 1842 botanical specimens, collected with Joseph Nicollet in Missouri and Illinois, in Silliman's *American Journal of Science and Art* as "twenty sets of one hundred fifty species of plants, which are offered at six dollars per set."[58] Upon Geyer's triumphant return to England a few years later, Hooker wrote that

Mr. Charles A. Geyer, who distinguished himself by the botanical collections he made with Nicollet in 1838 and 1839, between the Mississippi and Missouri

Rivers, has recently arrived in England with a very valuable and beautifully preserved collection of Plants, gathered in the Upper Missouri, on the Rocky Mountains, and in the Oregon Territory ... [for sale] at the rate of £2 the 100 species, all expenses included.[59]

Gray also made note of English horticulturalist Aylmer B. Lambert having purchased two significant herbariums "at a great expense."[60] Gray further located the collections of Frederick Pursh, which served as the basis of his *Flora Americanae Septentrionalis,*

with a few specimens brought by Lewis and Clark from Oregon and the Rocky Mountains, and a set of Nuttall's collections on the Missouri, and also of Bradbury's, so far as they are extant ... compose the most important portion of [Lambert's] herbarium, so far as North American botany is concerned.[61]

Lambert's collections later sold at auction in 1842 for £1,171 ($136,000 in today's dollars).[62]

Conclusion

The plant trade was the botanical equivalent of the fur trade. Botanists performed all aspects of fur trapping and trading except their product was plant, not fur. All other steps were quite comparable, from collection to distribution of the final product. However, it was the fur trade companies and other exploration sponsors (both private and government) who bore the brunt of initiating, organizing, and financing the journey.[63] The collection of plant specimens proved to be a far more self-sustaining business model than that of the fur trade, which devoured its own by turning its resource into pelts. Seeds and nursery plants could be multiplied endlessly, while skins were literally a dead-end street. Had the fur trappers and traders stopped to consider the naturalists' long-range plan, perhaps they would have understood the monetary value of all those scientific specimens, and even seen the method to Thomas Nuttall's madness.

Carol Kuhn holds degrees in Botany, Zoology, and Studio Art. She is a managing member of K&K Environmental LLC, an environmental consulting company in Leavenworth, Kansas, specializing in archaeological investigations, cultural resources, endangered species, and wetlands. K&K also hosts occasional K&K History Wagon Tours of eighteenth- and nineteenth-century historic sites in Missouri.

NOTES

1 Thomas Nuttall, "A Catalogue of a Collection of Plants made chiefly in the Valleys of the Rocky Mountains or Northern Andes, towards the sources of the Columbia River, by Mr. Nathaniel B. [sic] Wyeth, and described by T. Nuttall," *Journal of the Academy of Natural Sciences of Philadelphia* 7, part 1 (1834): 5-60. Despite a catastrophic loss of the majority of plants Wyeth had collected during his 1832-33 expedition, he nevertheless gained high praise from Thomas Nuttall for the quality of the surviving collection. "The number of the species will therefore be duly appreciated, and particularly when it is known that this was the first essay of the kind ever made by Mr. W.; and yet I can safely say, that besides their number, there being many duplicates, they are the finest specimens probably, that ever were brought from the distant and perilous regions of the west by any *American* collector." The Wyeth collection contained 113 species of plants, 60 of which were new to science.

2 Elias Durand, "Memoir of the Late Thomas Nuttall," *Proceedings of the American Philosophical Society* 7 (1860): 297-315. Apparently unfamiliar with Wilson Price Hunt or the Astorians, Durand recorded that John Bradbury had a desire to botanize the West, Nuttall volunteered to accompany him, and the two of them "started together from St. Louis, with a party of trappers and traders."

3 Christine Chapman Robbins, "John Torrey (1796-1873) His Life and Times," *Bulletin of the Torrey Botanical Club* 95, no. 6 (Nov - Dec 1968): 528.

4 William Jackson Hooker, Introduction to Charles A. Geyer, "Notes on the Vegetation

and general character of the Missouri and Oregon territories, made during a Botanical journey from the State of Missouri, across the south-pass of the Rocky Mountains, to the Pacific, during the years 1843 and 1844," *The London Journal of Botany* 4 (1845): 479.

5   Francis B. Heitman, *Historical Register and Dictionary of the U.S. Army*, (Washington, DC: Government Printing Office, 1903), 1:965; C. S. Rafinesque to G. Cuvier, December 28, 1818, in Charles Boewe, *Correspondence of C. S. Rafinesque* (Philadelphia, PA: American Philosophical Society, 2011) CD-ROM, 612. "A national expedition under the command of Majr Long is going to leave from Pittsburgh next March, to explore for 3 years, the tributaries of the Missouri. Dr. Baldwin is joining as Botanist, Mr. Say as Zoologist, Dr. Torrey as Geologist; they will go with a flat-bottomed Steamboat: I am expecting a great deal from their research." On page 666 in the same volume, see C. S. Rafinesque to John Torrey, April 5, 1819: "I hardly knew if you was in Newyork, and I was told you had been proposed as Mineralogist in the expedit~ of Major Long up the Missouri but I have just heard a (P)hiladelphian Miner~ Mr Gessup [Augustus Edward Jessup] is gone instead of you, along with Mess. Say & Baldwin."

6   Robbins, "John Torrey," 540.

7   William Darlington, *Reliquiae Baldwinianae: Selections from the Correspondence of the Late William Baldwin, M. D. Surgeon in the U.S. Navy. With Occasional Notes, and a Short Biographical Memoir* (Philadelphia, PA: Kimber and Sharpless, 1843), 293.

8   Ibid., 11. Though ailing with "an hereditary predisposition to Pulmonary Consumption," Dr. William Baldwin had joined Stephen H. Long's Yellowstone Expedition. Baldwin died early in the expedition, near Franklin, Missouri, at the estate of John J. Lowry, now Wettershaw Manor. Dr. Baldwin's remains still rest in the Manor's gardens, and naturalists still come to pay their respects. See H. A. A. R. von Wetter, *A Short History of the life of Dr. William Baldwin and his death at Wettershaw Manor*. (Self-published booklet, 2008).

9   David Douglas, *The Oregon Journals of David Douglas*, 2 vols. (Ashland, OR: The Oregon Book Society, 1972), 2:148.

10   Thomas Drummond, "Sketch of a Journey to the Rocky Mountains and to the Columbia River in North America," *Botanical Miscellany* 1 (1830): 197. Drummond, after surviving a near-death experience with a female grizzly, discovered that his vasculum proved good defense. "I found, by future experience, that the best mode of getting rid of the bears when attacked by them, was to rattle my vasculum, or specimen box, when they immediately decamp."

11   One quire = 24 sheets of paper. John Bradbury, *Travels in the Interior of America in the Years 1809, 1810, and 1811* (London: Sherwood, Neely, and Jones, 1817), 53. When dried properly, and curated well in museums, these pressed plants became invaluable specimens for many decades, or even today, two centuries later. Many of these old plant specimens collected during the fur trade era are still housed in the cabinets of the primary repository herbaria of North America and Europe.

12   Prince Maximilian of Wied, "Travels in the Interior of North America," *Early Western Travels, 1748-1846*, 32 vols., edited by Reuben Gold Thwaites (Cleveland, OH: The Arthur H. Clark Company, 1904), 22:111.

13   William Stanton, *Introduction to American Scientific Exploration, 1803-1860*, American Philosophical Society online bibliography, http://www.amphilsoc.org/guides/stanton/front (accessed January 15, 2016).

14   Henry Marie Brackenridge, "Journal of a Voyage Up the Missouri River, Performed in 1811," *Early Western Travels*, 6:102. See also Ted Binnema, *Enlightened Zeal: The Hudson's Bay Company and Scientific Networks, 1670-1870* (Toronto, ON: University of Toronto Press, 2014), 258. Nineteenth-century Canadian missionary Emile Petitot noted that "lovers of science are, we say, all original and a bit cracked, but the naturalists that we meet in the wilds of America seem to march to the beat of their own drums."

15   Bradbury, *Travels*, 43. Entry for April 11-14, 1811. Bradbury was likely aware that his hosts were hurrying up the Missouri River to provision the overwintering Astorians at the mouth of the "Naduet" (Nodaway) River.

16   Ibid., vi. Bradbury's fellow traveler and pirogue commander Henry Brackenridge stated that they navigated the 1,440 river miles between the Arikara villages and St. Louis in just 14 days. See also Brackenridge, "Journal of a Voyage," 151.

17   Thomas Nuttall, "Observations on the Geological Structure of the Valley of the Mississippi," *Journal of the Academy of Natural Sciences of Philadelphia* 2, part 1 (1821): 16. This proves incorrect the oft-repeated suggestion that Nuttall simply abandoned his contract with Dr. Barton (to botanize and bring back plants of the Northwest) to choose instead the more interesting offer of joining the Astorians.

18   John Howard Redfield, "Some North American Botanists: Dr. William Baldwin," *Botanical Gazette* 8, no. 6 (June 1883): 236.

19. William Baldwin to William Darlington, July 22, 1819, in Darlington, *Reliquiae Badwinianae*, 320.

20. Ibid., 296. John C. Calhoun to William Darlington, January 6, 1819. Calhoun wrote, "The original object of the [Stephen H. Long] expedition was to extend the knowledge of the Geography of our country; but it has been determined to make it as subservient to science, as possible. With this view, the expedition will be accompanied by citizens eminent in the several branches of knowledge, which you have enumerated. In serving our country, it will always afford me pleasure to contribute to the advancement of science." However, at nearly the same time that Calhoun wrote this glowing letter in honor of all things science, John Torrey, assigned as the expedition's mineralogist, vehemently questioned the terms of the naturalists' participation in Long's expedition. See John Torrey to Amos Eaton, February 16, 1819, in Andrew Denney Rodgers, III, *John Torrey: A Story of North American Botany*, (New York, NY: Hafner Publishing Company, 1965), 47. "I have given up the idea of accompanying Major Long. I & all my friends have been very much misinformed respecting the expedition, or else the plan of it has been changed. Three or four weeks ago, I received a letter requesting me to provide myself with apparatus & everything necessary for the expedition which I had engaged to accompany upon the [Missouri]! This startled me and I immediately wrote to Major Long, requesting of him full information in regard to the intended expedition, its object & destination, & I lately received his answer. The terms are, — that the naturalists will be provided with board, & receive protection — the papers, drawings, etc. are to be given up to government, who are to have the entire disposal of them — the naturalists to furnish themselves at their own expense. The object of the expedition is to traverse the [Missouri] its tributaries and subtributaries, embracing an extent (as Major Long supposes) of about 30,000 miles! The time occupied in making the researches will probably be from three to five years. The party will consist of three naturalists, of three young officers, & a crew of 12 to 14 men! No compensation will be allowed the naturalists. I need hardly ask you, how you would have determined … in my situation."

21. Journal entries May 26-31, 1827, in David Douglas, *Journal kept by David Douglas during his travels in North America 1823-1827*, (London, England: Royal Horticultural Society, 1914), 269. http://www.biodiversitylibrary.org, (accessed January 15, 2016).

22. The lack of genealogical connection betweem Thomas Drummond and William Drummond Stewart was explained by Thomas Fothringham, current Laird of Murthly Castle and Stewart family genealogist, via email, May 3, 2016. Drummond, "Sketch of a Journey," 183.

23. These departure dates explain the rarity of spring specimens in early botanical collections, as the collectors were still journeying westward with their travel providers. Indeed, one of the very few New Mexico locations with representative spring plant collections from the first half of the nineteenth century is Santa Fe, this thanks to August Fendler's having arrived there in October, 1846, well past the growing season. Having been tasked with the collection of vast quantities of specimens, he remained in Santa Fe through winter and thus was waiting with vasculum and shovel in hand when the beautiful Santa Fe flora awoke the next spring. Thomas Drummond to William J. Hooker, July 19, 1831, in William Jackson Hooker, "Notice Concerning Mr. Drummond's Collections, Made in the Southern and Western Parts of the United States," *The Journal of Botany* 1 (1834): 57.

24. Thomas Drummond to William J. Hooker, December 14, 1831, ibid., 59.

25. John K. Townsend, *Narrative of a Journey Across the Rocky Mountains, to the Columbia River and a Visit to the Sandwich Islands, Chili, &c. with a Scientific Appendix* (Philadelphia, PA: Henry Perkins, 1839), 28. See also Townsend's May 31, 1834, entry on journal page 64.

26. Douglas, *Journal in North America*, 57.

27. Clifford M. Drury, "Botanist in Oregon in 1843-44 for Kew Gardens, London," *Oregon Historical Quarterly* 41, no. 2 (June 1940): 186.

28. Ibid., 187. One wonders if at least some of the Douglas firs recorded as being planted at Murthly in 1847 are part of Mr. Geyer's travel agreement. A 1900 inspection of the Murthly Castle gardens identified a Douglas fir planted in 1847, measured at 97.4 feet in height, with a circumference, at five feet above ground, of 9.1 feet. See E. T. Cook, "Conifers [including Pines] in Ornamental Planting – Conifers at Murthly Castle," *Trees and Shrubs for English Gardens* (Covent Garden, England: Country Life and George Newnes, Ltd., 2nd Ed., 1908), 125-129.

29. Peter Skene Ogden to John McLeod, February 25, 1837, "Arrival of Steamer Beaver," *The Washington Historical Quarterly* 2 (April 1908): 260. Susan Delano McKelvey suggests that the nuisance group included Thomas Nuttall and John Kirk Townsend. Susan Delano McKelvey, *Botanical Exploration of the Trans-Mississippi West, 1790-1850* (Jamaica Plain, MA: Arnold Arboretum, 1956), 388. However, letters written by Nuttall place him elsewhere.

30. Binnema, *Enlightened Zeal*, 129.

31. Townsend, *Narrative*, 25, 75. It should be noted that Townsend's disdain may have been

31 fueled in part by his illness, as eight days later he describes the camp as "most lovely in every aspect." Ibid., 26.
32 Ibid., 101n.
33 Douglas, *Journal in North America*, 67.
34 Ibid., 248-249.
35 Ibid., 258.
36 Ibid., 61-62. *Narthecium* is a lily, common name bog asphodel. Mr. McKenzie is fortunate to have suffered merely "some inconvenience," as *Narthecium* can cause severe kidney damage. See U.S. Food and Drug Administration Poisonous Plant Database, http://www.accessdata.fda.gov/scripts/plantox/ (accessed January 15, 2015).
37 Townsend, *Narrative*, 224.
38 Benjamin Silliman, "The Herbarium of the Late Zaccheus Collins of Philadelphia," *The American Journal of Science and Arts* 23, no. 1 (October 1832 - January 1833): 398. In 1833, announcement was made in Silliman's *Journal* of the sale at auction of the late botanist Zaccheus Collins's herbarium, which likely brought significant monetary reward to the grieving family, thanks to a "complete set of the plants collected in Arkansaw by Mr. Nuttall, together with many from the Missouri ... included in the herbarium." Unlike furs, herbariums were sold and re-sold, divided and combined. Collins had purchased the William Baldwin herbarium at a reported cost of $200 (ca. $5,800 in today's dollars). See Ronald Stuckey, "The first public auction of an American herbarium including an account of the fate of the Baldwin, Collins, and Rafinesque Herbaria," *Taxon* 20, no. 4 (August 1971): 447-452. The Collins Herbarium was broken into three groups, which sold for a grand total of $330 ($9,600 today). In 1834, the Baldwin Herbarium was donated to the Academy of Natural Sciences in Philadelphia, where it gained in scientific value through time, as more and more species were named from it, thus making the collection full of invaluable "type" specimens critical for use in systematic botany today.
39 Jim Hardee, *Obstinate Hope: The Western Expeditions of Nathaniel J. Wyeth, Volume One: 1832-1833* (Pinedale, WY: Sublette County Historical Society, 2013), 305.
40 The specimen can be viewed online at the New York Botanical Gardens website: http://sweetgum.nybg.org/science/vh/specimen_details.php?irn=629987
41 John Bradbury to William Roscoe, September 9, 1808, in H. W. Rickett, "John Bradbury's Explorations in Missouri Territory," *Proceedings of the American Philosophical Society* 94, no. 1 (1950): 60.
42 Boewe, *Life of Rafinesque*, 231.
43 James L. Reveal, *Gentle Conquest: The Botanical Discovery of North America with Illustrations from the Library of Congress* (Washington, DC: Starwood Publishing, Inc., 1992), 114.
44 John Claudius Loudon, "History and Geography of Trees, Part 1, Chapter II. Of the History and Geography of the Trees and Shrubs Now in the British Islands" in *Arboretum et Fruticetum Britannicum; or, The Trees and Shrubs of Britain* (London: Longman, Orme, Brown, Green, and Longmans, 1838), 1:126.
45 William Jackson Hooker, "A Brief Memoir of the Life of Mr. David Douglas, with Extracts from his Letters," *Companion to the Botanical Magazine* 1 (1836): 140.
46 Perley Spaulding, "Investigations of the white-pine blister rust," *Office of Investigations in Forest Pathology, United States Department of Agriculture, Bulletin No. 957* (Washington, DC: Government Printing Office, February 6, 1922), 7-10.
47 Loudon, *History*, 127.
48 Ibid., 125-126.
49 Thomas Nuttall, *A Journey of Travels into the Arkansas Territory During the Year 1819*, edited by Savoie Lottinville (Norman, OK: University of Oklahoma Press, 1980), x-xvi. Nuttall had known Bernard McMahon since about 1808, and was back in Philadelphia in 1815, the year before McMahon died.
50 Reveal, *Gentle Conquest*, 114.
51 William Jackson Hooker, "Notice Concerning Mr. Drummond's Collections, Made in the Southern and Western Parts of the United States," *The Journal of Botany* 1 (1834): 50-60, 183-202.
52 William Jackson Hooker, "Botanical Information," *Companion to the Botanical Magazine* 2 (1836): 185.
53 Ibid. Hooker incorrectly placed St. Louis on the Missouri River, rather than the Mississippi.
54 Representative plant catalogues and journal advertisements: 1) William Prince, Proprietor, *Wholesale Catalogue of American Trees, Shrubs, Plants, and Seeds, Cultivated and for Sale at the Linnaean Botanic Garden and Nurseries, Near New York*, (New York, NY: T. & J. Swords, 1827). Prince's 1827 catalog lists several agents in Europe and England "who will forward orders to the Proprietor." To further enable this fledgling American industry, "Consuls of the United States will forward any communications for the Proprietor." William Prince and his sons published catalogs from 1815 to 1850; 2) *Curtis's Botanical Magazine*, published continuously since 1787 by the Royal Botanic Gardens, Kew; 3) Sir Joseph Paxton, *Paxton's Magazine of Botany and Register of Flowering Plants*, (London: Orr & Smith, 1834-1849); 4)

Fraser Brothers' Catalogue; 5) J. C. Loudon, Conductor, *The Magazine of Natural History, and Journal of Zoology, Botany, Mineralogy, Geology, and Meteorology,* (London: A. & R. Spottiswood, 1829-1837).

55 William Jackson Hooker, "Notice of Mr. Fendler's Botanical Journey to Santa Fe, in North Mexico. (Extract of a Letter addressed to Dr. Asa Gray, from Dr. Engelmann of St. Louis George Engelmann to Asa Gray," *The London Journal of Botany* 7 (1848): 45-46. Hooker's *The Journal of Botany* appears to have ended in 1842 and emerged under a new publisher using this title. A full detail of the specimen sets: "about 10 sets of something like four or five hundred (perhaps more) species, ten more of about three hundred, and twenty more of 200 species, most of them in the best possible preservation, and well selected, a few being only incomplete (in some oaks, willows, &c.), that the price is ten dollars a hundred, transportation from St. Louis to be paid by the subscriber; and that a printed catalogue with descriptions of new species will be sent to every subscriber." Assuming that all sets sold, converting those 1848 dollars into 2014 dollars reveals an astounding $221,200 worth of plant specimens from one excursion (assessing commodity real price using www.measuringworth.com).

56 Asa Gray (identified as "A. G."), "Notices of European Herbaria, particularly those most interesting to the North American Botanist," in Sir W. Jardine, et al., *The Annals and Magazine of Natural History, including Zoology, Botany, and Geology* 7, no. 43 (1841): 132.

57 Ibid., 179. These HBC officers included Alexander Caulfield Anderson, who after much encouragement by Archibald McDonald, sent a package to Sir William Jackson Hooker in 1845, with various seeds, fruits, tubers, and bulbs which he had collected while at Fort Alexandria in New Caledonia (see Jean Murray Cole, ed., *This Blessed Wilderness – Archibald McDonald's Letters from the Columbia, 1822-44* (Vancouver, BC: UBC Press, 2001).

58 Asa Gray (identified as "A. GR."), "Notice of Botanical Collections," in Professor Silliman and Benjamin Silliman, Jr., eds., *The American Journal of Science and Arts* 45, no. 1 (April-June 1843): 225-227.

59 J. Orin Oliphant, "The Botanical Labors of Reverend Henry H. Spalding," *The Washington Historical Quarterly* 25, no. 2 (April 1934): 96. At today's prices, a hefty $20,640 dollars, assuming all lots sold.

60 Asa Gray (identified as "A. G."), "Notices of European Herbaria," *The Annals and Magazine of Natural History* 7, no. 43 (1841): 140.

61 Ibid.

62 Hortense S. Miller, "The Herbarium of Aylmer Bourke Lambert: notes on its acquisition, dispersal, and present whereabouts," *Taxon* 19 (August 1970): 489-656.

63 Louise Barry, *The Beginning of the West: Annals of the Kansas Gateway to the American West 1540-1854* (Topeka, KS: Kansas State Historical Society, 1972), 130. Barry estimated that Ashley and Smith compiled a $20,000 outfit for their 1825 trek to the Rockies, including approximately 60 men, horses, mules, and supplies.

Appendix A: Selected Sales of Botanical Specimens, 1840s

Collector	Dealer	Specimen Packets	Price and Year	2015 Adjusted Estimated Value*
unspecified[1]	Hooker	1 lot of 200 specimens 1 lot of 100 specimens, North American plants	1840 12 florins[2] per 100 specimens 100% sales = 36 florins	100% sales = $403
Nuttall[3]	self	100 per group (presumed pressed plants)	1841 $10 per 100 specimens	$280 per 100 specimens
Lewis & Clark, Bradbury, Fraser, Nuttall, Scouler, Douglas, Pursh, etc.[4]	Sotheby's auction of Lambert's herbarium	Pressed plants	1842 100% sales = £1,171	100% sales = $136,000
Geyer[5]	Gray	20 sets of 150 specimens	1843 $6 per set 100% sales = $120	100% sales = $3,600
Geyer[6]	Hooker	20 sets of specimens x average 425 specimens per set = 8,500 specimens	1845 £2 per 100 specimens 100% sales = £1,700	100% sales = $207,000
Fendler[7]	Engelmann & Gray, advertised by Hooker	A. 10 sets of 400-500 (perhaps more) pressed plant specimens; B. 10 sets of 300 pressed plants; C. 20 sets of 200 pressed plants Total of 7,900 specimens = 790 sets of 100 specimens	1848 all pressed plants @ $10 per 100 specimens plus shipping 100% sales = $7,900	$280 per 100 specimens 100% sales = $221,200

1 Sir W. J. Hooker, *The Journal of Botany* 2 (June 1840): 33.

2 florin : British florin, issued 1838-1887, silver coin valued between half-crown and shilling (0.10 £) (Herbert Appold Grueber, *Handbook of the Coins of Great Britain and Ireland in the British Museum* (London: British Museum, Department of Coins and Medals, 1899), 156.

3 Letter, A. Gray to W. J. Hooker, January 15, 1841, in *Letters of Asa Gray,* edited by Jane Loring Gray, 2 vols. (Boston, MA: Houghton, Mifflin and Company, 1894), 1:278.

4 Hortense S. Miller, "The Herbarium of Aylmer Bourke Lambert: notes on its acquisition, dispersal, and present whereabouts," *Taxon* 19 (August 1970): 489-656.

5 *American Journal of Science and Arts* 45 (1843): 73-77, as noted in McKelvey, 772n5.

6 Sir W. J. Hooker, Introduction to Charles A. Geyer, "Notes on the Vegetation and general character of the Missouri and Oregon territories, made during a Botanical journey from the State of Missouri, across the south-pass of the Rocky Mountains, to the Pacific, during the years 1843 and 1844," *The London Journal of Botany* 4 (1845): 479-492.

7 "Notice of Mr. Fendler's Botanical Journey to Santa Fe, in North Mexico" (extract of a letter addressed to Dr. Asa Gray, from Dr. Engelmann of St. Louis), *The London Journal of Botany* 7 (1848): 44-46.

* 2015 adjustments based upon real value of commodity. See http://www.measuringworth.com/uscompare/relativevalue

Appendix B: Representative Expeditions with Accompanying Naturalists

Year	Naturalist	Expedition	Location
1811	John Bradbury	Wilson Price Hunt - Overland Astorian Expedition	Lower Missouri River
1811	Thomas Nuttall	Wilson Price Hunt - Overland Astorian Expedition	Missouri River: St. Louis to Mandan Villages
1811	Henry Marie Brackenridge	Manuel Lisa – St. Louis Missouri Fur Company	Lower Missouri River
1819-1820	William Baldwin Thomas Say Edwin James	Stephen H. Long Expedition	Lower Missouri River
1820	Henry Schoolcraft	Cass Expedition	Upper Mississippi
1824-1825	David Douglas	Hudson's Bay Company	Pacific Northwest; Columbia River
1824-1825	John Scouler	Hudson's Bay Company	Pacific Northwest
1825-1827	Thomas Drummond	Franklin's Second Arctic Expedition – Northwest Passage	Rocky Mountains (Athabaska Pass, Carlton House, York Factory)
1831	Thomas Drummond	Private expedition	Southern and Western United States
1832-1833	Nathaniel J. Wyeth	Nathaniel J. Wyeth	Travel to Pacific Coast
1832-1834	Prince Maximilian Karl Bodmer	Prince Maximilian's expedition	Upper Missouri River
1834-1836	Thomas Nuttall John Kirk Townsend	Nathaniel J. Wyeth	Travel to Pacific Coast
1838	Peter Banks Robert Wallace	Hudson's Bay Company	Columbia River
1839	Frederick A. Wislezenus	American Fur Company	1839 Green River Rendezvous
1841 or 1842	William Gambel	William Gambel	Southwest (Santa Fe; Mexico)
1842	John C. Frémont	Frémont's First Expedition	South Pass via Platte River
1843	John James Audubon	Private expedition	Missouri River
1843	John C. Frémont	Frémont's Second Expedition	South Pass, Oregon, southern Rocky Mountains
1843	Charles Mersch, Friederich Luders, Charles Geyer, Alexander Gordon	Stewart's Rendezvous Expedition	Rocky Mountains
1845	John Charles Frémont	Frémont's Third Expedition	Arkansas River source, southern Rocky Mountains, California
1846-1847	Frederick A. Wislizenus	Doniphan's Expedition to Northern Mexico [return trip]	Santa Fe region

Expedition Sponsor	Naturalist Sponsor	Goals/Achievements
Pacific Fur Company	Pacific Fur Company	Collect plant specimens, live plants, seeds; establish New Orleans nursery; propagate and ship plants to England
Pacific Fur Company	Pacific Fur Company	Collect plant specimens for his Genera of North American Plants; seeds for propagation
St. Louis Missouri Fur Company	Self	General naturalist collections
US Government	US Government	Collect natural history data, specimens for Long's Expedition publication
US Government	US Government	Record geology, mineralogy, flora, fauna of recently acquired land
HBC	Horticultural Society of London	Harvest of plant specimens and seeds for shipment to England
HBC	HBC, British Government	Surgeon/naturalist
British Government	Sir William Hooker, Kew Gardens	Collect plants for Hooker's Flora Boreali Americana
Sir William Hooker, benefactors, and subscriptions	Sir William Hooker, benefactors, and subscriptions	Collect specimens in areas not previously explored, for sale to subscribers in England
Nathaniel J. Wyeth	Nathaniel J. Wyeth	Plant collector for Thomas Nuttall
Prince Maximilian	Prince Maximilian	General naturalist collection, recordation and observation
Nathaniel J. Wyeth	Nathaniel J. Wyeth	Plant collection for Nuttall's Flora; bird collection for Audubon
HBC	Chatsworth Garden (Sir Joseph Paxton), private subscriptions	Collect regions of the Northwest not previously traveled by David Douglas
American Fur Company	Self, subscriptions	Plant collection for George Engelmann
Private subscriptions	Private subscriptions	First botanist to collect in New Mexico
US Government	US Government	Collect plant specimens for US botanists John Torrey, Asa Gray, George Engelmann
Private funding	Subscriptions	Collect specimens for Viviporous Quadrupeds of North America
US Government	US Government	Collect plant specimens for John Torrey to identify for US Gov't publication
Sir William Drummond Stewart	Sir William Drummond Stewart	Geyer: collect plants and seeds in Pacific Northwest
US Government	US Government	Collect plant specimens for John Torrey to identify for US Government publication
US Military	George Engelmann, John Torrey, subscriptions	Plant collection for Torrey's Flora

Mountain Men and the Taking of California, 1845-1847

by Larry E. Morris

A sketch made c.1848 by US Navy gunner William H. Meyers depicts the Battle of San Pasqual, fought December 6, 1846. COLLECTION OF THE OAKLAND MUSEUM OF CALIFORNIA

On the afternoon of July 29, 1845, five companies of the renowned 1st US Dragoons, led by Colonel Stephen Watts Kearny, approached Bent's Fort on the Arkansas River, just north of the border between the United States and Mexico. First came a lone scout, then the commanding officer, his orderly, chief bugler, and staff officers. Following them came one company of two-by-two dragoons mounted on black horses, then one on greys, one on bays, one on sorrels, and the fifth company on blacks again, all spaced to keep the dust down.

Next came two horse-drawn 12-pound howitzers, then the teamsters with supply wagons, trailed by a drove of cattle and sheep. The main guard brought up the rear.[1]

The forty-five-year-old guide riding a quarter-mile ahead of the colonel was the veteran mountain man and explorer Thomas Fitzpatrick. In the twenty-two years since ascending the Missouri River with William Ashley in 1823, the Irish-born Fitzpatrick had been virtually ubiquitous in the Rockies, playing a vital role in advancing the fur trade and establishing the Oregon Trail.

After a short stay, Colonel Kearny continued on to Fort Leavenworth on August 1, but Fitzpatrick stayed at Bent's Fort, scheduled to guide a group of soldiers on a scientific expedition.

On August 4, a patchwork battalion of military volunteers, Delaware Indians, and mountain men approached Bent's trading post. Among the mountain men were Lucien Maxwell, Basil Lajeunesse, Alexander Godey, and Auguste Archambeault, each furnished with "1 whole-stock Hawkens rifle, two pistols, a butcher knife, saddle, bridle, pistol holsters & 2 pr. blankets."[2] Their leader was John C. Frémont, a thirty-two-year-old brevet captain in the army's Topographical Corps of Engineers, now on his third expedition [see Carol Kuhn article, this volume].

With Frémont was Lieutenant James W. Abert, son of Colonel John Abert, Frémont's superior officer. In a few weeks, young Abert would lead the scientific expedition, guided by Fitzpatrick, out of Bent's Fort and down the Canadian River on a loop that would take it as far as today's Oklahoma before returning to St. Louis in November.[3]

By 1844, Frémont had led two expeditions along the Oregon Trail and as far west as the Pacific coast, and would soon be dubbed "The Pathfinder." Guided by former mountain men, Frémont surveyed and documented regions discovered decades earlier by the likes of fur trader Jedediah Smith.

After the Mexican War, Colonel Stephen Watts Kearny (1794-1848) served briefly as governor of both Vera Cruz and Mexico City. But he returned to St. Louis after contracting yellow fever, which took his life within weeks. LIBRARY OF CONGRESS

Kit Carson had served Frémont on the first expedition, in 1842; the second journey, in 1843, enlisted both Carson and Thomas Fitzpatrick as trailblazers. Having been co-commander of the second expedition, Fitzpatrick no doubt welcomed the captain warmly. Nor would he have been surprised to know that Frémont was asking about Kit Carson's availability as a guide. After Frémont had met Carson on a Missouri River steamboat in 1842, the two had become fast friends.

Called "Kit" from an early age, Carson was born in Kentucky in 1809. He had run away from his Missouri saddle-making apprenticeship in 1826 and joined a Santa Fe-bound wagon train. In New Mexico, he cut his trapping teeth with Mathew Kinkead and Ewing Young, traversing much of the Southwest. In

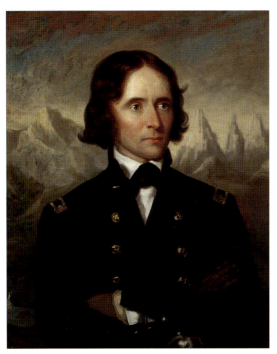

In 1848, John C. Frémont (1813-1890) was found guilty of insubordination for actions in California during the Mexican War. Although President Polk commuted the sentence, Frémont resigned his commission. This undated portrait of Frémont was painted by George Peter Alexander Healy. OIL ON CANVAS 30X25.5 INCHES. COLLECTION OF THE UNION LEAGUE CLUB OF CHICAGO, ULI895R.4

1831, he was hired by Fitzpatrick, who was headed for the northern Rockies.[4] Carson trapped with Jim Bridger, Joe Meek, and others in the vast fur-trade country centered in Wyoming before returning to Taos.

Upon his arrival at Bent's Fort, Frémont learned that Carson and his wife, Josefa, had made a home in the Cimarron Valley just six months before. But Carson had promised to join Frémont "in case he should return for the purpose of making any more exploration." When a letter from Frémont arrived, requesting help, Carson and his colleague Dick Owens sold out and hurried to Bent's Fort.[5]

Fitzpatrick and Carson had thus piloted Kearny and Frémont, the two most influential military figures in the West. Now, they were about to join their old fur trade companions in a new drama. Though neither guide knew it, they were harbingers of another turning point in American history, when the United States would go to war with Mexico and ambitiously expand to the south and west. Over the next two years, a host of experienced mountaineers would follow Fitzpatrick and Carson, playing vital roles as guides and messengers in the US military's taking of California. They would also find themselves embroiled in an epic conflict between Kearny and Frémont.

Mountain men lead Frémont to California

Frémont's official orders tasked him with exploring the upper Arkansas and Red rivers, which required him to travel no farther west than Colorado. Frémont had left St. Louis in June 1845 and had ignored the Red, but when he left Bent's Fort on August 16, 1845, he indeed ascended the Arkansas. The company, now led by Kit Carson, followed that river toward its headwaters, where it was perfectly positioned to take measurements, collect plant specimens, record observations, and create maps. Frémont, however, showed little interest in conducting a comprehensive survey – quite the contrary, because he soon hired another guide, trapper Bill Williams, whose area of expertise was not the upper Arkansas River.

Old Bill, as he was called, had been born in 1787 in North Carolina, and at 58 was now another mountaineer who knew the frontier well. His hiring was one more sign that Frémont intended to continue west. As Carson matter-of-factly noted, the men soon trekked from the Arkansas to the Colorado, which Carson called the Grand.[6] They crossed the Continental Divide onto the Pacific watershed, explicitly disregarding orders from Frémont's superiors to explore "streams which run east from the Rocky Mountains."[7] Clearly, Frémont, Carson, Williams, and many others on the

Christopher "Kit" Carson (1809-1868), photographed c.1845. Carson's career as a trapper, scout, guide, Indian agent, and soldier took him throughout the West and made him famous. PRIVATE COLLECTION / PETER NEWARK AMERICAN PICTURES / BRIDGEMAN IMAGES

expedition knew exactly where they were and where they were headed – California.

Traveling with so many mountaineers would not necessarily have spelled trouble, but Williams had brought along his Ute wife. One of the men wrote that Lucien Maxwell visited her "at very unfashionable hours and when Bill was not there." One night, Williams returned to his tent to find Maxwell talking to the woman. An onlooker reported that

> as soon as Old Bill saw him, he brought his gun to his shoulder and drew a bead on [Maxwell] and there is no doubt but whart he would have killed him, had I not sprag forward just in time and struck the gun up, so the bullet passed through the top of the tent, it did not take Maxwell long to evaporate from that tent.[8]

The incident was hushed up, and Frémont was told the firearm's discharge was an accident. As for Maxwell, he was not seen near the tent after that.

Sometime in September, Frémont descended the White River into present northeastern Utah and found another veteran explorer, Joseph Rutherford Walker. Hardly a chance encounter, according to his biographer Walker was actually "camped and waiting for [Frémont]. They met, it seems, by prearrangement."[9] Like Fitzpatrick and Carson, Walker was yet another mountain man who had served previously with Frémont, having accompanied him on the 1843 second expedition.[10]

Born in Tennessee in 1798, Walker had traveled the Santa Fe Trail and trapped the Arkansas River as early as 1822. Three years later he was in the same area with Old Bill Williams and others. It was Walker's 1833 journey for Benjamin Bonneville, however, that made him invaluable to Frémont. That July, Walker had led forty men from a Green River camp to Great Salt Lake, where they stocked up on buffalo meat. From there, Walker's clerk Zenas Leonard reported taking "a westerly course into the most extensive and barren plains I have ever seen."[11] Following the Humboldt River through present Nevada, Walker's party eventually managed to cross the Sierra Nevada Range before winter set in. This group ventured all the way to the Pacific at Monterey, California, then circled to the south before finally returning north, back across Nevada and Utah. No one else in Frémont's group had traveled this northern route to California. Now, unsurprisingly, Frémont named Walker head guide. Walker had known Carson and Fitzpatrick for decades, and having guided Frémont for part of the second expedition, was

Opposite page: Territories, landmarks, and routes at the start of the Mexican conflict.
MAP BY CLINT GILCHRIST

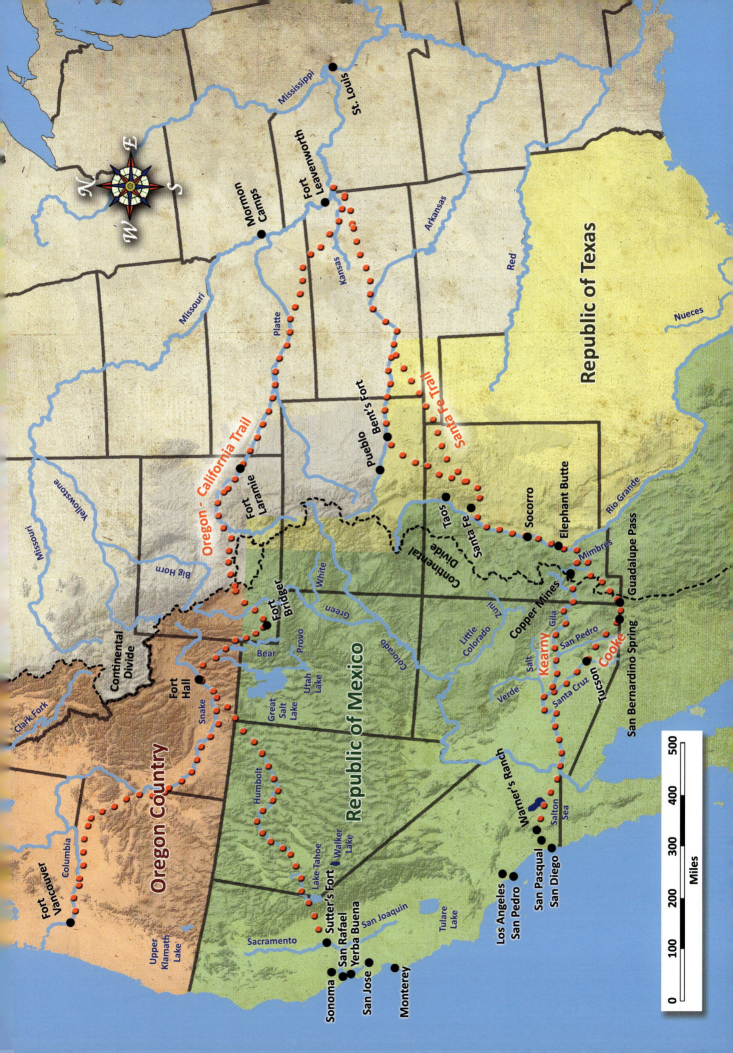

already known to many of Frémont's crew.

While no extant document grants Frémont official permission to enter California, there is no doubt that Frémont's powerful father-in-law, Senator Thomas Hart Benton, knew of, and likely encouraged, Frémont's plan to go all the way to the Pacific. On October 24, 1845, President Polk wrote,

> *Some conversation occurred [with Senator Benton] concerning Capt. Frémont's expedition, and his intention to visit California before his return.*[12]

Neither Benton nor Polk ever offered details of that conversation, but the prearranged meeting with Joseph Walker, the best California guide of all, is solid evidence, if not proof, that as early as 1844, as Walker was leading Frémont's second expedition back toward St. Louis, that Frémont had plotted an excursion across the Sierra Nevada.

Now, in September 1845, Walker led Frémont's sixty-man party to the head of the Provo River, which they descended to Utah Lake and then to Great Salt Lake. They had barely arrived when Williams and Walker began to quarrel over the route. One night things got heated and Williams sulked off to his tent. The next morning, Old Bill was gone, along with two of Walker's best horses, but Walker showed no interest in trying to catch Williams.[13]

Around the first of November, west of Great Salt Lake, the expedition divided for purposes of exploration and discovery.[14] Frémont took Carson, Maxwell, Archambeault, Lajeunesse, and about ten others and swung to the south, while Walker guided the main party down the Humboldt. The two groups met briefly at what is now called Walker Lake, then split up again. Frémont advocated crossing the Sierra by ascending the Truckee River. However, it being mid-November, Walker advised that if the entire expedition attempted this route, there was great risk of its being caught in deep snows.

Walker's group therefore took the pack animals south toward today's Walker Pass. Frémont, Carson, and the other mountaineers pushed over the Sierra, arriving after about three weeks at Sutter's Fort [for background on Sutter, see Jim Hardee article, this volume]. The troupe enjoyed the good luck of an exceptionally mild winter.[15]

Reuniting the entire brigade proved complicated. On December 27, 1845, Walker's group reached the south side of Tulare Lake, expecting to meet Frémont. When Frémont did not appear, Walker decided there had been a misunderstanding and took the party north in search of the captain. Eventually, they met yet another former trapper, this one by the name of Bill Fallon, also known as Le Gros, who told them Frémont had been in the area but had returned to Sutter's Fort. After further confusion, all of the men finally came together there.[16]

After several weeks at Sutter's Fort, Frémont received permission from Mexican authorities to proceed farther south. Pledging to leave California as soon as he resupplied his men, Frémont instead persevered to Yerba Buena (San Francisco), San Jose, and Monterey. Jose Castro, the military commandant at Monterey, had soon seen enough. In a March 5, 1846, letter, he warned Frémont:

> *The party under your command have entered the towns of this Department, and such being prohibited by our laws I find myself obligated to advertise you that on the receipt of this you will immediately retire beyond the limits of this same Department.*[17]

Rather than complying, Frémont led his men to a flat promontory outside Monterey, where they hastily erected a semblance of a fort and the next day raised an American flag. "We have in no wise done wrong to the people or the authorities of this country," Frémont blustered in a March 9, 1846, letter to US consul Thomas Larkin in Monterey, "and if we are hemmed in and assaulted, we will die every man of us, under the Flag of our country."[18]

Castro condemned Frémont's group as a band of robbers and began gathering forces, rifles, and artillery. Meanwhile, Larkin urged Castro to hold off and pressed Frémont to leave. Frémont, apparently looking for a way to retreat gracefully, found it:

> *Late in the afternoon of the third day, the pole bearing our flag fell to the ground. Thinking I had remained as long as the occasion required, I took advantage of the accident to say to the men that this was an indication for us to move camp.*[19]

That night, Frémont headed north to Oregon country, which was jointly held by Britain and the United States. He left under cover of darkness, likely saving his men from imprisonment or death. Yet Frémont's mountain men stood by him, ready to do anything asked of them. Frémont often turned to them for important missions.[20] In the midst of the tension with Castro, for example, Alexander Godey had acted as a courier of dispatches between the captain and Larkin.[21] Walker, however, had been itching for a fight. He was so disgusted with the retreat, that notwithstanding his loyalty to Frémont, he withdrew from the expedition.

Invasion of Mexico

By now, the prospect of war with Mexico had loomed for nearly two years. In April of 1844, when the US signed a treaty of annexation with the Republic of Texas, Mexico proclaimed the treaty an act of war and severed diplomatic ties with the US. Then, on March 1, 1845, outgoing president John Tyler had signed the resolution to annex Texas. Three days later, in his inaugural address, James K. Polk spoke of the acquisition of California. A month after that, Polk ordered General Zachary Taylor and his Army of Occupation to move into the disputed territory between the Nueces River and the Rio Grande. No hostilities had broken out, but relations between the US and Mexico had grown dangerously tense.

In November 1845, President Polk dispatched John Slidell on a peace mission to Mexico to attempt to purchase New Mexico and California. But at the end of December 1845, before Slidell met with any Mexican officials, General Mariano Paredes led a bloodless coup against President José Joaquín Herrera, took control of Mexico, and refused to meet with Slidell. Within days, Texas was admitted to the Union. On January 13, 1846, President Polk, who had received word of Slidell's rejection the previous day, ordered General Taylor's army to advance to the Rio Grande, a move Mexico would certainly see as an act of war.

Finally, on May 13, 1846, as Frémont's men lingered in Oregon, the US declared war on Mexico.[22] On May 26, Kearny, then at Fort Leavenworth, received a dispatch from Washington informing him of the declaration of war and ordering him to organize the Army of the West to march on Santa Fe. Kearny and his staff immediately began the countless chores required to move several hundred men, hundreds of wagons, and thousands of horses, mules, and oxen more than eight hundred miles across plains, rivers, and mountains.

On June 18, Kearny received additional orders:

> *It is known that a large body of Mormon emigrants are en route to California, for the purpose of settling in that country. You are desired to use all proper means to have a good understanding with them, to the end that the United States may have their cooperation in taking possession of, and holding, that country. It has been suggested here that many of these Mormons would willingly enter*

into the service of the United States, and aid us in our expedition against California. You are hereby authorized to muster into service such as can be induced to volunteer; not, however, to a number exceeding one-third of your entire force.[23]

Early in June, Jesse C. Little, a Mormon church representative in the East, had arranged a meeting with President Polk to see if the Mormons and the Federal government could help each other. Polk wrote,

I told Mr. Little that we were now at war with Mexico, and asked him if 500 or more of the Mormons now on their way to California would be willing ... to volunteer and enter the US army in that war.

Little answered with an enthusiastic yes.[24] Kearny promptly ordered Captain James Allen

to proceed to [the Mormon camps in Iowa] and endeavor to raise from amongst them 4 or 5 Companies of Volunteers to join me in my expedition to [California] ... They will under your command follow on my trail in the direction of Santa Fe, & where you will receive further orders from me.[25]

Attempts to recruit Mormons were initially met with skepticism but the men began enlisting in droves after church leader Brigham Young urged them to do so. Military pay would help finance hundreds of families going west in 1847. The enlistment would also calm fears about Mormon loyalty to the US and secure permission for the remaining Mormons to winter on Indian land.

In recruiting Mormons, Allen had requested able-bodied men, ages eighteen to forty-five. He got more than he bargained for. The oldest of the 496 recruits was sixty-seven, the youngest fourteen. Virtually all of them proceeded on foot, often in scorching heat those first several weeks. There were 35 women and 44 children also present. With Allen and his staff riding on horseback, and many of the women and children riding in wagons, the group Allen dubbed "the Mormon Battalion" departed for Fort Leavenworth on July 20, 1846.

Death in Oregon, chaos in California

Two months after Frémont's retreat from Monterey, on May 8, 1846, he was camped in Oregon country near Upper Klamath Lake when two men on horseback made their way through falling snow to his camp. They had ridden ahead of Lieutenant Archibald Gillespie of the US Marines, who had messages from Washington for Frémont.

The next morning, Frémont "took ten picked men, traveled about 60 miles, and met [Gillespie] encamped for the night."[26] Among the ten were mountaineers Carson, Owens, Godey, Lajeunesse, and four Delaware Indians. As the men warmed themselves around a fire, Gillespie told his story. The previous October – the same month as the conversation between the President and Benton, which hardly seems coincidental – Gillespie had been assigned as a confidential agent for Navy Secretary George Bancroft and had sailed from New York to Mexico. He entered that country using false papers. At Mazatlán, Gillespie had given Commodore John Drake Sloat a letter ordering him to seize the port at Yerba Buena and as many other ports as possible, if he learned of fighting between US and Mexican forces.[27] Gillespie then boarded a Navy ship and sailed to Monterey, arriving in mid-April 1846. After memorizing a letter from Secretary of State James Buchanan and destroying the original, he now dictated it to Larkin in Monterey, California. Information from Larkin allowed Gillespie and a few companions to track Frémont to Upper Klamath Lake.

Mystery surrounds the meeting between Frémont and Gillespie, because the discussion went largely undocumented, and most of the letters Gillespie reportedly delivered to Frémont have been lost. For Frémont, who had apparently loitered in California hoping for such news, the conclusion was clear:

The information through Gillespie had absolved me from my duty as an explorer, and I was left to my duty as an officer of the American Army with the further authoritative knowledge that the Government intended to take California.[28]

Convinced Indians were not nearby, Frémont posted no guards that night. He read the letters delivered by Gillespie till about midnight. According to Carson,

Shortly after Frémont had laid down, I heard a noise like the stroke of an axe striking, jumped up, saw there were Indians in camp, gave the alarm. The Indians had then tomahawked two men, Lajeunesse and a Delaware.

Another man was killed by arrows before Carson and the others drove off the attackers. Of the three men killed, Carson wrote of his fellow mountain man, "Lajeunesse was particularly regretted. He had been with us on every trip that had been made."[29]

Frémont and his men were now bent on revenge, and using typical frontier tactics, retaliation was random. Over the next few days they killed several non-hostile Klamath Indians without any evidence of their involvement in the earlier assault. When Carson and several others quietly discovered a Klamath village, they attacked without warning, executing several before the remainder fled.[30]

Frémont then traveled south to the Sacramento Valley, where American settlers urged him to lead an uprising, which later became known as the Bear Flag Revolt. Of particular interest to these settlers was the town of Sonoma, where Mexican General Mariano Vallejo was supplied with arms, ammunition, and horses but very few soldiers. Frémont listened sympathetically to the rebels, but professed that he had no authority to start a war with Mexico. On the evening of June 14, fanatical American Ezekiel Merritt led thirty-odd rebel settlers to surprise a sleeping General Vallejo. The mob took him, his wife, and two junior officers prisoner, then marched them to Frémont's camp.

In the first clear sign that he had joined with the revolutionaries, Frémont accepted the prisoners and transferred them to Sutter's Fort, treating John Sutter, who had once been friendly with Frémont, quite harshly and threatening serious consequences if the prisoners escaped.

Frémont and his men rode toward Sonoma. In an Indian battle along the way, Frémont saved Carson's life by charging his horse at an Indian after Carson's gun misfired. Carson reported that Archambeault, Maxwell, and Godey all acquitted themselves quite well in Indian skirmishes during the trip to Sonoma.

By June 25, Frémont, approaching Sonoma, learned that American insurrectionists had outraced him to the destination and captured the Mexican military post at Sonoma. He also learned that two settlers, Thomas Cowie and George Fowler, had been taken prisoner by Mexican guerrillas, tied to a tree, and tortured to death. Frémont later wrote,

Both the settlers and the men under my command were excited against the Californios *by the recent murder of the two Americans, and not by the murder only, but by the brutal circumstances attending it.*[31]

Each day after that, Frémont sent scouts out in search of Californios. On June 28,

Robert Field Stockton (1795-1866), in a daguerreotype c.1845-50. Stockton replaced US Navy Commodore John Drake Sloat in July 1846. CHICAGO HISTORY MUSEUM

Carson and two companions saw a small boat heading for shore at San Rafael. They intercepted the skiff as it landed and held the three passengers (twenty-year-old twins Ramon and Francisco de Haro, and their uncle Jose de los Berreyesa), at gunpoint. The three were then shot and killed in cold blood, though the exact details of the murder remain a matter of considerable controversy.[32]

Carson mentioned the murder of the two Americans in his memoirs but said nothing about the killing of the three Californios in the boat. Decades later, Frémont wrote,

My scouts, mainly Delawares, influenced by these feelings [about the murder of Cowie and Fowler], made sharp retaliation and killed Berreyesa and de Haro.[33]

Ten years later, when Frémont ran for US president, the killing of the three Mexicans would be an issue in the campaign. Mountaineer Alexander Godey defended Frémont, saying that Carson had shot the men when they resisted arrest. Archibald Gillespie, however, claimed that after the men were shot, Frémont had said, "It is well."[34] Early California settler William Boggs would document that in the early 1850s, he had asked Carson about the incident. Carson had admitted to the killings:

He had reported them to Frémont and he told him to do his duty ... and Kit said his reason for the killing of these three Californians was to retaliate for the horrible manner in which the Californians treated these two Americans [Cowie and Fowler].[35]

Frémont and Carson apparently treated the murders of the Mexicans as they had the deaths of innocent Indians: merely as a fact of life that in no way hampered the July 4, 1846, celebration in Sonoma. The cannon was fired, the Declaration of Independence read, and the revolutionists' Bear Flag raised. Frémont was selected as leader of the well over one hundred armed men, which he organized into four companies. Carson's old trapping friend Dick Owens was named captain of the company consisting largely of men who had accompanied Frémont into California.[36]

Frémont, Carson, and the others had returned to Sutter's Fort by July 10, when an express arrived with thrilling news. Three days earlier, Commodore Sloat, who must have learned of battles between US and Mexican forces, had raised the Stars and Stripes at Monterey's main plaza, proclaiming it US territory, as the letter delivered by Gillespie had instructed. US flags had subsequently been raised in Yerba Buena and Sonoma, and so Frémont did the same at Sutter's Fort. The Bear Flag rebels' Republic of California had lasted less than a month.

Based on his meeting with Gillespie in Mazatlan, Sloat assumed that Frémont carried secret orders from the War Department.

Lithograph of Santa Fe, from a report by Lieutenant James W. Abert c.1846-47. Stephen Watts Kearny marched his troops into Santa Fe on August 18, 1846, claiming it for the United States.
COURTESY OF FRAY ANGÉLICO CHÁVEZ HISTORY LIBRARY

Sloat, "a man who believed in an ironclad chain of military command," had therefore followed Frémont's lead. Now, however, when he asked Frémont by what authority he was acting, Frémont replied, "I acted solely on my own responsibility, and without any expressed authority from the Government to justify hostilities." Sloat was outraged and their meeting ended abruptly. The two men did not meet again.

The ailing Sloat was anxious to be relieved of his command. On July 23, Commodore Robert F. Stockton replaced him. Stockton promoted Frémont to major, assigned him official command of the "California Battalion," and ordered Frémont and his men to San Diego, where they fully expected to see their first action against Mexican soldiers. They sailed from Monterey on July 26.[37]

The Army of the West moves west

One month earlier, on June 29, 1846, now Brigadier General Kearny entered the Mexican American War, leading 1,600 soldiers out of Fort Leavenworth on the way to New Mexico. He had already summoned Thomas Fitzpatrick, in St. Louis after completing Abert's expedition, to act as a guide for the journey to Santa Fe and an expected excursion on to California. Within weeks, Fitzpatrick learned he had been appointed as a federal Indian agent but would be allowed to continue with Kearny for the duration of the campaign.

On July 31, 1846, Fitzpatrick wrote to his friend, mountaineer Andrew Sublette:

Late news which we received from Santa fee would indicate that we shall have no fighting, and indeed it has always been my opinion that there would not be a blow struck at Santa fee, whatever may be the case elsewhere. I know not, but from what I can learn the campaign will not end in New Mexico.[38]

Fitzpatrick's prediction proved accurate; Kearny took New Mexico without firing a shot, marching his troops into Santa Fe on August 18.

Philip St. George Cooke (1809-1895) served as a Union cavalry general during the Civil War and retired in 1873 after almost fifty years of military service. LIBRARY OF VIRGINIA

On September 25, Kearny and three hundred dragoons rode south out of Santa Fe, bound for California by way of the Gila River. Fitzpatrick was their guide and Antoine Robidoux served as their interpreter. Born in St. Louis, fifty-year-old Robidoux had been prominent in the fur trade for twenty years and was well known to Fitzpatrick, Carson, and many of the others. Robidoux knew the Southwest well, having operated trading posts in western Colorado and northeastern Utah. Most important to Kearny, he was a naturalized citizen of Mexico who spoke fluent Spanish. Qualified aides such as Fitzpatrick and Robidoux were crucial to Kearny, because he had been unable to obtain a single map of the Southwest.[39]

Also with Kearny at this time was Jean Baptiste Charbonneau, a forty-one-year-old mountain man and the son of Sacagawea, the famed Shoshone woman who had accompanied the Lewis and Clark Expedition. Charbonneau had spent a few years in Europe and spoke English, French, Spanish, and German, as well as several Indian languages. Between 1825 and 1845, he seemed to appear everywhere – at the Platte River with Joe Meek, at the Green River with Jim Bridger, on a buffalo hunt with Kit Carson, and more. A traveler who saw him working out of Bent's Fort in 1844 said he was known as "the best man on foot on the plains or in the Rocky Mountains."[40]

Two weeks after Kearny's departure, the advance company of the Mormon Battalion fixed their bayonets, drew their swords, and marched into Santa Fe's public square. "The first [company] of the Battalion arrived at Santa Fe on the evening of October 9th, 1846," wrote Battalion member Daniel Tyler.[41] They soon met their new commander, Lieutenant Colonel Philip St. George Cooke, "who received [them] with much courtesy & conversed freely."[42]

Yet the Mormons viewed their new commander warily – and he them. Cooke would later write:

Every thing conspired to discourage the extraordinary undertaking of marching this battalion eleven hundred miles, for the much greater part through an unknown wilderness without road or trail, and with a wagon train. It was enlisted too much by families; some were too old, some feeble, and some too young; it was embarrassed by many women; it was undisciplined; it was much worn by traveling on foot and marching from Nauvoo, Illinois; their clothing was very scant; there was no money to pay them or clothing to issue; their mules were utterly broken down; the quartermaster department was without funds and its credit bad; and mules were scarce.[43]

To deal with at least some of these realities, Cooke ordered that the sick men and twenty laundresses, their husbands and children be escorted to the new Mormon settlement at Pueblo where ten women and thirty-three children had previously been sent.

During this time, General Kearny and his dragoons had followed the Rio Grande south. On October 6, at the town of Socorro, Kearny was surprised to meet a party of mountaineers on their way to Santa Fe. One of Kearny's men wrote,

> *Came into camp late and found Carson with an express from California, bearing intelligence that the country had surrendered without a blow, and that the American flag floated in every port.*[44]

Carson and his companions had departed Los Angeles on September 5. Carson told a shocked Kearny how Stockton had taken San Diego without firing a shot and had employed sailors, marines, and Frémont's "Mounted Riflemen" to also take Los Angeles. Convinced the war was won, Stockton announced that all of California was now US territory and appointed Frémont "Military Governor." Stockton and Frémont had then tasked Carson and fifteen riflemen to deliver letters as quickly as possible to Senator Benton and President Polk announcing the victories.

Hearing this news, Kearny made two decisions. First, he convinced Carson to trade places with Fitzpatrick; Carson would lead Kearny to the Pacific, leaving Fitzpatrick to deliver dispatches to Washington. Although Fitzpatrick was fully capable, Carson had just made his way across the desert and could easily reverse his route, saving time and supplies. Moreover, his first-hand knowledge of the situation in California would be valuable. Second, Kearny sent two thirds of his men back to Santa Fe with Fitzpatrick, thinking they would no longer be needed since fighting in California had ended. The 100 dragoons Kearny retained would provide ample protection from Indians.

One historian wrote that sending the 200 soldiers back to Santa Fe "was a decision that came close to costing the general his life."[45] Only three months later, Kearny would lose some of his best officers in a hard-fought battle that could have turned out entirely differently – or not happened at all – if his two hundred missing dragoons had been present. Moreover, Carson's course reversal would ignite a series of events that would inspire Frémont to near-mutiny if not borderline civil war, and would dramatically impact the lives of both Kearny and Frémont.

Carson leads Kearny across the desert

"An excessively bad route today," wrote dragoon Captain Henry Smith Turner on October 9, "the country more broken than any I have ever seen traveled over with wagons." Indeed, Carson had said the previous day that it would take four months to travel from Socorro to California with wagons.[46] Kearny had resisted leaving the wagons, but finally did so on October 10, reluctantly using pack mules to haul supplies.

Up to this point, the dragoons had descended the Rio Grande southward, but now they turned west, crossing "extremely precipitous" ravines that "would have been wholly impracticable for our wagons." On October 19, they crossed the Continental Divide at the western edge of New Mexico and camped on a tributary of the Colorado called the Rio Gila, "a beautiful stream – perfectly clear water, and about 30 steps across, timbered with cotton wood."[47]

Carson frequently warned the men about the rough road ahead and sparse graze for livestock. On October 25, Carson spotted a horse and mule he had left behind on his eastbound trek, but the two animals were well rested and so wild that they could not be caught. Kearny's troops, now more than 400 miles from Santa Fe, descended the Rio Gila across today's Arizona. "After getting out of this kanyon we are promised … a good road into California, still some 400

On June 10-12, 1852, John Russell Bartlett sketched the junction of the Gila and Colorado rivers, viewed from the west bank of the Colorado. Bartlett was appointed United States Boundary Commissioner to carry out the provisions of the 1848 Treaty of Guadalupe Hidalgo.
COURTESY OF THE JOHN CARTER BROWN LIBRARY AT BROWN UNIVERSITY

miles distant," wrote Turner in the first week of November, "but as for grass, our guide says there is literally none." The next day Turner added, "Had quite a rain last night – the first since leaving Santa Fe," and then depicted the average day

> wading streams, clambering over rocky, precipitous mountains or laboring through the valleys of streams where the loose earth or sand cause animals to sink up to their knees at almost every step – then, our frugal meals, hard bed, & perhaps wet blanket.[48]

On November 19, "Mr. Carson killed a mountain sheep as we were passing the point of a mountain." As the day ended, Turner noted 787 miles had been traveled thus far.[49] On the 23rd, as Kearny's army approached the mouth of Rio Gila, they learned "that the Mexicans about the Pueblo de Los Angeles, had revolted and were in possession of that part of the country," information confirmed when Kearny's men arrested a dispatch-bearer and read letters intended for General Castro in California.[50] This was sobering news; Kearny's present army was less than one hundred men strong because a few had died of natural causes or accidents on the way. The cocksure Stockton and Frémont had unintentionally misled Kearny, who had acted on their word. The two hundred men idled in Santa Fe would have been of inestimable value now, as would the Mormon Battalion marching several weeks behind him. Forging ahead, Kearny realized, was his only option; he had to get to California as soon as possible.

The army forded the Colorado River on November 25. Turner wrote,

Had a most laborious march of 32 miles, arrived about 7 at night at a salt lake [Salton Sea] which was too briny for our animals to drink, and not a spear of grass in its vicinity – lost many animals on the road today from fatigue and exhaustion. 917 miles.[51]

A week later the dragoons concluded their desert trek, and began halting at ranches where ample feed and water for their animals could be requisitioned. The morning of December 1 was cold, and they wore their coats for the first time since leaving Fort Leavenworth. The next day, they arrived at Warner's Ranch, a popular stopping place for westbound travelers, and confirmed that the Mexicans were still in arms at Los Angeles. They also met Englishman Edward Stokes, who was going to San Diego the next day and offered to take a letter to Commodore Stockton.

Kearny took advantage of the proposal and wrote a quick note to Stockton, not revealing too much for fear the letter might fall into enemy hands. He informed Stockton that he had come by order of President Polk, that New Mexico had been annexed to the US and that the dispatches sent with Carson had likely reached Washington ten days earlier. He requested Stockton send a party to meet him but said nothing about Carson being back in California.[52]

On December 5, as Kearny's men rode through a heavy downpour, they saw a band of horsemen approaching, the Stars and Stripes fluttering above the riders. Kearny gave a friendly welcome to the leader of the thirty-nine men, who introduced himself as Captain Archibald Gillespie of the Marine Corps. Gillespie carried a return post from Stockton, informing the general that a force of about one hundred Mexican soldiers was reported to be close by at an Indian village called San Pasqual. Kearny should attack if he thought it advisable. Kearny pondered this as his men retired without any supper. A cold rain fell all night.[53]

Mountain men lead Cooke to the Colorado River

On October 19, 1846, Cooke's Mormon Battalion had left Santa Fe on its way to California to support Kearny. "My guide," Cooke wrote "is Mr. Weaver, sent to me by the general, who met him coming by the Rio Gila from California." Learning that Kearny had abandoned his wagons, Cooke considered:

I have brought road tools and am determined to take through my wagons. But the experiment is not a fair one, as the mules are nearly broken down at the outset. The only good ones (above twenty, which I bought near Albuquerque) were taken by Mr. Fitzpatrick [then on his way to deliver Stockton's and Frémont's dispatches to Washington], who brought an order for the twenty-one best in Santa Fe.[54]

"Mr. Weaver" was forty-nine-year-old Powell "Pauline" Weaver, a half-Anglo, half-Cherokee Tennessean, who had trapped and traded in the Rocky Mountains in both the US and Canada, spent several years in New Mexico, and trekked across Arizona and California as early as 1831.

The day after leaving Santa Fe, Cooke met another guide sent by Kearny – Jean Baptiste Charbonneau. Because Charbonneau had scouted for Kearny during the previous month, he knew the general planned to follow the Rio Grande to Elephant Butte, then go west to follow the Rio Gila into Arizona. However, Cooke knew that Charbonneau

had examined a route different in part and farther than that taken by the general, viz., to descend the [Rio Grande] river farther and fall into a road from

El Paso to the Copper Mines. The report is favorable; but [Charbonneau nor the other guides] did not make a thorough examination by any means; and the practicability of the route from the Copper Mines to the Gila is still a problem.[55]

On November 1, Cooke noted that Weaver was dangerously sick. Luckily, a third guide arrived from Kearny the next day. "Of the guides sent me by the general," wrote Cooke, "only Leroux joined me this afternoon; the others have come up tonight more or less drunk."[56] Born in St. Louis about 1801, Joaquin Antoine Jacques Leroux was a well-educated French-Canadian who had been a boyhood friend of Antoine Robidoux. Leroux, a former Henry-Ashley man, had gone up the Missouri River in 1822 with such luminaries as Smith, Fitzpatrick and Bridger. He settled in Taos, married a Mexican woman, and became a Mexican citizen. In the late 1820s he trapped in southern Colorado with the Robidoux brothers. In the 1830s he trapped in both Arizona and Colorado. By 1845, Leroux knew the Southwest so well that Cooke named him head guide.[57]

On November 3, Cooke made first mention of the last of his four main guides, calling him "Doctor Foster, the interpreter."[58] At twenty-six, Stephen Clark Foster was much younger than the other scouts but had a noteworthy background. A native New Englander, he had graduated from Yale College, studied medicine in Louisiana, and practiced medicine in several states. Unusually versatile, he served as interpreter, surgeon, and scout for Cooke.

Foster was a greenhorn, but Weaver, Charbonneau, and Leroux had crisscrossed the Southwest. They were familiar with such trails as those blazed by trapper Ewing Young along the Rio Grande, Rio Gila, and Colorado River in 1827, and along the Zuni, Salt, and Verde rivers in 1831. Cooke, however, was asking for something that had never been asked of any Southwest scout: to chart an extensive course *for wagons*. When Cooke complained about his guides, it was not because they were lost, but because they were understandably befuddled about how to get wagons, not to mention hundreds of men and hundreds of animals, across an unforgiving terrain.

By November 9, Cooke had listed several obstacles facing the Mormon Battalion: mules in miserable condition, twenty-two men on the sick report, many people needing to be transported in wagons, many men weak or old or debilitated, and insufficient rations. He ordered fifty-five of the sick, and enough men and rations to supply them, back to Santa Fe.[59] Fewer than 350 Mormon soldiers now remained in the battalion.[60]

Cutting the road as they went made ten miles a hard day's march, the equivalent of twenty-five miles on a good road. Despite his discouragement, Cooke was determined to blaze a route more than 300 miles long to the San Pedro River, a tributary of the Gila in today's southern Arizona, "of which the guides know little or nothing – know not if there be water sufficient."[61]

Scouting ahead on November 13, Leroux fixed a note to a pole, telling Cooke to go west, away from the Rio Grande. Two days later, with a bitter gale blowing all day, "raining, snowing, and shining alternately," Leroux, Charbonneau, Foster, and Weaver reconnoitered the country ahead.[62] The maps they had could be "depended on for nothing." On November 20, at the Mimbres River, north of present Deming, New Mexico, Cooke and all four guides climbed a hill and "had a long and anxious consultation."

Kearny had wanted the Mormon Battalion to follow the Gila, which would have meant going northwest into a mountain range, but Cooke's pilots, feeling doubtful about the troupe's wagons, agreed to a man that they "would not attempt it." Instead, the foursome proposed, and it was ultimately agreed, to reach the San Pedro by a different, much longer route that dipped southwest, adding perhaps 150 miles to their trail. The men continued southwest toward San Bernardino Spring, a well-known oasis on the present Arizona-Mexico border – a much better route.⁶³

The search for water was continual, sometimes for days at a time, and November 22, 1846, found Leroux and Charbonneau doing what they always did. Cooke wrote,

*Suddenly, at four o'clock, exactly before us, at perhaps fifteen miles we saw a white smoke spring up. I knew then that it was Leroux, who had spoken of making a little smoke at the little water hole.*⁶⁴

That night, well after dark, Charbonneau straggled into camp on foot carrying his saddle, his mule nowhere to be seen. He reported coming to a grassy area where he let the tired mule eat and rest. Half an hour later, when Charbonneau tried to bridle the mule, the stubborn animal kicked him and ran off. He followed it for several miles but could not catch it. Finally, to keep his saddle and pistols from falling into the hands of Apache Indians – and partly, conjectured Cooke, from anger – Charbonneau shot it.⁶⁵

On November 25, the men woke to bitter cold temperatures dipping to twenty degrees or less. A seven-mile march brought them to a long, rocky defile that took two and a half hours to get the wagons across. Charbonneau killed an antelope before the column reached a nearby mountain, and not long after that, Cooke saw his scout near the summit in pursuit of grizzlies:

*Saw three [bears] far up among the rocks, standing conspicuously and looking quite white in the sun, whilst the bold hunter was gradually approaching them. Soon after, he fired and in ten seconds again; then there was a confused action, and we could see one fall and the others rushing about with loud and fierce cries that made the mountains ring ... the young bears were close by, I was much alarmed for the guide's safety; and then we heard him crying out in Spanish, but it was for more balls; and so the cubs escaped. The bear was rolled down and butchered before the wagons had passed.*⁶⁶

At the end of November, as the Mormon Battalion made its way over Guadalupe Pass, in the southwest corner of New Mexico, Leroux told Cooke they were less than one hundred miles from the San Pedro River. They reached San Bernardino Spring on December 2, staying over to rest, wash clothes, and trade with the Indians. Mormon William Coray recorded, "the San Pedro River was within 30 miles. The pilot, Weaver, professed to be acquainted all the way."⁶⁷ They reached the river on December 9.

Leroux proved his value when he returned to the camp three days later with important reconnaissance on the garrisoned town of Tucson – it held two hundred Mexican soldiers. He and the other scouts had concluded that rather than following the San Pedro north, "over a trackless wilderness of mountains and river hills," it would be best to cross west to Tucson, then follow the Santa Cruz River to the Gila.⁶⁸ Based on reports from his mountain men, Cooke concluded that any road other than the one through Tucson would be a hundred miles out of the way. He therefore needed a plan to march through Tucson peaceably and without being detained.

Battalion member Daniel Tyler reported that Leroux proposed an inventive deception to accomplish this goal. Leroux and Foster would go ahead of the Mormon Battalion and tell the Mexican commander at Tucson that

an army of Americans are en route to California; that the front guard is about three hundred and sixty men, and if it stops to drill it will be to give time for the main army to come up.

Should either man fail to return by an agreed-upon time, it would mean that he was being held prisoner in Tucson.[69] Leroux and Foster then left for Tucson; Leroux returned later, but Foster did not. Cooke soon learned that Foster was indeed a prisoner.

Cooke initiated the charade the afternoon of the next day, December 13, with an inspection of arms and a lengthy drill, principally at loading and firing, and column formations.[70] Meanwhile, Leroux slipped ahead, made contact with a few soldiers at a guardhouse, and reported back to Cooke. According to Tyler,

The Colonel learned that a rumor of a large force of American soldiers had reached the town and great excitement prevailed. Of course, the Colonel … took no pains to disabuse their minds, and thus expose our little army to unnecessary peril.[71]

The bluff worked. Foster was freed through Cooke and Leroux's negotiations, and Cooke marched through Tucson without incident.

By December 28, the Mormon Battalion was following the same trail along the Rio Gila taken by Kearny's dragoons six weeks earlier. Confident he could continue without his full complement of guides, Cooke sent Leroux, Charbonneau, and three men to communicate with Kearny.[72] Cooke would not see Charbonneau again until January 20, and Leroux not for some time after that.

As he descended the Rio Gila, Cooke knew he would soon have to cross the Colorado River to continue west into California. On January 7, 1847, he sent Weaver and Foster ahead to check the difficulty of the road and to see if any troops had come from Sonora or if anyone was approaching from the west. All was clear, and Cooke forded the Colorado on January 10 and 11. Fifteen miles beyond the river, Cooke found a note "on the high bank above the well, stuck on a pole, 'No water, 2nd January. Charbonneau.'" The note concerned Cooke,

not only for the full success of my party, but almost for their safety, for they had rode their tired animals hard so far, were disappointed for water here, and would be for fifty-seven miles farther.[73]

"Our great loss in action"

On January 13, men and mules fought their way through sand, covering thirteen miles in seven hours. Cooke consulted with Weaver about Indians in the area and on what route to take near the Salton Sea. Two days later, Cooke headed out before sunrise to reach the Pozo Hondo ("deep well"), where he was met by Major Jeremiah Cloud, one of Kearny's officers. Cooke wrote that his pleasure at seeing Cloud

was sadly changed to the most sorrowful feelings on hearing of our great loss in action of Captains Moore and Johnston and twenty-one dragoons.[74]

Cooke learned that well before dawn on December 6, Kearny had attacked a mounted patrol of Californio lancers. Kearny led about 150 troops in a poorly executed fight that quickly degenerated into a desperate mounted skirmish. Heavy rain the night before had dampened the dragoons' gunpowder, making what should have been superior weapons ineffective. Kearny had divided his force into several columns but as they met the foe on the flats near San Pasqual, the officers lost control and the fight became a brawl. Bested initially, the Americans eventually gained the upper hand. The Californios retreated, taking their dead and wounded along. The American "victory" was a hollow one because they had suffered more casualties.[75]

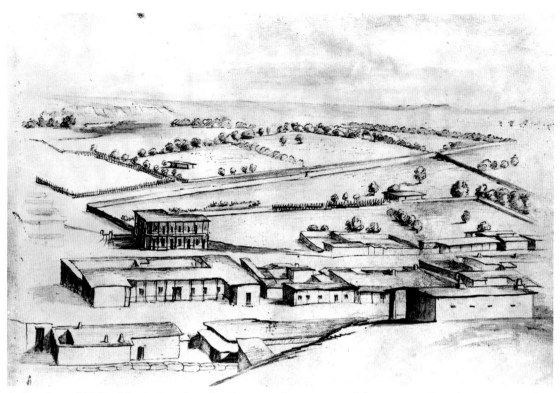

A drawing of El Pueblo de Los Angeles in 1847 shows part of the town and outlying vineyards. When Kearny led his troops out of Bent's Fort in 1845, Los Angeles was a Mexican settlement. By 1848, California would belong to the United States. SECURITY PACIFIC NATIONAL BANK COLLECTION, LOS ANGELES PUBLIC LIBRARY

Lieutenant William Emory wrote in his journal two days after the conflict:

Robidoux, a thin man of fifty-five years, slept next to me ... The loss of blood from his wounds, added to the coldness of the night, 28° Fahrenheit, made me think he would never see daylight, but I was mistaken. Robidoux woke me to ask if I did not smell coffee, and expressed a belief that a cup of that beverage would save his life, and that nothing else would.

Emory did not think there was any coffee in camp and thought the veteran trader was imagining things, but to his surprise found the cook heating coffee over a small fire of wild sage. Emory wrote,

One of the most agreeable little offices performed in my life, and I believe in the cook's, to whom the coffee belonged, was, to pour this precious draught into the waning body of our friend Robidoux.[76]

Within two more days, the enemy force had grown to over two hundred lancers. Kearny and his surviving officers agreed that their only option was a fight to the death. Luckily, Stockton had sent reinforcements, and on the night of December 10, when approximately two hundred marines and sailors arrived, the lancers disappeared into the desert. Kearny then joined with Stockton, and the combined American force won crucial battles in Los Angeles and San Pedro on January 8 and 9, 1847.[77]

Frémont and his California Battalion were not involved in these hostilities. In fact, though they had been active in various war maneuvers since the previous summer,

Four unidentified members of the California Battalion, in a photograph labeled "Friends of J. C. Fremont." SEAVER CENTER FOR WESTERN HISTORY RESEARCH, LOS ANGELES COUNTY MUSEUM OF NATURAL HISTORY

they had not seen combat. By January 11, Frémont, who had been farther north, was camped with his troops at the mission in present San Fernando, north of Los Angeles. When Frémont heard that some of the Californios defeated by Stockton and Kearny had fled to the area, he sent an emissary with peace overtures.[78] Kearny had taken Santa Fe, and the war in California was over, with relatively minor battles having given the US control of a huge area that now includes all or parts of the American Southwest.

It was a different world in Mexico. For example, in February 1847, six weeks after hostilities ceased in California, General Zachary Taylor and his 4,500 men would defeat Santa Anna and his 15,000 at the Battle of Buena Vista, in which hundreds of men on each side were killed. Similarly, at the Battle of Chapultepec, in September 1847, General Winfield Scott and 3,500 men would defeat a Mexican force of equal size, with thousands of men killed or wounded.[79]

Now, with the fighting in Mexico raging on, a personal battle of wills was about to break out between the commander of the Army of the West and the Pathfinder.

"He would unquestionably ruin himself"

When Frémont arrived in Los Angeles on January 14, 1847, he and Carson were quickly reunited. "As soon as Frémont joined," wrote Carson, "I left Kearny and joined him."[80] Frémont was glad to see Carson, but he was livid that Kearny had not allowed Carson to carry the dispatches to Washington. This was only one of several points of conflict between the two officers, but Frémont took this one personally, and his preoccupation with it would culminate in his court martial, which would come early in 1848.

In his memoirs, Frémont made it clear how important it was to him that Carson fulfill the mission. The mountaineer had been selected

> *to insure the safety and speedy delivery of these important papers, and as a reward for brave and valuable service on many occasions.*

There is no doubt Frémont felt great affection for Carson and that he hoped Carson could reunite with his family in Taos, see Washington for the first time, and have the honor of meeting Senator Benton and President Polk. At the same time, having Carson represent him was in Frémont's self-interest. He could not have had a better advocate than the former trapper, who could fully provide Benton and Polk with "the incidental detail always so much more interesting than the restricted official report." Still, his fondest hope was seeing Carson "going off at the head of his own party with carte blanche for expenses and the prospect of novel pleasure and honor at the end."[81]

Carson felt similarly about Frémont. "I have heard that [Frémont] is enormously rich. I wish to God that he may be worth ten times as much more," he said in 1856.

> *All that he has or may ever receive, he deserves. I can never forget his treatment of me while in his employ and how cheerfully he suffered with his men when undergoing the severest of hardships.*[82]

Little wonder that Frémont was hurt so deeply by Kearny requiring that Carson abandon his mission and lead Kearny's soldiers west to California; Frémont felt Kearny had betrayed him as well as Carson. Frémont also viewed the decision as a sign of Kearny's failed leadership. He would question Kearny about it when defending himself at his own court martial.[83]

On January 15, Kearny learned that Stockton was organizing a civil government with Frémont as governor, in spite of the fact that Kearny had already shown Stockton his War Department authorization to act in such matters. The higher ranking officer was clearly Kearny, a brigadier general, not Stockton, a brevet commodore whose permanent rank was only captain. The two were corresponding by letter even though their offices were within easy walking distance, and in one dispatch Kearny asked by what authority Stockton was operating. Stockton responded with a letter of his own, declaring he was not responsible to Kearny, outlandishly announcing that Kearny should consider himself suspended from command of US forces in California.[84]

On January 16, an exasperated Kearny had one of his officers take a message to Frémont ordering him to stop making military appointments without Kearny's permission. When no reply came, Kearny sent word to Frémont that he wished to see him "on business," so Frémont showed up at Kearny's office the next day.

When Kearny received Frémont on January 17, he assumed he was dealing with a junior officer who had a huge chip on his shoulder, but in reality, Frémont's ego was about to unfurl. Frémont acknowledged he had received the order and had written a response. Moments later, Carson walked in delivering the freshly copied letter to Frémont, who proofed it, signed it, and handed it to Kearny. One passage stood out:

> *I feel therefore, with great deference to your professional and personal character constrained to say that, until you and Commodore Stockton adjust between yourselves the question of rank, where I respectfully think the difficulty belongs, I shall have to report and receive orders, as heretofore, from the Commodore.*

Frémont had the audacity to have signed the letter, "Lieutenant Colonel, United States Army and Military Commandant of the territory of California," as if he, and not Kearny, were in charge.[85]

Kearny must have been speechless. A junior officer in the United States Army was telling a general with full authorization from the Secretary of War that he would be answering to a brevet commodore in the Navy. Had it been anyone else, Kearny would have arrested him on the spot, but this junior officer was arguably the most famous man in America and the son-in-law of a powerful senator who also happened to be a friend of Kearny's. As Captain Henry Turner wrote in a letter to his wife,

Genl. K. is evidently timid with respect to Frémont. He fears to do his duty lest some offense should be given to Col. Benton.[86]

Rather than losing his temper, Kearny told Frémont that if he took the letter back and destroyed it, all would be forgotten. Frémont declined, confident Stockton would support him. Kearny warned Frémont that if he persisted, "he would unquestionably ruin himself." At that, Frémont marched out of the office, Carson hard on his heels.[87]

That same day, Kearny wrote two letters, the first to the War Department:

I am not recognized in my official capacity, either by Com Stockton or Lieut. Co Frémont. Both of [them] refuse to obey my orders or the instructions of President, and as I have no Troops in the country under my authority, excepting a few Dragoons, I have no power of enforcing them.

The next letter he addressed to Stockton:

And as I am prepared to carry out the President's instructions to me, which you oppose, I must, for the purpose of preventing collision between us & possibly a civil war in consequence of it, remain silent for the present, leaving with you the great responsibility of doing that for which you have no authority & preventing me from complying with the President's orders.[88]

Kearny set out with fifty dragoons for San Diego the next day. Like the privates, Kearny marched the entire way on foot while a sick solider with severely blistered feet rode Kearny's horse. The following day, January 19, in the midst of these difficulties, Kearny received the best possible news: Lieutenant Colonel Cooke and his Mormon Battalion had reached Warner's Ranch. In a few days, it would no longer be true that Kearny had no troops outside of a few dragoons.

Kearny sent a letter to Cooke, an officer he knew well and trusted, ordering him to march the battalion to San Diego. On January 29, Cooke rode by moonlight and reported to the general.[89] A few days later, Kearny ordered the Mormon Battalion to San Luis Rey, where it would begin official combat training, something the men had not had a chance to do when they enlisted six months earlier. Kearny wanted the Mormon soldiers to be ready in case hostilities broke out. With Cooke and his troops safely in California, the services of Dr. Foster and mountain men Leroux, Charbonneau, and Weaver were no longer needed. They were presumably paid and discharged, but Cooke's journal is silent on such matters. Charbonneau remained in the area as late as April, and later traveled north to the Sacramento Valley, where he settled. Foster remained in southern California and eventually became mayor of Los Angeles. Leroux and Weaver made their way back to Taos, and both were active as military and civilian guides well into the 1850s.[90]

Hoping to use diplomacy and leverage rather than force, Kearny and a few staff officers boarded a US warship on January 31 to sail to Monterey. This would give Kearny the chance to meet with Consul Larkin and gain his support. Army reinforcements from New York were also expected to land at Monterey soon.

Kearny arrived at Monterey on February 8 to more good news. Commodore W. Branford Shubrick had arrived two weeks earlier aboard the *USS Lexington* to replace Stockton. Shubrick had orders from the Secretary of the Navy authorizing him to form a civil government, but when Shubrick saw Kearny's similar orders, he promptly accepted him as the military and civil commander in the area. A week later, 113 US soldiers, mostly from the Third US Artillery out of Maryland, arrived. Among them were Colonel Richard Mason (Kearny's replacement as commander of the 1st US Dragoons), and a junior officer named William Tecumseh Sherman. On March 5, 500 members of the First New York Volunteer Regiment reached Monterey. Kearny now had more than a thousand men at his command, and Stockton was no longer on the scene. Nor was Carson, whom Frémont had sent to Washington with dispatches once again.[91]

Still, Frémont did not budge from his position. Of all the forces available to him, Kearny ordered the inexperienced Mormon Battalion to perform the dangerous mission of confronting Frémont's volunteers. On March 19, four companies of the Mormon Battalion marched to Los Angeles.[92] Confiscating the arms and ammunition from Frémont's men became Cooke's responsibility, because Frémont had thus far refused to obey the order to stand down. Frémont was still in Monterey, so Cooke met with Frémont's second in command – none other than mountain man Dick Owens. Not surprisingly, Kit Carson's old friend refused to comply.

"The general's orders are not obeyed?" the incredulous Cooke asked rhetorically in his report. "To be refused [ordnance and artillery] by this Lieut. Colonel Frémont and in defiance of the orders of the general? I denounce this treason or this mutiny."[93] Nevertheless, Cooke maintained patience. Over the next few weeks, he continued to drill his men, who were aware of the conflict with Frémont. One of them wrote:

Last night we were called up and ordered to fix bayonets, as the Col. [Cooke] had sent word that an attack might be expected from Col. Frémont's men before day.[94]

Fortunately, there was no attack. By the end of April, Frémont finally gave in, handing over arms and ammunition. He offered to resign, but Kearny refused to accept the resignation. On June 16, a peculiar military cohort departed California for Fort Leavenworth. Kearny led Cooke, about fifty US Army soldiers and fifteen members of the Mormon Battalion eastward. Frémont and his loyal mountain men and some of the California volunteers followed a few hundred yards behind in a separate group. Reaching the fort in August, Kearny promptly arrested Frémont.

Epilogue

Less than a month after Kearny and Frémont arrived at Fort Leavenworth, Mexico City fell, and the major fighting ended. Five months later, in February 1848, the Treaty of Guadalupe Hidalgo ended the war and brought a vast territory officially into the US – all of the present states of California, Nevada, and Utah, and portions of Arizona, New Mexico, Colorado, and Wyoming.

About a dozen former mountain men had played an important role in the taking of this territory, right or wrong. The fact that some of these frontiersmen ended up on the Kearny side of the conflict and others on the Frémont side was largely a matter of chance. Nevertheless, it is safe to say that the great majority of these mountaineers proved themselves to be loyal, responsible, and skillful.

The beaver men who guided the Mormon Battalion were faced with a severe challenge. Yet their reaction to that test was particularly praiseworthy. They brought Cooke's wagon company to California a month faster than Carson thought possible and helped prevent a civil war from breaking out among American troops. These feats were genuinely appreciated by Philip St. George Cooke, who wrote:

> History may be searched in vain for an equal march of infantry. Nine-tenths of it has been through a wilderness where nothing but savages and wild beasts are found, or deserts where, for want of water, there is no living creature. There, with almost hopeless labor, we have dug deep wells which the future traveler will enjoy. Without a guide who had traversed them, we have ventured into trackless prairies where water was not found for several marches. With crowbar and pick and ax in hand we have worked our way over mountains which seemed to defy aught save the wild goat, and hewed a passage through a chasm of living rock more narrow than our wagons ... Thus, marching half naked and half fed, and living upon wild animals, we have discovered and made a road of great value to our country.[95]

Leroux, Charbonneau, Weaver, and Foster well deserved such praise – an impressive reflection on a generation sometimes called a "majority of scoundrels."[96] All of these retired mountain men used skills they honed during the Rocky Mountain fur trade to further serve their country and advance its borders across the continent.

Larry E. Morris is a writer and historian from Idaho Falls, Idaho. He has published three books on the early American West. His latest volume is The 1959 Yellowstone Earthquake, *published by The History Press. Larry and his wife, Deborah, live in Salt Lake City, Utah.*

NOTES

1. From an account by Lieutenant J. H. Carleton, who was in charge of the commissary, cited in LeRoy R. Hafen, *Broken Hand: The Life of Thomas Fitzpatrick, Mountain Man, Guide and Indian Agent* (Denver, CO: The Old West Publishing Company, 1973), 211-212. Kearny had been ordered to reconnoiter the Oregon Trail from Fort Leavenworth to South Pass and determine the plausibility of establishing forts to protect emigrants. The difficult 2,200-mile journey was completed in fourteen weeks, then the troops returned to Fort Leavenworth. In his report, Kearny recommended that rather than establishing military posts along the Oregon Trail, "a military expedition, similar to the one of this season, be made every two to three years ... to keep the Indians, perfectly quiet, reminding them of (as this one proved) the facility and rapidity with which our dragoons can march through any part of their country." S. W. Kearny, "Report of a Summer Campaign to the Rocky Mountains," in Senate Executive Documents, 1, 29th Congress, 1st Session, Document No. 2, found in David A. White, ed., *News of the Plains and Rockies, 1803-1865* (Spokane, WA: The Arthur H. Clark Company, 1998), 4:120-124.
2. Thomas Salathiel Martin, "Narrative of John C. Frémont's Expedition to California in 1845-46," MS, The Bancroft Library, University of California, Berkeley, 3, cited in Ferol Egan, *Frémont: Explorer for a Restless Nation* (Reno, NV: University of Nevada Press, 1977), 282.
3. Hafen, *Broken Hand,* 218-224.
4. Fitzpatrick had just come west on the Santa Fe Trail with his old friends, Jedediah Smith, Bill Sublette, and David Jackson, and had been the last person to see Smith alive before his death at the hands of Comanche warriors in the Cimarron Desert.
5. "The Kit Carson Memoirs, 1809-1856," in Harvey Lewis Carter, *"Dear Old Kit": The Historical Christopher Carson* (Norman, OK: University of Oklahoma Press, 1968), 95-96. All quotations from Carson's memoirs are taken from *Dear Old Kit* because Carter transcribed the original manuscript dictated by Carson in 1856 with a minimum of change. Milo M. Quaife's edition, on the other hand (entitled *Kit Carson's Autobiography* and first published in 1935) took liberties with the primary text, sometimes rendering it into clearer and more correct English. See Carter, *Dear Old Kit,* 3-37, for a detailed review of the adventures of Carson's memoirs.
6. Carter, "Kit Carson Memoirs," 96.
7. Letter, J. J. Abert to Frémont, February 12, 1845, Donald Jackson and Mary Lee Spence,

eds., *The Expeditions of John C. Frémont* (Urbana, IL: University of Illinois Press, 1970), 1:396.

8   Thomas Breckenridge Manuscripts, University of Missouri, Western Historical Manuscript Collection, Columbia, cited by Bil Gilbert, *Westering Man: The Life of Joseph Walker* (New York, NY: Atheneum, 1983), 211.

9   Ibid., 212.

10 Egan, *Frémont*, 140-158, 251-260.

11 Hiram M. Chittenden, *The American Fur Trade of the Far West* (Lincoln, NE: University of Nebraska Press, 1986), 1:408.

12 Diary entry for James K. Polk, October 24, 1845, Milo M. Quaife, ed., *The Diary of James K. Polk During His Presidency*, 1845-1849 (Chicago, IL: A. C. McClurg and Company, 1919), 71-72.

13 Gilbert, *Westering Man*, 212. Carter adds: "The belief that it was impossible to cross this desert was responsible for Old Bill Williams's desertion at this point." Carter, "Kit Carson Memoirs," 99n177.

14 David Roberts, *A Newer World: Kit Carson, John C. Frémont, and the Claiming of the American West* (New York, NY: Simon and Schuster, 2000), 143.

15 Gilbert, *Westering Man*, 213.

16 Ibid., 213-214.

17 Letter, Jose Castro to John C. Frémont, March 5, 1846, Jackson and Spence, *Expeditions of Frémont*, 2:74-75.

18 Letter, John C. Frémont to Thomas Oliver Larkin, March 9, 1846, Jackson and Spence, *Expeditions of Frémont*, 2:82.

19 John Charles Frémont, *Memoirs of My Life* (Chicago, IL: Belford, Clarke & Company, 1887), 460.

20 Roberts, *Newer World*, 143.

21 Jackson and Spence, *Expeditions of Frémont*, 2:73, 74n3.

22 Sherman L. Fleek, *History May Be Searched in Vain: a Military History of the Mormon Battalion* (Spokane, WA: The Arthur H. Clark Company, 2006), 8, 52.

23 William L. Marcy to Stephen Watts Kearny, June 3, 1846, House Executive Document, No. 60, 30th Congress, 1st Session, 520, reprinted in its entirety in David L. Bigler and Will Bagley, eds., *Army of Israel: Mormon Battalion Narratives* (Spokane, WA: The Arthur H. Clark Company, 2000), 38-39.

24 Diary entries for James K. Polk, June 3 and June 2, 1846, Quaife, *Diary of James K. Polk*, 445-446, 444.

25 Letter, Stephen Watts Kearny to James Allen, June 19, 1846, Kearny Selected Papers, MIC A139, National Archives, reprinted in its entirety in Bigler and Bagley, *Army of Israel*, 41.

26 Carter, "Kit Carson Memoirs," 103.

27 Tom Chaffin, *Pathfinder: John Charles Frémont and the Course of American Empire* (New York, NY: Hill and Wang, 2002), 336-337.

28 Frémont, *Memoirs of My Life*, 488.

29 Carter, "Kit Carson Memoirs," 105.

30 Ibid. Just a few weeks earlier, based merely on rumor, Frémont had sanctioned – but not participated in – an attack on an Indian village in which approximately 150 villagers were massacred. "The number I killed I cannot say," wrote Carson. "It was a perfect butchery." Ibid., 101.

31 Frémont, *Memoirs of My Life*, 525.

32 Egan, *Frémont*, 355-56.

33 Frémont, *Memoirs of My Life*, 525.

34 Jackson and Spence, *Expeditions of Frémont*, 2:186-187n6.

35 LeRoy R. Hafen, ed., "The W. M. Boggs Manuscript About Bent's Fort, Kit Carson, the Far West and Life Among the Indians," *The Colorado Magazine* 7, no. 2 (March 1930), 62-63.

36 Jackson and Spence, *Expeditions of Frémont*, 2:164n2.

37 Chaffin, *Pathfinder*, 341-342.

38 Letter, Thomas Fitzpatrick to Andrew Sublette, July 31, 1846, Sublette Collection, Missouri History Museum Archives, St. Louis, MO, cited in Hafen, *Broken Hand*, 233.

39 Dwight L. Clarke, *Stephen Watts Kearny: Soldier of the West* (Norman, OK: University of Oklahoma, 1961), 163.

40 Hafen, "The W. M. Boggs Manuscript," 67.

41 Daniel Tyler, *A Concise History of the Mormon Battalion in the Mexican War, 1846-1847*, n.p., 1881.

42 Diary of John D. Lee, October 11, 1846, cited in Bigler and Bagley, *Army of Israel*, 135.

43 Ralph P. Bieber, ed., "Cooke's Journal of the March of the Mormon Battalion, 1846-1847," *Exploring Southwest Trails, 1846-1854* (Glendale, CA: The Arthur H. Clark Company, 1938), 69n144.

44 W. H. Emory, *Notes of a Military Reconnoissance*, 1846-1847, House Executive Document, No. 7, 30th Congress, 1st Session, 505, reprinted in full in Ross Calvin, *Lieutenant Emory Reports* (Albuquerque, NM: University of New Mexico Press, 1951), quoted excerpt on p. 87.

45 Roberts, *Newer World*, 174.

46 Henry Smith Turner, diary entry, October 9, 1846, Henry Smith Turner Papers, Missouri History Museum Archives, St. Louis, MO. The diary (June 30-December 4, 1846) is reprinted in full in Dwight L. Clarke, ed., *The Original Journals of Henry Smith Turner: With Stephen*

Watts Kearny in New Mexico and California, 1846-1847 (Norman, OK: University of Oklahoma Press, 1966), 81, 80.

47 Ibid., 84, 87.
48 Ibid., 105, 106.
49 Ibid., 115.
50 Ibid., 118.
51 Ibid., 119-120.
52 Clarke, *Stephen Watts Kearny*, 190-191.
53 Ibid., 192-194.
54 Bieber, "Cooke's Journal," 70.
55 Ibid., 74-75.
56 Ibid., 85-86.
57 "When, in 1853," writes David J. Weber, "Antoine Leroux testified [in a letter to Senator Thomas Hart Benton] that he had 'trapped the whole country, every river, every creek, and branch from the Gila to the head of the Grand River fork,' his exaggeration was probably slight." David J. Weber, *The Taos Trappers: The Fur Trade in the Far Southwest, 1540-1846* (Norman, OK: University of Oklahoma Press), 1971, 97.
58 Bieber, "Cooke's Journal," 89.
59 Ibid., 94-95.
60 Norma Baldwin Ricketts, *The Mormon Battalion: US Army of the West* (Logan, UT: Utah State University Press, 1996), 20, 31-33, 79; Tyler, *Concise History*, 169.
61 Bieber, "Cooke's Journal," 95.
62 Ibid., 101.
63 Ibid., 105, 107, 106. Cooke, who bitterly resented Kearny's and Fitzpatrick's taking all the best mules, added: "If I had been supplied with *good* fat mules, it might be safe to keep directly on in this wilderness." (106, italics in original)
64 Ibid., 110.
65 Ibid.
66 Ibid., 116.
67 Diary of William Coray, cited in Ricketts, *The Mormon Battalion*, 93.
68 Bieber, "Cooke's Journal," 147, 146.
69 Tyler, *Concise History*, 224.
70 *Cooke's Journal* 147.
71 Tyler, *Concise History*, 225.
72 Bieber, "Cooke's Journal," 180.
73 Ibid., 207.
74 Ibid., 213-214.
75 Sherman L. Fleek, "The Kearny/Stockton/Frémont Feud: The Mormon Battalion's Most Significant Contribution in California," *The Journal of Mormon History* 37, no. 3 (Summer 2011): 241-242. Some have blamed Kit Carson for the misfortunes at San Pasqual, claiming that Kearny intended to avoid the Californios and move on to San Diego but changed his mind when Carson assured him the lancers would not stand; Clarke, *Stephen Watts Kearny*, 204-207. These claims are suspect because they generally come from late, hearsay reports, but, in any case, General Kearny was the commanding officer and the one responsible for the decision to attack.
76 Emory, *Notes*, 172-173.
77 Fleek, "Kearny/Stockton/Frémont Feud," 243.
78 Chaffin, *Pathfinder*, 363-364.
79 K. J. Bauer, *The Mexican War* (New York, NY: Macmillan, 1974), passim.
80 Carter, "Kit Carson Memoirs," 116.
81 Femont, *Memoirs of My Life*, 567.
82 Carter, "Kit Carson Memoirs," 120-121.
83 At Frémont's court martial, Kearny described his initial meeting with Carson thus:

Question. [from Frémont] Did the express [Carson] remonstrate against being turned back and did you insist and assert the right to order him back?

Answer. [from Kearny] The express was Mr. Carson, who was at first very unwilling to return with me; he being desirous of proceeding to Washington, to convey letters and communications to that place, which he had received from Lieutenant Colonel Frémont and Commodore Stockton. He told me that he had pledged himself that they should be received in Washington. I at last persuaded him to return with me by telling him that I would send in his place, as bearer of those despatches Mr. Fitzpatrick, who was an old friend of Lieutenant Colonel Frémont, and had traveled a great deal with him. Mr. Carson, upon that, was perfectly satisfied, and told me so. "The Proceedings of the Court Martial in the Trial of Lieutenant Colonel Frémont," April 7, 1848, Senate Executive Document No. 33, 30th Congress, 1st Session, p. 42.

Carson's account was brief and to the point: *On the 6th of October, '46, I met General Kearny on his march to California. He ordered me to join him as his guide. I done so, and Fitzpatrick continued on with the despatches.* Carter, "Kit Carson Memoirs," 112.

One of those present when Carson and his fifteen fellow horsemen arrived at Kearny's camp, Captain Abraham Johnston, offered this report in his journal:

The general told him (Carson) that he had just passed over the country which we were to traverse and he [Kearny] wanted him [Carson] to go back with him [Kearny] as a guide; he [Carson] replied that he [Carson] had pledged himself to go to Washington, and he could not think of not fulfilling his promise. The general told him [Carson] he [Kearny] would relieve him of all responsibility, and place the mail in the hands of a safe person to carry it; he [Carson] finally consented and turned his face to the west again, just as he was on the eve of entering the settlements, after his arduous trip and when he had set his hopes on seeing his family. Abraham R. Johnston, "Journal of the March of the Army of the West, 1846," cited in Clarke, *Stephen Watts Kearny*, 171.

Johnston, who was killed in battle two months later, looks to be an impartial judge, making no apparent effort to favor one side over the other. If anything, his account leans in Carson's favor because he closes it thus: "It requires a brave man to give up his private feelings thus for the public good; but Carson is one such! Honor to him for it."

The claim later made by Thomas Hart Benton that Kearny essentially coerced Carson to return to California and told Carson many times that he himself intended to appoint Frémont governor of California cannot be taken seriously because it does not square with any other account, including Carson's (quite significant when one considers that Carson did not testify at the court martial, even though he certainly would have done so if Frémont asked).

84 Fleek, "Kearny/Stockton/Frémont Feud," 244.
85 Ibid., 246.
86 Letter, Henry Smith Turner to Julia Turner, March 16, 1847, Clarke, *Journals of Henry Smith Turner*, 160. Benton indeed took offense. During and after Frémont's court martial, he went to great lengths to destroy Kearny's reputation, even though the two had been friends.
87 Chaffin, *Pathfinder*, 370; Fleek, "Kearny/Stockton/Frémont Feud," 246-247.
88 Fleek, "Kearny/Stockton/Frémont Feud," 229-230.
89 Bieber, "Cooke's Journal," 238.
90 Ricketts, *The Mormon Battalion*, 134; http://politicalgraveyard.com/bio/foster.html, (accessed on March 28, 2016); Forbes Parkhill, *The Blazed Trail of Antoine Leroux* (Los Angeles, CA: Westernlore Press, 1965), 106; http://archive.azcentral.com/travel/articles/20140108arizona-explained-pauline-weaver-mountain-man.html, (accessed on March 28, 2016).
91 Fleek, "Kearny/Stockton/Frémont Feud," 249.
92 Ibid., 251.
93 Ibid., 252.
94 Ibid., 254.
95 Bieber, "Cooke's Journal," 239-240. Cooke's "road of great value" approximates today's Interstate 25 south from Santa Fe to Hatch, New Mexico, then cuts southwest into Arizona, dips into Mexico, goes northwest to Benson, Arizona, follows I-10 and I-8 to Yuma, dips into Mexico again, enters California near Calexico, and loops northwest to Warner Springs and Mission San Luis Rey de Francia before following the coast southeast to San Diego, California.
96 Letter, Nathaniel J. Wyeth to Francis Ermatinger, July 18, 1833, in Nathaniel Wyeth, "The Correspondence and Journals of Nathaniel J. Wyeth, 1831-6," F. G. Young, ed., *Sources of the History of Oregon* (Eugene, OR: University Press, 1899), 1:69.

REVIEWERS

J. Ryan Badger is the Living History Coordinator at The Alamo. He has worked with the National Park Service, Forest Service, Smithsonian National Museum of the American Indian, and private organizations to present the culture and history of the American West.*

Stephen V. Banks of Dubois, Wyoming is a lecturer and re-enactor of the Rocky Mountain fur trade. Banks studied western history at the University of Wyoming, has written several articles and produced a website for Wyoming's K-12 schools about this time period. Banks is a retired IT consultant for the Dubois School District.*

Vic Nathan Barkin is an active member of the American Mountain Men and volunteers as a living history interpreter for national and regional historic sites, including Fort William, Bent's Fort, and Fort Lupton. His studies of the Rocky Mountain fur trade include the Taos and Santa Fe traders. Barkin owns a consulting business in Louisville, Colorado.*

Nathan E. Bender is a former professor of the University of Idaho Library special collections and archives. He has built historic research collections at the Buffalo Bill Historical Center, Montana State University, West Virginia University, and the University of Oklahoma. Publishing on western history, folklore, and American Indian studies in a variety of research journals, he is currently an independent scholar in Laramie, Wyoming.*

Dr. Roger Blomquist earned his Ph.D. from the University of Nebraska-Lincoln in American Frontier History. He is an expert in Wyoming saddles of the Old West and an award winning saddlemaker. He is also a documentary filmmaker and an author of young adult historical fiction novels.

Barry Bohnet lives in Michigan. A Navy and Vietnam veteran, he is currently retired from the State of Florida where he worked as a supervisor in the Juvenile Probation Department. He is an artist and designer, lifelong black powder shooter and gun builder. Bohnet's booklet *The Golden Mean, an Art Historical Approach*, was published by the National Muzzleloading Rifle Association.*

Dr. Jay H. Buckley is Associate Professor of History at Brigham Young University. He is the author of the award-winning *William Clark: Indian Diplomat* (University of Oklahoma Press, 2008). Buckley has co-authored volumes on Meriwether Lewis and Zebulon Pike. His current book project is *A Fur Trade History of the Great Plains and Canadian Prairies* (Plains Histories series, Texas Tech University Press).*

Allen Chronister is a retired attorney and independent researcher with a lifelong interest in the history and people of the American West. He maintains particular interests in the history and ethnology of Native Americans and the material culture of the fur trade.

O. Ned Eddins is a Doctor of Veterinary Medicine in Afton, Wyoming. He has extensively researched the Plains Indians and mountain men of the Rocky Mountain fur trade. Dr. Eddins has written two historical novels, *Mountains of Stone* and *The Winds of Change*. His website, www.thefurtrapper.com, features well-documented history on America's western expansion.*

Jerry Enzler is a historian of the West and is completing a new biography of Jim Bridger. He is the founding director of the National Mississippi River Museum & Aquarium, a Smithsonian affiliated museum, and has created several museum exhibits including "Lewis and Clark's Excellent Adventure" and "The Rivers of America." He is a frequent speaker at national forums and has appeared on national media. He lives along the Mississippi River in East Dubuque, Illinois.*

REVIEWERS

John W. Fisher is a retired Idaho high school science teacher who has a second career researching the material culture of the Lewis and Cark Expedition. He has presented to thousands of people across the expedition route and published articles and book reviews about the expedition. Fisher has assembled the most extensive period artifact collection representing those items carried on the expedition, on display at the Fort Mandan Museum in Washburn, ND.

Todd Glover recently retired after twenty-five years in the military. He has participated in numerous living history events and spends much of his time researching, experimenting and recreating the lifestyle of the historic Rocky Mountain mountaineers. He is a Hiverano member of the American Mountain Men.

Willam Gwaltney serves as the Director for Interpretation and Visitor Services for the American Battle Monuments Commission, which maintains and protects 25 overseas military cemeteries and 26 American monuments around the world. Previously, he served 33 years with the National Park Service, specializing in historical interpretation at a number of parks, including Bent's Old Fort and Fort Laramie. He currently makes his home in Paris, France.

Gene Hickman has pursued historical interpretation for many years, focusing on Lewis and Clark, Indian Sign Language, and the Western fur trade; he has written numerous articles related to those topics. Hickman is a Hiverano in the American Mountain Men and currently serves both as the Booshway for the Manuel Lisa Party and the Brigade Booshway for Montana and North Dakota.

Keith Moki Hipol has lived and worked in the mountain West for thirty years. He has always been interested in the history and involvement of Hawaiians in the American fur trade, and has also studied the material culture of the Native American and the horse culture of the mountain men. Hipol is currently the Western Segundo of the American Mountain Men, and resides in Evanston, Wyoming.*

Mark William Kelly has twenty-four years experience as a professional archaeologist, architectural historian and historian in cultural resources management. He is also a practicing attorney to Native American clientele. He has written numerous articles, papers and current publications.

Mike Moore is a lecturer and author, with over 150 articles to his credit and four books on the early American West. He has appeared on the History Channel and has been a staff writer for *On the Trail Magazine* for thirteen years.

David F. Morris holds graduate degrees in historic preservation, library science, and park & resource management. Morris has been involved with historic preservation in several locations across the country, including volunteering with the National Park Service, the USDA Forest Service, and Kootenai County, Idaho. He is currently a librarian at Grand Canyon National Park.

Dr. David J. Peck is a retired physician and author of *Or Perish in the Attempt: The Hardship and Medicine of the Lewis and Clark Expedition* (Bison Books/University of Nebraska Press, 2012). He is producer of the film documentary of the same name for the Lewis and Clark Foundation of Great Falls, Montana.

Dean Rudy is a member of the American Mountain Men, and the creator of the "Mountain Men and the Fur Trade" website (www.mtmen.org). He holds degrees from Cornell University and the University of Utah and currently lives in Park City, Utah.

Dr. Mark Schreiter holds a Ph.D. in history from the University of Idaho and specializes in environmental and Native American history of the Pacific Northwest. His fur trade studies focus on trappers' relationships with tribes of the upper Missouri. A long-time wilderness ranger and fire lookout for the U.S. Forest Service, Schreiter is currently professor of history and humanities with the University of Alaska at Kodiak College.

Dr. Darby Stapp has spent thirty years studying the history and archaeology of the Pacific Northwest. For much of that time, Stapp worked on understanding and protecting important cultural and historic resources at the Hanford Reach National Monument, Mid-Columbia River, in Washington State. Stapp established Northwest Anthropology LLC to conduct cultural resource impact studies for tribes and agencies in Washington, Oregon, and Idaho.

Dr. William R. Swagerty has taught college-level American history since 1977 and has presented papers at many fur trade symposia over the past thirty years. Swagerty is especially interested in the labor and social histories of fur trade personnel, and the material culture of the fur trade, specifically blankets and trade cloth. He is director of the John Muir Center and professor of history at University of the Pacific, Stockton, California.

Tim Tanner was educated at Utah State University and the California Art Institute, and embarked on a career as an illustrator in 1989. His artwork has graced the pages of national best-sellers and many popular magazines. An avid historian and fur trade re-enactor since the late 1970s, Tanner is a member of the American Mountain Men, and a founding member of the American Longrifle Association. Tanner is on the art faculty at Brigham Young University/Idaho.*

Melissa Tiffie of Durant, Oklahoma, has spent her life from childhood re-enacting fur trade history and has mastered many skills of the early West with a focus on women's roles in the Rocky Mountain region. She has also edited fur trade articles and related books. Tiffie is a regional nurse coordinator and emergency communication specialist in southeastern Oklahoma. She holds a BA from Southeastern Oklahoma State University in Criminal Justice and Sociology.*

Dale Topham, a native of Orem, Utah, received his B.A. and M.A. degrees from Brigham Young University. He is presently a doctoral candidate in American History at Southern Methodist University in Dallas, Texas.*

Dr. Mark van de Logt is an assistant professor of history at Texas A&M University at Qatar. He received an M.A. degree in American Studies from Utrecht University and his Ph.D. in history from Oklahoma State University. His particular interests are Pawnee and Arikara Indian culture and history. In 2010, he published *War Party in Blue: Pawnee Indian Scouts in the United States Army* (University of Oklahoma Press). He has also published on Ponca history as well as other Plains Indian cultures.*

Scott Walker became fascinated by the Rocky Mountain fur trade as a child. Since then he has followed the trails of trappers and traders through their writings, and gained a hands-on sense of their lives as a member of the American Mountain Men. Walker is currently studying British Isles and American fiddle music of the early nineteenth century to recreate tunes of the rendezvous period in a style those trappers would have heard around camp fires and trading posts.*

E. Rick Williams is currently serving as an administrator for Brigham Young University, and is a member of the American Mountain Men. He has also participated in Living History Days presentations to school children in May at the Museum of the Mountain Man.*

THE MUSEUM OF THE MOUNTAIN MAN

The Museum of the Mountain Man is in Pinedale, Wyoming, in the heart of Rocky Mountain fur trade country. Its mission is to preserve and interpret the history of the Rocky Mountain fur trade. The Green River Valley was a favorite location for fur trappers' rendezvous in the 1830s, and accordingly many important historic events occurred here. Numerous renowned fur trade personalities passed through this area for more than three decades.

Opened in 1990, the Museum of the Mountain Man has gained a national reputation for its interpretation of one of America's legendary eras. In addition to noteworthy exhibits, the museum offers educational programs and experiential learning opportunities for all ages. Visiting scholars deliver engaging presentations and hands-on demonstrations that explore and define the history of the mountain man, Plains Indian culture, and the area's natural history. To further its intellectual mission, the museum collaborates with eminent scholars and historians from around the country. The museum's peer-reviewed publication, the *Rocky Mountain Fur Trade Journal*, represents an annual culmination of that effort.

The museum collection includes a comprehensive and expanding fur trade library containing more than 7,000 volumes, available to scholars for in-house research. The museum is open to the public daily May 1 through September 30 and weekdays during October. The museum's staff conducts special projects and regular business year-round.

THE SUBLETTE COUNTY HISTORICAL SOCIETY

The mission of Sublette County Historical Society (SCHS) is to collect, preserve, and interpret the history of the Upper Green River Valley and Sublette County, Wyoming. Established in 1935, SCHS is the oldest historical society in Wyoming. In 1936, the SCHS inaugurated a living history pageant to celebrate the history of the fur trade era and the historic mountain man rendezvous, which evolved into an annual event that has endured to the present day.

For more information about the Museum of the Mountain Man and the Sublette County Historical Society, visit www.MMMuseum.com or call toll free: 877-686-6266

David Wright has been painting memorable moments in American history for more than forty years. Wright's paintings have been featured in television documentaries and as covers and illustrations for numerous books and magazines. He has appeared on television as a historical consultant and served as Art Director for Native Sun Productions' award-winning film *Daniel Boone and the Westward Movement*. He also provided art direction for the History Channel film, *First Invasion – The War of 1812*, for which he received a Prime Time Emmy nomination.*

Dr. Ken Zontek is an ethnic and environmental historian teaching at Yakima Valley Community College (YVCC). His monograph *Buffalo Nation: The American Indian Effort to Restore the Bison* (University of Nebraska Press, 2007) won the American Library Association's Best of the Best University Press Award in 2008. Zontek also founded YVCC's Afghan Women's Education Project, a by-product of his ongoing military service in Afghanistan.*

*Published in a previous volume of the Journal.

More information about the role of a peer reviewer can be found at:
www.MMMuseum.com/journal